SECRETS OF POWER CONVERSATION

Talk Your Way to Riches, Respect & Romance

Lawrence E. Bjornson

ISBN 0-9709719-2-3

Printed in the United States of America

Contents

Introduction

Human beings are social animals. Although there are a few hermits out there, most of us choose to sacrifice some elements of our freedom in order to gain the benefits of living and working with our fellows. Our vast civilizations exist and function only because each of us has learned to control our behavior in very intricate ways. Still, some of us have a better grasp than others of the complex systems in which we live. Those who have the deepest awareness and understanding of the core rules are the ones who will succeed and prosper. This is a book of rules, rules many people live and die without ever fully comprehending.

Society's rules aren't always obvious. The rules that allow us to get by and survive are fairly simple (don't run red lights, don't make bank robbery a career). But other rules, the ones that confer real success, not mere survival, can be as difficult to detect as black holes in deep space.

When your career progress bogs down, when your relationships are weak or troubled, when you have a hard time making friends, when you have difficulty making yourself heard, and when people take advantage of you, it is because you have an imperfect comprehension of those shadowy rules that allow you to focus social power to your advantage.

No one in our world succeeds strictly on his or her own. True accomplishment requires that you efficiently influence those around you in positive ways. The primary tool of influence is communication, and like society itself, communication has rules that few fully understand.

This book of communication rules is organized around one over-arching and seemingly paradoxical concept, a concept only life's true winners master—inducing others to meet your needs, requires you to pay unfailing and detailed attention to their needs.

Now let's begin our discovery of the secrets of power conversation.

Chapter 1:
Listening

Why would a book about talking begin with a chapter about the opposite of talking, namely, listening? Because listening is the sun around which all other conversational skills orbit like planets. Without that sun, these planets grow cold and die. Enjoyable and productive conversation is fueled by the information we take in through listening. There is no more significant chapter in this book.

So, you think you're already a good listener. That's highly doubtful. I'm sorry, but very few people are truly good listeners.

If you've ever wondered what to say next, or why you can't persuade well, or how you got into an argument, or why you're so often misjudged, you probably need to work on your listening skills.

All too often, conversation is conducted as a competitive event, not a cooperative effort. A speaker can hold the floor only as long as he can defend it from conversational predators who want to seize it from him. The listener only listens when he isn't mentally putting together his own next comment or plotting the overthrow of the current speaker. Few of us actively encourage others to talk about themselves or fully explore and explain their ideas. And yet, the quality of our friendships, romances, family life, and business relationships depends on the information we could get if we would only make the effort to listen.

Enormous power is at the fingertips of anyone who trains himself to listen. It is a core competence for those who aspire to influence others. Why? Because it is through careful listening that we discover what other people want. Once we know what others want, we can adapt our message to persuade them far more effectively. By careful listening, we discover the keys that unlock their vaults.

Despite this easy access to real power, listening remains an underdeveloped skill for most of us, especially in America. The natural inclination of Americans is to solve problems and influence others through talk and action. We'd rather assert ourselves than sit quietly and listen. Listening just seems so passive, so weak. But, of course, you and I want to be listened to, we're dying to be heard. When someone listens intently to what we have to say, it makes us feel great. So great, paradoxically, that we're even less inclined to yield the floor and do the same favor for others.

Ever notice how common it is for people to talk to a dog or a cat, a goldfish, even houseplants? We know they don't understand a syllable, but we do it anyway because they don't try to interrupt, and we can easily pretend they are listening intently. We want to be heard so badly that even this simulated listening is valued.

Here's another indication of the powerful need people have for a good listener. Why do so many functional, sane people go to psychiatrists? A psychiatrist is a trained listener. He stays out of your way, let's you fully explore your thoughts and feelings, and smoothes the road for self-revelation. For a sizable fee, a psychiatrist does what all our friends, girlfriends, boyfriends, spouses, and relatives won't do— he listens.

People want to be listened to, need it, crave it. It is a rewarding experience to speak to someone who listens deeply and makes an effort to understand. It is an incredible flattery. When you listen well, you tell people that you are interested in them and respect them. It has been said that President Kennedy, by careful listening and thoughtful questioning, could make a person feel like he was the only other person in the world. Those who had spoken with him said afterward that even though he was the President of the United States, they were convinced they had 100% of his attention while they spoke. People don't forget an experience like that.

When someone respects you enough to listen intently to what you have to say, without interruption or wandering eyes, that is the stuff of friendship and solid business relationships. We are interested in those who are interested in us. In contrast, we are more likely to distrust and dislike those who won't take the time to listen or try to understand our point of view. If you want to have minimal impact on people, if you want to be disliked, if you want people to laugh at you and insult you behind your back, then talk incessantly and refuse to listen. It won't be

long before people are giggling at whispered comments such as—
"Talking with John is easy. It's like attending a lecture."

The goal of conversation is not simply to talk but to keep all parties engaged and involved. The best way to discover topics that are interesting and meaningful to others is to listen carefully. A good conversationalist's gift is his ability to pull people out of their shells. He discovers their interests by listening and then makes it easy for them to talk about those things. Few people notice how little a good listener says. They do notice the appropriateness and intelligence of the comments he does make. And afterwards, they will remember him warmly and praise him as a wonderful conversationalist even though he may actually have said very little.

One of the basics of good conversation is the search for subjects that interest the other party. More often than not, people want to talk about some aspect of their personal experience. If you provide a willing ear and allow them to say what's on their mind, they will be eternally grateful (just as you would be if someone did you the same favor).

Good listening also increases the quality of what speakers say. When a speaker senses that you are listening closely, his energy level goes up. Suddenly, his speech is quicker and more animated, his comments more forceful and fluid, his jokes cleverer. If you doubt this, check out your own reaction the next time you're talking to a person who seems truly interested in what you have to say. I guarantee that the confidence this gives you will invigorate your fluency and wit. A person who has a fascinated audience becomes, almost magically, more fascinating.

On the other hand, check out your reaction when you have a listener who is bored, distracted, or clearly wants to be elsewhere. You begin to feel uncomfortable and frustrated, your pace slows, you hesitate and lose your train of thought. You can't concentrate on what you're saying because mental energy you might have used to formulate your comments is being redirected to assessing the reactions of your uncooperative listener.

What are some other advantages of good listening? The primary advantage is the strengthening of your relationships, both business and personal. People are inclined to like and trust someone who works hard to comprehend their feelings and ideas. A friend is someone who understands us, and there is no better way to understand a person than to listen to him. A trusted business associate is someone who hears us out and makes an effort to see a problem through our eyes.

Careful listening also solves the great majority of our what-do-I-say-next problems, especially when we try to converse with someone we don't know well. You can always find a subject for discussion by listening to and keying off the other person's comments, but only if you let him speak and you hear what he says. More on this later.

A good listener is less likely to get into trouble by speaking impulsively. How often have you blurted out something disastrous, something that a little more thought and a few more facts would have prevented you from saying? Or, how often have you argued with someone only to eventually discover that the two of you have been in agreement all along? It's easy to hold the same view and argue if neither party pauses long enough to discover what the other is saying. Before long someone does catch on and yells in exasperation, "Hey, that's exactly what I've been saying all along!"

The most angry, impatient, complaining person can be subdued merely by letting him fully vent his position and feelings. Most people who are angry and frustrated simply want to be heard. If you listen with an obvious desire to understand and without interruption until they are absolutely and completely finished, almost any tyrant can then be dealt with on a reasonable level. Too often we instead choose to interrupt and argue, which only drives tempers and blood pressure even higher.

Although this may seem hard to believe, it is just possible that by listening to others, you may actually hear a good insight or a valuable new way of looking at something. And, incredibly, it's even possible that someone could reveal the solution to a problem you've been attempting to solve. One thing is certain, you're less likely to encounter a new idea if you do all the talking.

One other advantage of listening concerns relationships. Many people believe, consciously or unconsciously, that quietly listening while a spouse, girlfriend, or boyfriend expresses needs or emotions is weakness. Because of this, many relationships deteriorate into ongoing verbal competitions rather than the supportive collaborations that were hoped for when the two individuals became a couple.

Listening to another person doesn't mean agreeing or caving in to his or her point of view. It does mean trying to appreciate how a problem or situation looks from that person's standpoint. Whether or not people ultimately agree on a given issue is often less important than the feeling of the parties that they have been heard. Once again, there is great value in being allowed to fully express oneself to someone who is genuinely trying to understand your experience. That value remains even if there is no ultimate meeting of the minds. When we feel we aren't being heard, the result is a resentment that slowly eats away at a relationship.

Now let's get into the nitty-gritty of how to listen. How to listen? What's so complicated about listening? Haven't we done it all our lives? Not really. Many of us mistake literal hearing or being able to repeat back what has been said with true listening. Real listening focuses on understanding, not just words.

As crucial as this skill is to a successful life, none of us ever receive formal training in the fine art of listening. We do receive considerable training in the avoidance of listening. Through hard experience, most of us came to believe early on that conversation is a competitive event in which only the loudest survive. We became like those around us—far more interested in our own thoughts and our own statements than those of others.

Listening takes effort and self-control. If you are ever to truly see the world through another's eyes, you have to beat back the strong natural inclination to focus on yourself. It takes patience to allow someone to explore his thoughts and feelings at his own pace. Usually, we want to hurry things along, jump in with a question, complete sentences, let our attention wander, change the subject, give advice, and most important of all, block the speaker from saying anything that makes us uncomfortable.

Consider this example. Bill goes to a party and runs into an old friend, Jane, whom he hasn't seen for a while.

Bill: Jane, I haven't seen you for over a year. What have you been doing?

Jane: I've been in France. My company transferred me there back in March.

Bill: No kidding. I've always wanted to go to France. What's it like?

Jane: Well, it wasn't easy at first. I don't know French, so I had to—

Bill: Oh, I know, I'm no good at languages either. I had five
            years of Spanish in school, and I couldn't speak it if my
            life depended on it. I remember one class I took, I didn't
            study at all until the last week, and then I tried to cram
            the whole semester into seven days. You can guess how
            that worked out. So the next semester…

Jane never did get the chance to relate her experiences in France,
even though they surely would have made fascinating material for
conversation. If Bill had in fact "always wanted to go to France," he
would have profited by listening, but his compulsion to focus on himself robbed him of the chance to learn something.

Listening is not so much a skill as an attitude. The real trick is to
want to listen and to be eager to help others open up their views. At
first, listening is an effort, later on it becomes a habit. Right now,
however, you're probably in the grip of a listening-evasion habit. It
won't be easy to break, especially since it is so much a part of who
you are. Still, it can be done if you train yourself in the rules of listening and then make an effort to carry them out. In the remaining
section, we will lay out the do's and don'ts of good listening.

Let's look first at the ways, intentional and unintentional, that we
discourage others from talking and revealing.

One result of poor listening is failure to contribute to the maintenance of the conversation. Conversation is a collaborative effort, every
participant has to do his share. Bewildered silence or comments that are
off the topic can kill a conversation. If you have allowed your attention
to wander and have lapsed into a series of automatic uh-huhs and yes's,
you may not be sufficiently tuned in to contribute properly. Poor listening can strangle an otherwise healthy conversation.

Another killer of healthy discussion is the personal filter. Filters are
biases formed throughout our life that cause us to close our mind and
prejudge people or ideas before we have all the facts. When someone
tries to tell us something that violates our personal filters, we ignore,
block, or fail to recognize the importance of the information.

There is a famous tale of the Swiss watch industry that demonstrates
the calamity that can befall a person or group that allows personal filters
to selectively exclude critical information. Roughly twenty-five years
ago, researchers for the Swiss watch industry invented the electronic
quartz-crystal watch. These electronic watches not only cost far less to

manufacture than traditional movement watches with all their tiny wheels and springs but also kept better time.

It seemed like a marvelous breakthrough, but senior watch industry executives were unimpressed. They declared that their customers would never trust a watch with no internal mechanics. For these executives, the tiny wheels and springs defined what a watch was; without them a watch wasn't a watch. And besides, the executives said, if we were to start building quartz-crystal watches, what would we do with all our thousands of craftsmen who painstakingly make all those tiny little parts for movement watches?

As soon as these executives saw the new electronic watches, their personal filters began to block any communication that violated their long held views about what a watch should be.

Incredibly, the Swiss sold the rights to quartz-crystal technology to the Japanese, who were soon selling the cheap, simple, but accurate watches by the millions. Within ten years, the entire Swiss watch industry, famous down through the centuries for its marvelous movement watches, was a shambles. Profits plunged and thousands of watchmakers were laid off. They discovered too late that their customers did not share their definition of what a watch should be. All the average person wanted from his watch was the time; he didn't care one whit about tiny springs and gears. The Swiss executives had deluded themselves and ignored information that could have saved their industry.

On a smaller scale, we all behave as the Swiss watchmakers did. We do it every day. A husband thinks that dwelling on the emotions behind family problems is too uncomfortable. A wife doesn't want to hear the dry facts of the family's situation when, as she sees it, simmering emotions are the problem. A father can't understand where his son gets "all these crazy ideas." A guy ignores his girlfriend's requests to spend more time alone. A businessperson won't listen to a co-worker's idea for a new workflow system. And on and on.

It is always easier to assume that our way is the only way and to filter out any messages to the contrary. Unfortunately, we court disaster when we do so. Failing to look at the world through the eyes of others is at the heart of divorce, short-circuited careers, lost friendships, and a thousand other potholes in the road of life. Only by careful, unbiased listening, can we truly understand other people's experience and respond appropriately.

In addition to ignoring or failing to perceive what others say, we as listeners have many tactics for cutting off messages we don't want to hear. Among these are questions or interruptions that we use to change the course of a conversation. For instance, Jim and Rick are talking about Jim's imminent divorce from his wife of fifteen years. Note how Rick uses questions and interruptions to change the subject every time he senses that Jim is starting to get emotional about losing his wife. As a result, Rick avoids the discomfort and embarrassment of seeing Jim lose control, but Jim never really gets to express himself about the pain of his breakup.

Jim: I suppose we're going to get divorced. I don't really see any way out at this point. The kids aren't doing very well right now, and I'm not much help. God, I'm starting to fall apart. I just don't know what I'm going—

Rick: Hey, hey, Jim, the kids will do fine. They're more resilient than you think. What's going to happen to the house? Will you sell it?

Jim: Ah, man, I don't know. Every time I think about living in an apartment by myself, I just—

Rick: Stop worrying, it'll all work out. You'll meet all kinds of new women in one of those big apartment complexes.

Without really knowing why, Jim may come away from this conversation as lonely and troubled as ever. He will feel that somehow Rick failed him as a friend when he needed help the most.

There are multitudes of other techniques that listeners use to avoid listening to something uncomfortable. Here are some other examples of listener responses that halt open and trusting communication.

A judgmental response tells speakers you have already made up your mind about what they are about to say.

Are we going to talk about that again?
What is it now?
Now what have you done?

Reassurance is a seemingly supportive response that we use to stop speakers from saying more than we want to hear.

Cheer up.

Let's not dwell on all this depressing stuff.

Hey, it's no big deal. Stop worrying about it.

A month from now it'll all be over, and you won't even remember it.

We also tend to jump in with advice when we want to get a speaker off of a troublesome topic.

Waiting by the phone all day won't help. Go out and have some fun.

It's not worth ruining your day over. What's the point of that?

You worry too much. Look at the bright side.

The primary task of a good listener is to stay out of the speaker's way. Try not to use responses that block or redirect the conversation. Give speakers the time and the room they need to explore their thoughts at their own pace. By doing so, you will allow them to clarify their own views as they speak, and they will feel comforted by having had the opportunity to do so. Sometimes this takes a lot of patience. Sometimes things are said that are hard to hear. In the end, though, you'll understand the people around you better, and your relationships will be closer and healthier.

Now that you know what not to do, let's spend some time on what you should do to encourage open expression through good listening.

Good listening is encouraged by a non-distracting environment. When possible, that means finding or creating a quiet place to talk where you won't be disturbed. It means going to a private room, putting down the newspaper, turning off the TV, telling your secretary to hold your calls, and generally stopping whatever it is that you're doing in order to give the speaker your full attention.

Good body language is also part of good listening. It tells speakers that you are receptive and encourages them to open up. The most important element of body language is eye contact. Good eye contact tells speakers you are listening carefully. It says, "Go ahead, I'm with you."

We've all had the experience of speaking to someone whose eyes look over our shoulder or around the room as we speak. We're pretty sure this person isn't enthralled by what we're saying. It's disconcerting. Is he listening or not? Is he bored, thinking, asleep? Who knows? Often we perceive this behavior as a put-down, and it disrupts our thoughts, slows our speech, and sometimes stops us cold.

Of course, eye contact doesn't mean an unbroken stare. That can be disturbing after a while. The acceptable duration for eye contact varies from country to country, but with Americans seven seconds is about right. At that point, look away briefly. If something funny has been said, you can glance away as you laugh. If the conversation is serious, you can briefly stare thoughtfully into the distance. You may feel uncomfortable looking someone directly in the eyes. Many do. If this is the case, it may help to consciously focus on the bridge of the speaker's nose or lower forehead.

Other indicators of attention are a smile (unless funeral arrangements are being discussed) and a posture of leaning slightly forward, both of which communicate interest and anticipation.

Verbal feedback, a periodic uh-huh, yes, really, or no kidding, tells the speaker that you are tuned in. However, don't get carried away. You may have run into people who say yes or uh-huh every second or two. That's overkill, and it's distracting.

Don't appear overeager to please by laughing too much. Don't jump in and complete the speaker's sentences every time he or she pauses to think or take a breath. Also, avoid fidgeting movements that divert the speaker's attention or communicate restlessness such as foot tapping, finger drumming, pencil twirling , teeth picking, whatever. Instead, move in response to the speaker, make your movements harmonious with what is being said. Finally, show enthusiasm. Give the speaker a reaction. Make your interest and curiosity visible. Doing so reassures your conversation partner and also makes you look good. Remember the old saying—To be interesting, you have to be interested.

Sometimes good listening involves more than just passive listening. If one of the goals of giving your full attention is to encourage the speaker to open up, occasionally you have to take a more active role. In essence, you deliver an invitation to the speaker. You throw the doors open and invite him to step through. You do not, on the other hand, seize him by the collar and drag him through.

One method you might use to urge another to talk is to take note of his or her body language, expression, or manner and comment on it.

You don't look too happy today. Anything going on?

You can't seem to sit still. What's up?

You are frowning. Does that mean you don't have a lot of confidence in this plan? What's your opinion?

Resist the urge to convince or coerce others to talk when they are reluctant. Let them reveal or not reveal at their own pace. Pushing people when they aren't ready may result in distrust or concealment.

> Come on, get it off your chest. What's the point in holding it in? Tell me what's going on.

If in the course of a conversation, the speaker seems to falter or hesitate, you can use a number of methods to encourage him to continue. For example, make a statement that assures him that you are interested and want to hear more.

> I'm following you. Go on.
> I never thought of it that way.
> This is interesting. What happened then?
> And then?
> Give me an example.

Another method of moving a speaker forward is to highlight one or two key words from his comments. This urges him to expand on the meaning those words hold.

Jill: I'm not sure whether to take the job or not. It's a big risk.
Jack: Risk?

OR—

Bob: I never knew that having kids would be so stressful.
Susan: What kind of stress worries you most?

Self-disclosure is a great way to draw people out, especially if they are hesitant or embarrassed. Here you attempt to build trust by revealing something personal about yourself or explaining that you have been in a similar situation.

> I guess this is pretty hard to talk about. It would be for me.
> I think you're handling this better than I did. I wasn't as decisive when I went through this with Bill.

There are many other methods that can be used to prompt people to communicate freely (we'll review them in later chapters), but for now, we'll discuss one last technique—silence. While not necessarily true in all cultures, conversational silences are uncomfortable for most Americans. For us, silence is embarrassing. We interpret it as a failure to maintain the flow of talk, and most people will search frantically for something to say whenever a silence lasts more than a few seconds. Frequently, listeners will jump in and fill even the slightest gap in a speaker's comments, even though he may only have paused to organize his thoughts or formulate a sentence.

Most listeners are overly active, asking too many questions and interrupting too often. A speaker may pause, preparing to reveal important information, only to be cut off by some irrelevant, space-filling listener comment. Despite our cultural training to obliterate silences as soon as they occur, we can retrain ourselves not only to tolerate silences but also to use them to nudge speakers to open up. By allowing a silence to persist, we give speakers time to think, feel, and then express more thoughtfully. Additionally, their own discomfort with silence may overwhelm any inclinations they might have to end their disclosures.

One way to become more comfortable with silences is to give yourself something to do when they occur. Mentally review your body posture and expression to make sure they invite further discussion. Uncross your arms, lean forward, and soften your expression. Next, observe the speaker. Try to determine his mood by examining his body language. Think about what he has said, look at the situation from his point of view, and sort out what his feelings are likely to be. In other words, use conversational pauses to analyze what's going on.

If the speaker avoids eye contact during a silence, he is probably formulating his next comment or considering whether to go on (if he looks at the listener, on the other hand, it probably means he has finished and wants a response). Your silence combined with body language that says you expect the speaker to continue is a strong inducement to talk. Try it and you'll find that it opens people up very rapidly.

One word of caution though—don't overuse silence. When it is your turn to contribute, do so. You don't want people to feel they are spilling their guts while you coolly refuse to reveal anything of yourself. After all, conversation is a two-way street.

Let's end by discussing those times when it is particularly crucial to fire up all your listening skills. Here are the top five.

When you meet someone for the first time—Good listening not only improves a new acquaintance's first impression of you but is also your best source of information about who a stranger is and what topics will be of interest.

When you come into contact with a person very different from yourself—Large differences between people, whether due to background, gender, ethnicity, nationality, or some other source, increase the possibility of misunderstanding. The best way to avoid error is careful listening.

Before you argue or criticize—Hear the other person out, put yourself in his shoes, and try to understand why he thinks or behaves as he does. You can often avoid saying something you will regret by listening before speaking.

Whenever the other person is experiencing strong emotions or needs to discuss a problem—Emotions such as anger can be cooled rapidly if the person is allowed to vent his feelings and thoughts fully. Listening with interest and concern is at the heart of friendship. Often, people with problems are not looking for solutions. They are trying to sort out their concerns through the very process of verbalizing their situation. They are also seeking recognition and validation of their feelings and emotions. Interrupting with solutions can be counterproductive

On encountering new, novel, or controversial ideas—It is very easy, as in the case of the Swiss watch executives, to dismiss ideas that don't fit with your preconceptions. Listening carefully does not mean that you must agree with the ideas being espoused; it only means that you will give them a fair hearing. Even if differences prevail, the information you acquire through listening may reveal how the other person arrived at his position (very valuable in negotiation or in planning how best to influence them). Keep your mind open as well as your ears; the cost of prejudging can be very high.

You can't learn who people are if you don't carefully study them, and listening is a key part of that learning process. If social and business success is based on having the best possible understanding of those around us, then listening is critical. How else can we learn to effectively influence others? The next time you are in a conversation, ask yourself the following question over and over—"Why is he/she saying this?" The answers to this question will tell you who that person is.

Chapter 2:
Drawing People Out

In this chapter, the focus is still on the listener's role. In the previous chapter, we concentrated on the more passive aspects of listening—keeping your mouth shut and concentrating on what the speaker is saying. Now we are going to move on to more advanced skills that require you to play an active role in encouraging people to open up. We will discuss three skills that are essential to good communication and relationship building—empathy, disclosure, and reflection.

Empathy

Empathy is the ability to see the world as another person sees it, to mentally stand in his shoes and look out through his eyes. A listener skilled in empathy constantly asks himself, "If I were this person, how would I feel about this?" Empathizing doesn't mean that you agree with the position or feelings of another. It does mean that you will try to understand the foundation of his outlook, the structure beneath the surface.

People respect a person who makes an effort to empathize with them. Empathy requires maturity, a willingness to put yourself aside for a moment and focus on another. When you look at the world through others' eyes, you signal that their views are worth hearing. You show that your purpose is to help and be with them, not to subdue or change them. You earn the respect of others by the respect you show them.

Never assume that others perceive the world as you perceive it. If you do, you are probably headed for divorce court, or a stalled career, or a million other kinds of trouble. To a large degree, empathy is based on constant self-querying designed to suppress the influence of your own outlook.

How will what I am saying or doing make this person feel or react?
How does this person see himself?
What is happening in this person's life right now, and how will it affect him/her?
What are his/her ambitions, hopes, dreams, goals, fears, passions?
What need or fear is this person coming from?
What is she really asking for?

Empathy is one of the key elements of strong friendships and relationships. When you show genuine interest in others, people are more inclined to like and trust you. Everyone has facades or false fronts that they use to protect themselves. Only trust can persuade people to lower those walls and reveal the hidden needs and concerns that make up their real selves.

Also, if you can't empathize with others, the implied lack of respect greatly reduces the likelihood that others will make an effort to understand you. If you aren't interested in them, they won't be interested in you.

The way the people in your life behave has underlying causes. Search out those causes, try to think like they do, and you will greatly advance your ability to make a difference in their lives. For instance, do you want to influence someone to do something? Then ask yourself why he would want to do it. Base your argument or message on your knowledge of his interests and concerns, not yours.

Suppose you work in a large office. You're just one cog in a giant wheel. How do you set yourself apart? How do you make the boss sit up and take notice? Study his needs. Find out what interests him, what worries him, and what priorities influence him. What does the boss's boss demand of him? With the answers to these questions, you can tailor your efforts to relieve the pressure on him. Make his priorities your priorities. When you do this, you will stand out from the crowd.

Here is a more specific example. A manager at a mid-size

manufacturing firm was looking for a new assistant. For over a month, he interviewed dozens of candidates, mostly recent college graduates, but he wasn't satisfied with any of them. Finally, just when he was about to give up, he decided to give one last applicant an interview.

This applicant was different. He asked about the manager's job and concerns whenever he got a chance. He asked about company goals, company methods, and company culture. These weren't idle questions. The young man used the information he obtained to do what none of the other candidates had done—he explained specifically how he would be able to help the manager solve his and the company's problems and concerns.

The young man got the job. Not one of the other applicants had empathized. Instead, they had focused on what the company and the job could do for them. If they did discuss what they could do for the company, they talked in vague generalities. Because they had never taken the time to discover exactly what the company and the manager needed, they dealt in assumptions, assumptions that were usually off target. You can't influence someone if you don't know what his hot buttons are. This young man found those buttons and pressed them.

If your communication with others isn't as productive as you would like, you are probably a poor empathizer. Perhaps you are failing to adapt your approach to others' values, beliefs, likely objections, emotional states, and so on. You are using your language, not theirs, addressing your needs, not theirs.

On a basic level, we all know how to analyze people and adapt what we say to fit. You would not speak to a junior clerk in the same way that you would speak to your superior. You would not talk with your father in the same way you would talk with your best friend. However, to be truly successful, we need to develop and fine-tune our rough empathetic abilities. We want to improve our speed and accuracy in analyzing others.

Successful salespeople are usually skilled in empathy. Ushered into a prospect's office or home, a good salesperson closely studies the surroundings for clues to the personality, interests, and values of his potential client. He quickly gathers additional impressions when interacting face to face and then formulates a selling message designed to fit that person's needs and personality.

If the prospect seems to be a practical individual, the salesperson makes a presentation that emphasizes facts. If the prospect seems to be driven more by his emotions, the salesperson's presentation stresses the human side. He modifies his tone and facial expressions in the same way. This contrasts with the mediocre salesperson who uses a nearly identical presentation with all comers and can't understand why he isn't more successful.

Please note that adapting your message to fit others' requirements doesn't mean deceiving people, nor does it mean ignoring your own needs. Certainly, one could use the insights derived from empathy to unfairly manipulate others. It's also true that people who are skillful in discovering the needs of others could ignore their own needs in an unhealthy effort to be all things to all people. Generally, however, there is no substitute for empathy. We can't interact effectively with others unless we maximize our ability to see the world as they see it and speak in a language they can understand.

It is all too easy for us to deny others' feelings and to belittle their problems. It is all too easy to draw quick conclusions and stereotypes, usually negative. As the other person speaks, we quickly find ourselves thinking (usually incorrectly), "Oh boy, I can read this person like a book." While these thoughts may occur internally, they show up externally in the expression, tone, and words that we choose to respond. Feeling the heat, the other party then clams up, gets angry, starts to argue, or goes away feeling resentful and belittled.

Since we rarely consider the feelings and ideas of others to be as important as our own, we rarely make a real effort to truly understand them. And understanding does take effort, real effort. Most speech is laced with hidden meaning, evasion, and incomplete messages that beg for a complete telling to a trusted, empathetic listener. More often than not, however, we listeners never notice the signs, never detect the clues, never follow the trails to their conclusion.

In addition, studies have shown that 70% of communication's meaning is non-verbal. Expression and body language are particularly effective in revealing underlying emotions, far more indicative than speech, and yet most of us rely excessively on speech to determine the feelings of others. Why? Because paying close attention to non-verbal messages requires a level of alertness we aren't willing to maintain. As a result, we may readily accept a statement that someone is "fine" even though his shoulders are stooped and his eyes dull.

Empathy is also the out and out best way to find good topics of conversation with a stranger. Suppose you meet someone at a party, and he tells you he just moved to Arizona after living all his life in upstate New York. From this one statement, empathetic thinking can give you enough topics to keep the conversation going for a month.

Asking yourself how this person must feel to experience such a major change in his life leads to all sorts of topics and questions. What is it like to leave all your friends and family behind? Do you miss all the trees and hills of New York? Do you find Arizona's hot, dry air hard to handle? What made you decide to take on such an upheaval in your life? What do you like most about Arizona? Least? And so on.

Empathy also allows you to respond appropriately to another's problem or situation. If a friend tells you that she just got a promotion, and you put yourself in her shoes, you automatically know the reaction she's hoping for. Even the most careless empathizing tells you that you would feel happy if you were promoted.

But, deeper empathy would point out the less obvious notion that you would also want people to reflect your excitement enthusiastically. If you respond to the promotion news with a bland "Oh, really" and a few perfunctory comments like, "I guess you won't have to worry so much about your bills," you've missed the empathetic point. This person probably wants a hearty, spirited response to her momentous development.

The emotional tone of your reaction needs to match her emotional state if she is to feel heard and appreciated. She wants to hear you laugh and yell, "WOW! That's terrific, congratulations!" and then excitedly ask for all the details of the story. This is a response that tells her you feel the joy she feels. We all want that. We all want others to understand our experience. A general rule of thumb is that your reaction should be based on what you would want to hear in a similar situation (although this might not always be accurate).

Careful listening combined with empathetic responses calms an emotionally upset humanoid better than any other known method. The next time you witness someone confronted by an angry boss, customer, or parent, watch what happens to the angry party when the target of his rage offers excuses, tries to explain, or, God forbid, decides to argue. All of these miserable efforts at self-defense have the opposite of their intended effect—they feed rather than extinguish the fires of anger. Only listening and empathy truly quell anger and absorb tension.

When people are angry, they are almost incapable of rationally listening to you. All they can do is talk (or yell) and vent. The only effective response (starting a fight is not effective) is to let them talk, without interruption, until they are absolutely out of gas, nothing more to say. Then you empathize, giving them respect by demonstrating that you do understand their position and complaint (this doesn't mean you agree with them). Only after this do you give your own point of view, because only now is the person calm enough to again listen to reason. We'll go into this in greater detail later on.

Here is another benefit of empathy. Suppose you observe someone doing something that seems foolish and ill considered. How often have you said to yourself, "What's wrong with him? I can't believe he did that?" More often than not there are hidden but logical causes and reasons for the undesirable behavior. To zero in on underlying causes, ask yourself how this person might benefit from such seemingly unwise behavior. Ask what fears, needs, or past experiences might motivate his failings and frailties.

Understanding root causes smoothes the interaction between people. Once you understand the cause of a behavior, you probably won't find it as irritating or senseless as you did when the reasons were a mystery. For example, suppose you know someone who never misses a chance to put herself down. You may find this annoying because she is actually quite smart and capable. However, when you discover that as a child this person's parents constantly told her that she was worthless and stupid, it is likely that you would be more understanding of her disfunctional attitude.

An empathetic listener stays alert to more than just the words of a speaker. Humans are very complicated and sophisticated communicators, and that obliges us to be broadly discerning listeners if we are to get the whole message. Speech is full to the brim with misleading, indirect, and hidden messages. It is critical to listen and watch for meaning and feeling, not just explicit words.

You can also empathize when you are the speaker. If you pay attention, you can assess your listener's reaction to you from his expression and body language. Is he smiling, frowning, uncomfortable, bewildered?

Is he nervously unable to maintain eye contact? Is he tapping his foot impatiently? Is he leaning toward you or away? As you gather impressions, you can alter your course, stop to answer questions or get reactions, rephrase your words, and so on. If you don't pay attention, you may never realize that your message is in trouble.

Most of us are far too literal. We blithely ignore subtleties, those communications that are implied, hinted, or revealed by body language and expression. We are impatient, dying to cut to the chase, even though serious communication often happens slowly or it doesn't happen at all.

Lack of awareness can be ruinous, but how do you sharpen your empathetic and observational skills? The first step is to make a commitment to do it. Whenever you enter into a conversation with anyone, your first thought should be to command yourself to pay attention, listen for meaning, and search for the feelings and motivations behind the facts.

Most of us never hone our observational skills because we never make an effort to practice them. Studies have shown that almost any new behavior repeated twenty-one times or more will become a habit. In other words, we are what we do. So, commit yourself to practice your listening and empathizing skills for the next twenty-one days. Once they become habitual, you'll find them increasingly automatic.

While practice may never quite make perfect, it will definitely move you a long way in the right direction. In time, you will develop that most marvelous of all human skills—gut instinct. There is wisdom in experience. With enough practice and effort, you'll find yourself sizing people up far more quickly and accurately. Your intuitive abilities will hone your empathetic smartness to an edge you never would have thought possible.

To increase the pace of your development, seek out opportunities for communication and serious discussion. Increase your exposure to a broad variety of people. You can't practice listening, empathy, and understanding any other way. Before long, you'll find that your ability to interpret the real concerns beneath people's indirect words is wonderfully improved.

But what do you do if despite careful listening and empathizing, a speaker remains wary and evasive? Sometimes a listener has to do more than just listen; he must take an active role in order to induce a conversational partner to trust and open up. The two techniques discussed next, reflection and disclosure, are the most potent tools available for encouraging speakers to clarify and expand their thoughts.

Disclosure

Providing your share of feedback and general fuel for discussion is a basic law of conversational fair play. Disclosure, however, goes beyond merely contributing conversational fodder when it's your turn to speak. True disclosure is about trust. If your partner pours his or her heart out, and you refuse to communicate on the same personal level, a trust problem arises. Openness requires that both parties in a discussion be willing to take some risk and reveal who they are.

Whenever you find yourself in a discussion with people who are reserved, you can use self-disclosure to pave the way for them to open up and let down their defenses. Disclosure begets disclosure, revelation begets revelation. It's only fair. By disclosing something about who you are, you tell others that you trust them. If you are willing to make a personal disclosure, others will not only feel safer doing the same but will also feel some degree of obligation to return the compliment.

So, what constitutes meaningful self-disclosure? Disclosures can range from small and lighthearted revelations all the way up a continuum to the deepest and most personal secrets. At the most basic level, they are simple personal facts, the kind you reveal to a stranger at a party, such as what you do, where you're from, hobbies, personal projects, background, your last vacation.

The next level of disclosure would be your personal opinions and preferences, your attitudes about the world. You might say that you believe Fords are better than Chevys, that you like women who are tall and brunet, or that you prefer an outside sales job to working in an office.

And finally, on the most intimate level, you reveal your feelings—your discomfort when your husband talks too long to other women, your love for someone, your anger and envy about a co-worker's promotion. Such disclosures of feelings are the most difficult to make, and the most likely to be spoken of indirectly or kept secret.

Disclosures revolve around your hopes, dreams, sorrows, loves, fears, and needs. They reveal your goals and struggles and give the people you meet something to identify with. They help others to empathize with you and find common ground. Disclosures let people know what is important to you, what excites you, and what you think about. After a disclosure, your conversation partner might suddenly exclaim, "Wow, I love soccer too!" or "Hey, I agree, Seinfeld was the funniest show ever." This is the jumping off point for a truly successful conversation

As with listening and empathy, disclosure is another important element in relationship building. Without self-revelation, relationships are bound to be shallow and weak. Disclosure establishes your humanity and approachability. Openness and a willingness to risk some vulnerability encourages trust, which encourages others to feel the same.

Unwillingness to disclose anything but the most mundane facts, on the other hand, tells people just the opposite. They may assume that you don't trust them, that you don't like them, or that you have something to hide. Secrecy reduces your opportunities for finding common ground with others and for dealing honestly with problems. Your family and business relationships will be less stable and more superficial. If you worry that people might use personal information against you, being reserved and private may feel safer, but in the long run the cost in stunted relationships is horrendous.

Disclosure doesn't mean that you reveal your deepest secrets and needs to your boss or someone you run into at a weekend party. It just means that you reveal enough info to give them a good picture of who you are and where you stand. Generally speaking, most of us think our secrets are more important than they really are. There are always going to be things best kept under wraps, but don't be paranoid about it. Give people the information they need to feed the kind of relationships you want with them.

There are a few guidelines to keep in mind when disclosing. In the normal give and take of light conversation, your main goal is to keep the discussion entertaining. Disclosures should generally be positive, not too heavy. And, don't get carried away, hogging the floor, telling your life story in minute detail. Keep it brief, and then give the other person a turn.

Also, avoid using disclosure to keep yourself in the spotlight. Some people can take any subject, no matter what it is, and bring it back to themselves.

Tina: Did you hear that there have been a couple robberies in

Bill: the neighborhood recently?

Bill: Yes, say, that reminds me, did I ever tell you about the time I was robbed back when I was in college? Well, I had gone to class and...

The topic here is local crime, but Bill brushes past that in order to hog the floor with some ancient personal tale about crime at his out-of-state college. This is disclosure out of control.

Be yourself. Don't skew your stories to exaggerate your good qualities while hiding your faults. Most people have finely tuned hog-wash detectors and will quickly brand you a phony. On the other hand, don't be overly afraid of boring others. There's no advantage in assuming that others don't want to hear what you have to say. You don't have to leave them awed or in stitches with every comment, that's not expected of you. Most conversation is pretty ordinary, and people are just glad to keep it going without any awkward silences. Share your life and get reactions, that's the point.

If your goal is to persuade someone to discuss an issue fully or be more revealing, disclosure is a great tool. You can use your own dis-closures to draw the other party out, encouraging that person to give you the fullest possible picture of his or her situation. In a case like this, you want to make sure that your disclosures don't change the subject or take over the conversation. They should be designed to make the other person feel more comfortable about revealing deeper thoughts or emotions. As such, it is critical to be brief and keep the focus on the other person.

Bill: You know, I'm really at a loss. I think Susan is the perfect girl for me, but I'm just not sure I'm ready for marriage yet.

Jake: I had the same problem once, but with me it was different because I wasn't sure Melinda was the right girl. Now that really puts the pressure on you. So, here's how I decided what to do. I spent a whole weekend...

Here Jake has shifted the conversation away from Bill's dilemma by veering off into a story he's probably told a million times, a story which will shed little light on Bill's problem. Below is a response that will open the door for Bill to discuss his situation.

Jake: I had the same trouble when I was trying to decide whether to marry Melinda. It's rough because your whole future is at stake, and it's hard to sort out how you really feel.

Bill: That's exactly it! I feel like I won't know if I've made the right decision until after I've made it.

This is much better. Jake's disclosure keeps the focus on Bill and serves to encourage him to dig deeper into his problem. This is how disclosure is supposed to work.

One way to supercharge your disclosures is to reveal how you felt in a given situation, as opposed to stressing what happened. Emphasizing feelings is more intimate and will therefore encourage a more intimate response from others. Here's a response that emphasizes facts versus feelings.

Jane: My boss is driving me crazy. She's so hard to please. It's so bad I'm thinking of looking for a new job.

Tanya: Oh, you think you've got it bad, my boss is the ultimate nut case. What a perfectionist! I have to do everything twice, and he's always looking over my shoulder. Last week, I had to re-copy a bunch of letters because of one missing comma.

In her response, Tanya concentrates on facts in her disclosure and implies that Jane's problem is no big deal compared to her own. None of this will make Jane feel comfortable about revealing her deeper concerns, such as her fears about looking for a new job. Below is a better response.

Tanya: Oh, that is terrible. I've been there myself. I've had bosses that made me feel worthless. I tried my best, but I always went home convinced I'd failed. It really got me down.

This response centers on how Tanya felt in a similar situation. It doesn't diminish Jane's problem, and it stays away from specific facts. This kind of response paves the way for Jane to discuss her problems more deeply.

Disclosure is a powerful method for building trust and convincing others that it's safe to reveal their intimate feelings and the underlying causes of their behavior. And, it is effective regardless of whether your conversational partner is a good friend or a stranger you met five minutes ago.

Reflection

Generally speaking, most of us don't like to be interrupted. We assume, and usually we are correct, that listeners interrupt because they aren't that interested in what we're saying. But there are interruptions that don't offend. These are ones that are intended to clarify what we've said. A listener is calling for a quick time-out to make sure he understands our meaning. The most common tool for clarifying is the question, but there is another tool that can be even more productive—reflection.

Few of us would be offended if a listener interrupted to say, "Let me make sure I understand what you've said." We want to get our message across, so we don't mind listeners stopping us to confirm our meaning. More often than not the listener follows up with questions, requests for facts or clarification. Questions can quickly seem like an inquisition to a speaker, and all too often the questions focus on what the listener is interested in, not the speaker's interest. In short, listeners frequently use questions to interrupt and redirect the conversation.

Reflection differs from questioning. In a reflective response, the listener restates the speaker's comments, both the facts and the feelings behind them, in his own words. He does this in a nonjudgmental and open manner that encourages the speaker to confirm or correct the reflection and then expand further. A conversational reflection has the meaning we normally associate with the word reflection—the listener mirrors back the speaker's meaning (although not his exact words).

Let's suppose, for example, that John is discussing a relationship problem with his girlfriend Linda. Linda has just stated a number of things that John has done that bother her. John has lots of options for responding. He can deny, argue, question, explain, walk out, etc. The problem with these tactics is that none of them make it clear to Linda that he has made an effort to understand her point of view. When a listener shows respect by putting aside his own concerns until he understands exactly what the speaker is saying, the effect is marvelously positive.

Assume that instead of arguing or denying or putting her off, John says, "Linda, let me make sure I understand you. You feel that I'm undependable because I'm often late when I pick you up from work." His tone is not sarcastic or condemning, he's just giving her an honest interpretation of what he thinks she has said.

How is Linda likely to respond? John has listened, made an effort to understand, remained calm, and treated her concerns with respect. All this remains true even if his reflection of her comments is incorrect. Linda can't help but be somewhat soothed by a response like this. There is a good chance that an argument will be avoided and that John and Linda will have a constructive discussion of their problems.

When you reflect someone's message fairly and non-judgmentally, it evokes a fair-play response from that person. People will treat you the way you treat them. If you argue and yell, they will argue and yell. Respect them and usually they will respect you. If they are very angry, they may not settle down immediately, but if you keep reflecting, showing concern, and playing fair, eventually most people will return that consideration. And, fair-minded reflection works with anyone—parents, kids, spouses, lovers, bosses, friends, irate customers, and that guy whose car you just backed into.

When you reflect someone's comments, you can reflect the facts of his message, the feelings of his message, or the overall meaning of his message (both facts and feelings).

If your boss has described a project he wants you to do, you'll probably reflect in a way that emphasizes facts. "Let me make sure I have this straight. You want me to call these ten clients, get their response to our new product, and give you a written report of their reactions by Wednesday. Correct?" In this situation, facts are critical, and feelings are relatively unimportant.

However, if your boss comes to you and says he's unhappy with the way you're doing your job, both facts and feelings may come into play. Both should be addressed in your reflection. "Let's make sure we're on the same track. You're worried that I'm spending too much time in the field, and you're angry that my absence overloads Fred here in the office."

Now the boss can discuss or correct your understanding of both the facts and the feelings of the situation. He might say, "Well, no, I wouldn't say I'm angry. I know your field work is important, but I am concerned that Fred is getting in over his head and needs more help from you." Now you have a better take on the boss's perception of the situation. And, you have avoided a misunderstanding of his feelings (he's not as upset as you initially thought).

Sometimes you may want to reflect feelings only, especially if feelings, and not facts, seem to be the heart of the matter.

Jane: I have four years of college, and I'm basically nothing more than a glorified clerk.

John: You're disappointed with your career progress.

Jane: Well, yes. I thought I'd be a lot further along by now. My sister has a great job, and she's younger than I am.

John: It feels like you're being left behind.

Jane: Right, and I hate to admit it, but I'm envious too.

All too often we ignore people's feelings, rushing past them to ask for more facts or to offer solutions. The problem is that people often bring up their problems not because they want advice but because they just want to talk and have someone listen. They want a little recognition that their troubles are upsetting and difficult to handle. Reflecting feelings, as John does above, is far more appropriate than giving Jane well-meaning advice. Jane is feeling small and unimportant right now, and John's empathetic reflection of her feelings tells her that she matters. At this moment, that is what she needs.

Let's look at some guidelines for reflecting.

Try to keep your reflections brief, stating the essence of another's message as concisely as possible. Stick with the essentials, the core issues. The main point of reflection is to show the speaker that you are listening and trying to understand. Accomplish this as quickly as possible and then promptly return the floor to the speaker. Don't launch into a long speech that derails the speaker's train of thought, or worse, takes over the conversation.

Don't just parrot the speaker. Reflection is not just repeating back the other person's exact words. Look for his meaning, his feelings, and then sum it up for him. Remember—your words, his meaning.

A typical structure for a reflective statement is as follows.

You are feeling (*emotion*) because (*reason*). Is this true?

For example—"You are feeling angry because you think I purposely ignored you. Is this true?" The formula's wording can be varied as long as the basics remain. "You believe I spent too much time talking to that blond at the party, and now you feel hurt, right?"

This formula is especially effective when something unsaid or unclear is bothering someone and you want to get everything out in the open. It states both the cause (the "reason") and the effect (the "emotion"). Nothing is left vague or hidden. The other party can agree with you or correct you. "Well no, I wasn't hurt. I was just bored because I didn't have anyone to talk to." After reflecting your impressions, you will very often find that the other person was not feeling or thinking what you had imagined. Now you can deal with the actual feeling or problem, not the assumed one.

As listeners, we are oftentimes oblivious to the emotional dimension of others' comments. Instead, we focus our listening on facts and ask questions as if we were newspaper reporters—who, what, when, where, and why. Often it is emotions that are the heart of the speaker's message, but we never realize it.

If a friend tells you that she never would have guessed she'd be as old as she is without ever marrying, a reflection focusing on feelings might go like this. "And that has you worried," or "You sound discouraged," or "You'd like to be married and you're confused about why it isn't happening." Commonly, however, we never progress beyond fact seeking. "Are you dating anyone now?" or "What happened to John?" or "Have you ever called one of those dating services?" We also like to reassure or advise. "Hey, you're lucky. Marriage is a pain, take it from me," or "Listen, you're too shy. You've got to get out there and meet more people."

Even when a speaker tells us nothing but facts, it's still wise to listen for the likely feelings that underlie those facts and then reflect your best guess.

Rick: I'm planning on taking some night classes. They'll help me get ahead at work, but, of course, I won't be able to spend as much time with my girlfriend.

Bill: You sound like you're afraid of what that might do to your relationship.

If Rick is torn between his desire to advance at work and his fears about shortchanging his girlfriend, Bill's response will probably get him talking.

Always make an extra effort to focus on feelings in your interactions with others. You need to perceive people's emotional reactions in order to fully understand their situations and have deeper relationships. Reading emotions accurately is a skill that takes practice to develop. Our culture has trained us to avoid feelings, and doing otherwise doesn't come naturally.

To begin with, focus on the feeling words in the comments of others, words like angry, depressed, afraid, love, proud, nervous, guilty, ignored, jealous, pressured, scared, stunned, happy, worried, and so on.

Also, watch their body language signals. Body language is usually a better communicator of feelings than words, which are often vague or purposely misleading ("I'm okay, it's nothing.").

Next, ask yourself how you would feel in a similar situation. This is a great clue to the reactions of others, but it's not always as accurate as you might think. People all have different backgrounds and personalities, and they react differently to similar situations. There are also likely to be influences and concerns unknown to you that can make people respond in unpredictable ways.

Teach yourself to analyze emotions and facts separately. Then put the two together in your reflective statement—"You feel (emotion) because (facts)."

> You feel used because I don't help with the housecleaning.
> You are relieved that I got the tickets early.
> You're angry because I made the decision without discussing it with you.

Try to use the most accurate and specific words possible to describe the person's emotional state. Most of us have a very limited vocabulary of feeling words. We rely on a handful of words with broad, general meanings and use them for almost all occasions, words such as *upset, depressed, worried, angry, excited,* and *happy.* To make these generic words more potent, we may tack on a *very, really,* or *extremely* when the emotion is greater than normal. Sometimes we even substitute non-feeling words for feeling words—"My life is really *busy* right now," or "Work is a real *challenge* these days."

Always try to use the most accurate words possible, the most descriptive words. For example, instead of saying, "You are upset," try to define the feeling more precisely. Is the person annoyed, blue, crushed, despairing, exasperated, infuriated, melancholy, pressured, heartbroken, shocked, or tense? The more accurate the word the greater its impact.

Sometimes you may think you are using reflection when you are not. Suppose you say, "I know how you feel." Is that a reflection? No, it is not. Simply saying that you know how someone feels doesn't make it so. Most people will doubt that you really do. Worse, they may believe that you are just giving them a habitual conversational response that has little real meaning.

Don't tell someone that you understand, prove it. Suppose someone relates a story about his troubles at work, and you respond with this reflection—"This situation sounds very tricky. You must be frustrated and worried." The person now knows that you understand because you described the nature of his problem and feelings correctly. Or, he knows that you missed the point and can correct you. Either way, he is convinced that you are interested and attempting to understand.

There is a temptation when reflecting to put words into the other person's mouth. Don't do it. Reflection is not telling others what they ought to have said or what you think of their situation. Your goal is to rephrase with as little distortion as possible the person's actual meaning, and to do it in a tone that is nonjudgmental. The purpose of reflection is to encourage others to speak freely. If your reflection reveals your opinion in tone or in content, this is hardly likely. Remember, when you reflect, you form a hypothesis about the other person's meaning and then test it's accuracy by verbalizing it and allowing the other party to confirm or deny.

Consider your assumptions and biases before you reflect. It's easy to unknowingly distort someone's message in a reflection that you believe is neutral. For instance, suppose you have a female friend, Elaine, who has a husband that you don't like or trust.

Elaine: Roger just doesn't spend a lot of time with me these days. Last night he came home at 11:00. Sometimes it's kind of difficult.

You: So, you think he's having an affair.

Elaine: What! No, no, he's just so busy with work right now. No, he'd never have an affair.

Because you don't trust Roger, you assumed that if he was out late, he was having an affair. He may be, but that's not reflection, and this assumption shuts down honest communication. From here on, everything Elaine says will be designed to prove that your conclusion was wrong. A true reflection would have gone as follows.

You: You're getting pretty lonely because you're spending so much time by yourself.

Now, if Elaine has any doubts about Roger's fidelity, she will be more likely to bring them up on her own.

Another reason that reflection is such a valuable conversational tool is that it often helps a speaker sort out his problems and move toward his own solution. You can promote this benefit if you actively urge the speaker to avoid fuzzy generalities and instead push him to describe his situation more specifically. For example, if someone says, "I'm not too pleased with the way things are going at work these days," he is being too vague for any productive discussion of the root causes of his unhappiness.

To understand or resolve their problems, people have to identify specific experiences, behaviors, and feelings. One way to encourage this is to begin by asking a few probing questions, such as "How did you feel? or "Can you give me an example?" This will bring out more specifics that allow you to reflect accurately.

In the example above, you might seek more information in this fashion—"In what way is work not going well? Give me an example." The response might be—"Well, the boss doesn't seem to want my opinion. I've been there the longest, but he keeps me out of the loop." Now you can reflect in a way that will bring out a more detailed discussion of experiences and feelings. "You're discouraged because the boss ignores your experience and instead goes to others who are less qualified." This kind of reflection cites an emotion, discouragement, and brings out into the open the implication that the boss takes counsel from others rather than the speaker. More than likely, this will cause the speaker to expand in more specific terms.

By continually urging others to be specific and concrete, you will lead them down a path of self-discovery and problem solving that they might never have taken on their own. They may not even be aware of what you are doing, but they will know intuitively that you have helped them find their way, and this will deepen your relationship.

Another method that can be used to induce people to reveal what's on their mind is to call attention to discrepancies between what their words say and what their actions, expressions, or body language say. The general formula for this is as follows—

You say/feel X, but you act/appear/do Y.

Kate: (slumped posture, sighs) I'm really very excited about my promotion and transfer to San Francisco.

Larry: You say you're excited, but you appear depressed.

If Kate has a problem and any desire at all to discuss it, this comment may very well get her talking. Larry has pointed out that her real feelings are showing through in her behavior. She now realizes that her cover is blown and further concealment is useless. She might as well disclose her reservations about her promotion and transfer.

One caution about this technique—it is generally best used with those who know and trust you. There is an element of confrontation here—you are telling people that their charade has failed and that you know they are hiding their true feelings. If you try this with someone you don't know very well, that person might resent your intrusion.

When reflecting, watch not only what you say but also how you say it. The kind of reflection that gets people to open up is firm, confident, and most of all, neutral. Always avoid telegraphing your opinion via tone or expression. You may feel judgmental, and you may be dying to jump in and straighten this person out, but resist the urge.

The more that people feel they are being evaluated or judged, the more false and self-protective they become. Regardless of whether you communicate it by word, tone, expression, or body language, a judgmental reflection is perceived as an attack, immediately throwing the other party into a defensive or counter-attack mode. His mental energy becomes focused on proving that you are wrong and he is right. All open discussion of true thoughts and feelings is abandoned. In fact, at this point the two of you are probably in the first stages of an argument.

Everything about your reflection should tell the other party that you will accept a wide range of answers, not just one. Your manner when reflecting should say that you don't regard your interpretation as the only reasonable one. You want to make it easy for the other person to say, "No, that's not what I meant." If you come across to others as faultfinding, superior, rigid, or all-knowing, you can hardly expect honesty.

Once you become skilled at reflection, you'll be amazed at how well it works. But why does it work? Words are imprecise tools for describing our experience. We often misunderstand what others tell us. Reflection allows us to check our understanding with the speaker and be confirmed or corrected.

Beyond the natural limitations of words, people are often reluctant initially to accurately express their true feelings or thoughts. The surface problem may not be the real problem. A part of us wants to hide rather than reveal. So, we are vague, indirect, and even downright secretive. This forces listeners to guess what is meant, to read between the lines, and frequently those guesses are wrong. Commonly, when we misinterpret, and don't reflect, neither side realizes there has been a misunderstanding.

The person you are speaking to may be influenced by strong emotion and not be aware of it. Reflection can help identify emotions and bring them out into the open—"To me, it seems you're saying that you are jealous of the amount of time he spends with his mother." By identifying the emotion, it can be discussed and dealt with.

Reflection can also solve another common communication problem—people often believe they have verbalized something when in fact they only thought about it. We've all done this. We're so aware of a particular fact or idea that although we never actually discussed it, we're sure we did.

For instance, Mary tells her secretary, Diane, that she has an important meeting at 3:30 and asks her to make sure that "the necessary files" are ready. Diane agrees. At 3:25, she hands Mary the materials, and suddenly Mary asks anxiously, "Where are the Fulton files?" Diane replies that the files aren't ready yet, and that she hadn't been aware that they were relevant to the upcoming meeting. Mary says, "I specifically told you I needed the Fulton files. Why aren't they ready?" Diane knows that Mary said no such thing but can't prove it. The result is hard feelings all around.

This disaster could have been avoided if Diane had specifically reflected Mary's initial request to have "all the necessary files ready." She might have said, "Okay, you want me to have the Smith and Jones files ready by 3:30. Is that all?" At which time Mary would have said, "No, I also want the Fulton files." Reflection is a great tool for avoiding situations in which one party says, "You never said that," and the other party says, "Oh, yes I did!"

As listeners, we all have biases that get in the way of accurate understanding. We have expectations that influence what we believe someone is saying. For example, a wife tells her husband about the beautiful new car the neighbors just bought. The husband, whose business is doing poorly, may get angry because he interprets her comment to mean that she is unhappy with the old cars they own. The wife, whose intention was only to pass on some neighborhood news, is surprised and irritated by her husband's attack and quickly retaliates—"Well, since you bring it up, our cars are wrecks. You'd think it'd kill you to own something nice for a change." Now the battle is on, and all because of a miscommunication.

If the husband had recognized that his emotional filters might be influencing what he was hearing and checked his wife's meaning with a reflection, the trouble could have been avoided.

Husband: You're dissatisfied because our cars are so old.

Wife: Oh, no, we need to save our money right now. We'll be able to afford a new car in the future when thing pick up.

Although reflection primarily serves to check accuracy and draw people out, it also works well as a memory aid. Reflection by a listener etches the message on his or her mind. If you listen carefully enough to reflect and then make the effort to paraphrase the speaker's message, it is unlikely that you'll forget anything that's been said.

There's no reason to reflect all the time. Reflection takes effort, and most of the time it's unnecessary. If someone says, "I'm going out to get a burger," there's no need to answer with a reflection—"You are saying that you feel hungry and need to purchase a burger to relieve that hunger." Reflection is best used when the issues are important, when there might be a misunderstanding, or when you want to draw someone out.

Here are some instances when reflection is particularly important. Reflect what a speaker has said—

- Before you take a significant action in business. Confirm your understanding of what others expect.

- Before you argue or criticize. Make sure you fully under stand the other's position and logic.

- When there are strong feelings or the need to share emotions.

- When the speaker wants to sort out his thoughts and is not looking for advice.

- When you are exposed to new or strange ideas. Make sure you fully comprehend an idea and empathize with the person espousing it before you criticize or dismiss. Reflection will help you do this.

You can also request a reflection from a listener. If you are not certain that someone has understood you, or if you think it's important to get feedback, you can ask the person to reflect what you've said. Asking for a reflection can be more respectful than asking a question, such as "Do you understand what I said?" When questioned like this, people might feel you're suggesting they aren't too smart. Naturally, they'll usually claim they understand whether they do or not. Requesting a reflection can be easier on the ego, especially if you put the onus for any misunderstanding on yourself—"Just to make sure I've been clear, would you please describe your understanding of my position?"

By the way, remember that the example phrases in this book, such as the one in the previous paragraph, are just general guides used to illustrate the basics of a concept. You may read some of them and think, "I can't talk that way. It's too formal, too unnatural. People will think I'm weird." Keep in mind that these formula phrases are for explanatory purposes and do sometimes sound unnatural. Feel free to alter their wording to fit your style of speaking if you can do so without damaging their effectiveness.

Also understand that these example phrases will initially be new and strange to you. With practice, you can learn to say them in a tone and modulation that sounds as normal as the rest of your speech. However, the main benefit of these techniques is better communication, more potent persuasiveness, and stronger relationships. These are things that are worth the effort of learning some new conversational tools.

Chapter 3:
Questioning

Asking questions is something we all think we know how to do. Generally, though, most people use this conversational technique poorly and excessively. Our questions are too frequent and very often inappropriate. More importantly, we become so dependent on questioning that we fail to develop other information-gathering skills such as listening, silence, reflection, disclosure, and simple statements.

Some people are addicted to questions. They are unrelenting in their probing, digging, and querying. The interrogation continues until the other party's defenses go up and the conversation degenerates into trivialities. Unfortunately, defensiveness only makes these questioners even more determined, and they redouble their prying ways until all hope of communication is dead.

Skilled questioning is a lost art in our culture. When our questions focus on our own needs rather than the needs of the speaker, they become a barrier to communication rather than a door. Most of our questions are constructed to yield information important only to us, thereby distracting speakers from their message. Or, they may also be used to deflect speakers' comments in directions we prefer rather than allowing them to explore their thoughts in their own way.

For example, six months ago Jim bought an expensive sports car that has proved to be harder for him to afford than he originally thought. He tries to discuss his thoughts about selling the car with Mike, but Mike doesn't seem to hear Jim's concerns about money. Mike's only interest is fantasizing about the joys of owning such a car, and his questions tend to sidetrack any discussion of the practical side of ownership—

Jim, how many girls have you dated since you got this machine?
Have you ever run this baby through the quarter mile?
What's the horsepower?

Mike isn't tuned in to Jim's financial concerns, and his questions direct the conversation to topics he wants to discuss. For Jim, the whole discussion becomes a waste of time, and he soon ends it by saying he has to leave for an appointment.

We may also use questions to divert a conversation from uncomfortable subject matter. If a speaker begins to talk emotionally about the pain of a divorce, the listener may become uneasy and begin asking questions that lead the talk onto safer ground—"So, are you going to stay in your house or move to a smaller one?" This gets the speaker talking about houses, moving hassles, driving distance to work, and other subjects that aren't as difficult as loneliness and heartbreak. The question has more to do with the listener's needs and fears than those of the speaker.

In many instances, questions aren't requests for information at all but a means of attacking or manipulating another. For example, when a mother says to a teenager, "Have you cleaned your room like I asked you to four hours ago?" she clearly knows the room hasn't been cleaned. This is no simple request for a status report on the cleanliness of the teenager's room—it is an accusation. The teenager knows he is being attacked and will respond accordingly. An honest discussion of the reasons for the room not being cleaned will never occur.

Questions are often used as a veiled attempt at manipulation or as an indirect means of giving someone your opinion. They become a devious substitute for more direct methods of communication. A father who says to his teenage daughter, "Are you still wasting time with that Smith kid?" is unlikely to receive any real information or have any real influence. He would be more effective if he were straightforward. "Honey, I'm worried about your relationship with Jason Smith. Tell me about him." This approach is honest, non-sarcastic, clearly not an attempt at manipulation, and communicates the father's genuine concern. The daughter will hear concern, not control, and answer less defensively.

Don't use questions to mask your real concerns. Others will react more honestly if you express those concerns directly instead of sneaking around asking questions full of innuendo and judgment. If your question is more than a simple request for information, phrase it as a statement. Put the real issues out in the open.

Ask one question at a time. Don't combine multiple queries into one utterance. Multiple questions sound like an inquisition and have a tendency to make people clam up or answer selectively. From an efficiency standpoint, people will usually forget the other questions by the time they finish answering the first one. They will stop and say, "Now what else did you ask me?" This disrupts the flow of the conversation, especially since the questioner has probably forgotten his other questions as well.

Another problem with multiple questions is that they are often not questions at all. They become speechifying statements of opinion, a backdoor attempt to take over a conversation. You often hear lawyers and politicians use this technique.

> Tell me, Mr. Jones, if you cared about your wife, why did you ignore her? Why would you spend so much time with your secretary? What were you thinking when you stayed out drinking every night until after midnight? Did it ever occur to you that your wife was being injured by your behavior? Did you ever think of anyone but yourself?

This is not questioning. It's bullying. Multiple questioning often has this feel, even when done innocently. The person being questioned smells attack and begins to clam up.

All too often our questions seek information that is irrelevant. We've all had the experience of talking with people who interrupt so frequently with trivial questions that the conversation becomes a chore and the original topic is lost in the clutter.

Pop: I remember the time I bought my first new car. It was about two years before we were married and—

Mom: No, no, wasn't it three years old when we were married?

Pop: It wasn't that old. I'm sure we'd only had it two years.

Mom: Didn't you own that car when you had that hernia operation? That was three years before we were married.

Pop: I owned that old Ford when I had the operation. I remember because it stalled on the way to the hospital. Boy, that operation was awful. I was laid up for almost two months and—

Mom: Was it late spring when you had that operation? Or was it
         early summer?

In this conversation, every story will be permanently derailed by a
maze of pointless questions and comments about peripheral matters.
While this is an exaggerated example, we've all distracted speakers in
this way at one time or another. Have patience. Ask yourself if the
question you are about to ask is pertinent to the primary issues. Some
details simply don't have to be perfectly understood or perfectly
accurate. Give speakers time to clarify before you disrupt their train
of thought and maybe ruin the story by interrupting. If your question
won't yield information of real value, skip it.

Of course, carefully thought out and relevant questions can help a
speaker clarify an important point or add critical facts that would
have been overlooked. If your confusion is intolerable, there is nothing wrong with asking questions to get back on track.

Now that we've reviewed the don'ts of asking questions, what are
the do's? What techniques will induce others to answer your questions as honestly and informatively as they are can?

The first rule, once again, is to check your attitudes, biases, and
assumptions at the door. For most people, it's a risky proposition to open
up and really tell you what's on their mind. It makes them vulnerable,
and they know it. An inflexible or judgmental manner on your part can
easily convince them to keep their true thoughts to themselves.

People won't unnecessarily expose themselves to peril. Before
speaking, they will assess the probable risk and then answer as openly or as defensively as the situation warrants. The more a speaker
feels he is being evaluated or judged, the more he will rely on a false
front. The more a speaker feels that only one answer is acceptable, the
more likely he will be to give that answer. The more a speaker per-
ceives his listener's goals and expectations, the more likely he is to
adjust his answers to those requirements.

The tyrannical boss provides the classic example of stultified
communication. A boss with a rigid, unforgiving attitude inevitably
convinces his employees that honesty is not the best policy. He
demands constant agreement, and he gets it. Unfortunately, the resulting lack of independent thought ultimately damages the organization.

In order to receive honest and open answers to your questions, the
key is to establish an atmosphere of trust and acceptance that puts

others at ease. If people feel their ideas will be given fair consideration, they'll be far more likely to speak freely. Whenever you discuss a sensitive matter with someone, move toward that issue gradually. Begin with easy, non-threatening questions and discussion. Move on to the more personal or troublesome issues only after you've built a solid rapport and a climate of fairness. This gives the other party time to assess your attitude and become more comfortable with you.

Here is another way to increase the odds of getting an honest answer when you ask a sensitive or controversial question. Preface your question with a statement that indicates you have an open mind and are not biased in favor of any one response.

An example—"Some employees feel we should ban smoking anywhere on company property. Others think that is too restrictive. What is your opinion?" Here the brief statements preceding the question reveal no prejudice and show the other party that you recognize there are differing views. Without this preface, the person might attempt to avoid disagreement by being vague or by attempting to discover what you wanted to hear.

Used skillfully, questions can help a speaker organize his thoughts and come to his own conclusions. This is a method commonly used by psychiatrists. Questions are asked in a way that assists patients in finding their own truths. Such questioning is the opposite of using queries to indirectly put forward advice or personal opinions.

For example, suppose a friend tells you that she doesn't want to go to a party because she might run into an old boyfriend. A skilled questioner might ask questions that help this person explore her feelings about the former love. "How would you feel if John showed up while you were there?" or "Are you still in love with John or just uncomfortable being around him?" or "How often do you alter your plans to avoid John?" People often act without really exploring their feelings. Questions like this can help them take a good look at the underlying reasons for their behavior.

The wording of your questions also plays a big role in the accuracy and relevance of the information you receive. Be as precise and concrete as possible in order to avoid listener assumptions. Vagueness forces others to guess what you mean, and such guesses are often incorrect. For example, suppose Bill wants to find out if a friend, Jill, would be interested in a blind date with a friend of his.

Bill: So, how's your social life? Are you meeting any eligible guys?

Jill: Oh, God, it's horrible! You're incredibly lucky to be married. I've had so many bad experiences, I've decided to quit dating for a while. I'm just sick of the whole scene.

Hearing this, Bill decides not to mention the blind date with his friend. However, in reality, Jill was just blowing off steam and didn't really mean what she said. She is lonely and would jump at the chance for a date with a man recommended by a trusted friend. Jill had assumed from Bill's vague question that he was asking her what it was like to be single, and she responded with a misleading answer about how horrible the dating scene is for her.

Try to provide the other party with an appropriate frame of reference for your question so that they understand what the subject is. Not "How are things?" but "How are you getting along with your new boss?" Or, using the example of the previous paragraph, "Would you be interested in meeting a single guy that's a friend of mine?"

This brings us to our next topic—leading questions. The way questions are phrased or structured can have a strong influence on the response. As we know, if a question is poorly worded, it can inadvertently encourage a dishonest answer in which the respondent tells you what he thinks you want to hear. On the other hand, calculated phrasing of questions can also intentionally lead people (hence, the term—leading question) to answer in a way you desire. You can use the form of your questions to force a frame of reference that makes it very difficult for people to answer in any way other than the one you want.

Leading questions, by their wording, push the respondent toward a very limited range of answers. A simple example would be, "This is the hottest it's been all summer, isn't it?" Technically, it may not be the hottest day of the summer; however, most people will answer yes and not argue. This is innocent enough, but some leading questions are more insidious.

Suppose you are at a party talking to several people who, from the nature of the discussion, seem to be Republicans. Suddenly, one of them turns to you and asks, "You aren't a Democrat, are you?" Your temptation will be to say no, even if you are a Democrat. Why? Because the wording of the question indicates that you won't be well received if you are a Democrat.

You would have been inclined to answer honestly if the question had been worded impartially, demonstrating that a candid answer would not be met with disapproval. "We need to hear all sides on this issue. Are you a Democrat?" If the object is to receive accurate and open answers, questions have to be phrased in a way that communicates to the respondent that he won't be punished for his true opinion. As discussed earlier, you can use an introductory statement ("We need to hear all sides…") prior to a question to indicate that you really do want an honest answer.

Of course, introductory statements can also be used to pressure a person into answering in a way you desire. For example—"You know I've been working a lot of overtime this week. Would you mind picking up Dad at the airport?" or "Tom, Jack, Bill and the boss have all agreed that this is a good plan. What's your opinion?" or "As you know, profits are down and all our employees need to contribute a little more to help us through these tough times. Would you be willing to work Saturdays?"

In the above examples, the introductory statement pressures the respondent to give an answer the questioner prefers. To ignore the message of the introductory statement and answer otherwise is to seem insensitive, troublemaking, or disloyal.

Another leading technique, one often used by lawyers, is to blend an opinion into a question. For example—"Did you know that driving 45 miles per hour on that street was dangerous?" This question assumes that 45 mph was in fact dangerous and only asks if the driver knew it. The assumption of danger is stated as if it were a fact—and that is the trap. Regardless of whether the driver answers yes or no, he will essentially be agreeing that 45 mph was indeed dangerous, thereby incriminating himself as an ignorant, inattentive driver. Thus the lawyer leads him to make a damaging admission.

The truly sneaky thing about leading questions is that the lead, or attempt to influence, may never be recognized as such by the person being questioned. Careful wording is used to subtly implant an idea or bias in the mind of another. One study showed that asking subjects how tall a basketball player was resulted in greater average estimates of height than asking how short a player was. When subjects were asked, "Do you get headaches frequently?" the estimates of headache occurrence were greater than when they were asked, "Do you get headaches occasionally?"

TV news reporters often use this technique to get people to make newsworthy statements. Instead of straightforwardly asking, "How did you feel about this?" a reporter will instead plant an idea or emotion with their question. For example, "Did you feel violated when the court ruled for the defendant? or "Were you outraged and disgusted to hear management make these claims?" More often than not, the person will cry out, "Yes, yes, I did feel outraged and disgusted!" Who knows how such people really feel? The reporter's only concern is getting a dramatic on-camera statement.

One of the most potent ways to influence not only how people answer but also how they think and feel is a shrewdly planned sequence of leading questions. Sometimes a single leading question can induce a person to answer in a specific way, but it may not influence his underlying beliefs. He might answer in a certain way to avoid trouble or embarrassment, but he doesn't really put much stock in what he's saying.

However, a calculated sequence of questions may influence what someone actually feels and believes by building step by step a rationale that supports the desired answer. A carefully designed sequence of questions can also be used to back a person into a logical corner so that he answers in the desired way to avoid looking foolishly inconsistent. Consider the following question and answer session.

Q: Do you believe that today's kids have too much unproductive time on their hands?

A: Absolutely.

Q: Do you think there aren't enough wholesome activities available for our kids?

A: Sure

Q: Would crime rates fall if kids were more closely supervised?

A: Yes.

Q: Are we as a society investing enough in our children's future?

A: Probably not.

Q: Would you be willing to vote yes on a new bond issue to fund after-school computer labs for our school district?

A: Yes, I sure would.

In this example, the victim has been skillfully manipulated by the questioner. Most people can be expected to answer yes to questions that ask if it's a good thing for kids to have activities and supervision. And, it would be hard to answer no to the final question after answering yes to all the previous questions. More important, however, is the fact that this series of questions, by the self-reinforcing logic of their organization, may actually have convinced the person that new labs are a good idea, even though he might not previously have supported such spending.

Now let's assume that this same person had instead happened upon a questioner who did not support computer labs. This new questioner asks an entirely different series of questions designed to elicit a different conclusion.

Q: Do you believe government spending is inefficient?
A: Yes.
Q: Do you think our taxes are too high?
A: Sure.
Q: Could most of our local governmental agencies and school districts make more efficient use of the money they already have?
A: Absolutely.
Q: Do you think our school district really needs additional monies to fund elaborate and expensive new computer labs?
A: Definitely not. They should find the money by cutting expenses.

Using this method, interviewees are lead through a series of questions that they will answer in a predictable way, thereby progressively boxing them in (you can be pretty sure, for instance, that most people will agree that taxes are too high). Then, once they have committed themselves to the suggested line of reasoning, you hit them with a final zinger, the question you've been setting them up for. Your questions have given them a frame of reference (government spending is out of control) that makes the answer you've been guiding them toward seem logical and reasonable.

Now let's look at two fundamentally different ways to phrase a question—*open questions* versus *closed questions*.

A closed question requires only a very short answer to satisfy it, typically yes or no, although other short answers are possible as well.

Are you going to school now?
Do you live in this town?

Which car is your favorite, the Chevy or the Ford?
Is this Wednesday or Thursday?

Closed questions are easy to answer and are a good way to get basic information quickly, but the answers are usually brief and minimal. In other words, the ball is soon back in your court, and you haven't learned much. Short answers can also be misleading. Asked the same closed question, ten people might answer yes but all have different reasons that go unstated.

Open questions are designed to encourage answers that are wider in scope. These are questions that don't restrict the way the other party answers. For instance, a closed question might be phrased like this—"Are satisfied with your new car?" a question that can be answered yes or no. An open question, on the other hand, would be phrased like this—"What is your experience with your new car?" a question that can't be answered with a simple yes or no. The open question encourages the new car owner to explain his car's strengths and weaknesses explicitly.

Here's an example of how a closed question can restrict a conversation when freedom and latitude are what is needed. A son approaches his father, who is reading the newspaper. The boy doesn't say anything, and after a moment the father puts down the paper and says, "Are you going to ask me about buying that motorcycle again?" In this case, the son actually wanted to talk about the trouble he was having in a math class.

The father's incorrect assumption directs the conversation to a sore point in their relations, and his use of a closed question makes it easy for the son to give a minimal response. The boy answers, "No, forget it," and walks out. If the father had asked an open, non-directive question such as "What's on your mind, son?" the conversation might have blossomed.

So, if you want to ask a question that requires only a quick answer ("Are you going to the store?"), or if you want to zero in on a specific subject ("Have you finished the Taylor letter?"), use closed questions. However, if you want to probe more deeply, find out what others think and feel, and carry less of the burden of maintaining the conversation, use open questions ("What kind of problems did you and John have at the meeting?").

When using open questions, remember the old newspaperman's

investigatory rule of thumb—ask who, what, when, where, why, and how. Also remember to use a combination of open and closed questions to get the fullest possible explanation. You can begin with open questions that elicit broad, big picture responses and then zero in on specific areas that interest you with closed questions. For example—

(1) "What's going on at home?" (open)
(2) "How did you get into an argument?" (open)
(3) "Why was she so upset about that?" (open)
(4) "Is she happy with your solution?" (closed)
(5) "Do you think the problem is solved?" (closed)

Note that once a conversation is rolling, people will often respond at length even if you use a closed question. In this type of situation, a closed question is a great tool for focusing and directing the course of the conversation.

Now let's look at specific types of questions designed to get at specific types of information.

Can you give me an example?—Urges the speaker to explain in real-world detail and to relate what has been said to day-to-day experience. This is a question that's very handy for getting a handle on statements that are too vague, general, or abstract to fully understand.

Why did you say (or do) that?—Attempts to discover the underlying reasons or motivation for someone's behavior. The goal is to get past surface action and find the real feelings, beliefs, and attitudes that motivate the person to act as he does. This is a great question for discovering who people truly are and often generates surprising and revealing answers.

I'm not sure I follow you. What do exactly do you mean? or ***Can you rephrase that?***—Used to get clarification or further explanation and detail about a confusing or ambiguous statement.

These may seem like simple and obvious questions, and they are, but all too often we fail to ask them. Instead, we make assumptions that end up being incorrect. Much of our and the world's troubles stem from assumptions about others that are incorrect. Make an effort to get clarification rather than relying on guesses.

One final point. The primary purpose of asking a question is to gather information. Frequently, however, we substitute questions for direct statements. For example, a woman asks her husband, "Why do you always have to watch so much football?" In this situation, a question is inappropriate. She's not actually looking for information; she's registering a complaint. What she really needs to do is make a clear statement of her concern—"I get lonely and bored when you spend so much time watching TV."

When we ask a question instead of making a direct statement of our needs, it is almost always less effective. Indirect questions offer the other party a way to avoid confronting the real problem—"No, I don't have to watch so much football. I do it because I like it." If the wife had stated frankly that she was lonely, it would have been a lot harder for the husband to deflect her concern with a flippant response. Her indirect question gave him an easy escape route.

To summarize, try to rely less exclusively on questions in conversation. Expand your repertoire of information eliciting tools to include listening, empathy, reflection, self-disclosure, and direct statements. This can be challenging at first, habitual questioning dies hard, but the improvement in communication makes it worthwhile. When you must ask a question, give more thought to its form, wording, and ultimate purpose.

Chapter 4:
Having
Your Say

Until now we have emphasized listening to others, drawing them out, and discovering their underlying thoughts and feelings. These are definitely core skills for a good conversationalist, but what about those times when you have something to say? What about those times when you are in a competitive environment such as the workplace where it's important to have your say and put your ideas out there? Are there ways of controlling the direction of a conversation and the length of time that you hold the floor? Can you survive in a competitive environment where others are pressing hard to drown you out and steal the floor from you? The answer, of course, is yes.

This is a chapter about conversational power—how to use it, and how to defend yourself from its use by others. I'm sure you'll be shocked to hear that there are people in this world whose only interest is to broadcast their own opinions and have an attentive, and silent, audience. Unfortunately, for them, there are times when you want to stop listening and speak your mind.

Studies of the dynamics of conversation have shown that dominant individuals tend to hold the floor longer and interrupt more frequently than others. Most are able to seize and hold the floor by fairly honest means. In other words, they are respected, have leadership skills, and know how to grab listeners' attention with interesting and involving talk. Others, however, are conversational pirates who board a conversation and hold all the participants at sword point, forcing them to listen whether they want to or not. This chapter will show you the techniques used by both types of assertive conversationalists, the good and the bad (and occasionally, the ugly).

While it's important to have your say, remember that conversation is primarily a cooperative effort. You may become quite adept at using some of the power techniques we're about to discuss, but if you use them to unfairly monopolize discussions, you violate the communal principles of good talk. When the other parties to a conversation feel they are being excluded or ignored, the conversation is heading toward a dead end. Think of conversational power techniques as tools you can use not to commandeer a conversation but to ensure that you are fully heard when you have something important to say.

Conversation usually moves forward through a reasonably organized system of turn taking. Generally, people are uncomfortable with simultaneous speech. If two people start talking at once, normally it isn't long before one of them will drop out and let the other have the floor. But what exactly are the rules of turn taking? Who gets to speak? When and how long? And once it's your turn, how do you hold and defend it against unreasonable interruptions?

Obviously, to get the floor you need to indicate your desire to speak. On the most basic level, this can be done in several ways—a well-timed intake of breath, a movement that draws attention such as gesturing with the hand or leaning forward, or simply forcefully beginning to speak. When you are in a group, the tricky part is to use such a method at exactly the right moment, just as the current speaker appears to be finishing his turn, and just ahead of others who may also be attempting to speak. If your timing is late, someone else will grab the floor before you. If your timing is early, you will be interrupting the current speaker before he has finished.

To improve your timing, observe the speaker closely, looking for signs that he is ending his turn. Paying close attention will give you an edge over less vigilant members of the group. When the time comes, start fast and strong. You can use one of the recognized conversational indicators of turn initiation such as *Well, But, Listen,* or even a sharp *Uh* or *Ahh.*

You can strengthen your effort by preceding your verbal initiation with physical gestures such as motioning with the hand or moving forward in your seat. These are useful in that you can use them just before the current speaker ends his comments without actually interrupting.

If someone else gets the jump on you and grabs the floor, and if you are determined to have your say right now, you can gain the floor by raising a problem of understanding with a previous statement. For example, if John grabs the floor ahead of you, you might say, "Excuse me, John, but I'm not sure I understand what Rick meant when he said blah blah blah. If he means that we should blah blah blah, then I have to disagree. I think…" Now, like a pirate, you have seized the floor.

When you begin your turn, your initial speech needs to be assertive. You should speak a little louder and quicker than normal. This serves primarily to get everyone's attention, but it also has another purpose. If you hesitate, pausing to organize your thoughts, or if you speak in a low voice, someone may use this as an opening to push you aside. Strong, rapid speech tells everyone that you have the floor and don't intend to give it up. This discourages the takeover artists who bully the more timid souls among us.

Also, avoid eye contact for a few moments, especially if you are in a competitive conversational environment. Gaining eye contact is one of the key methods that people use to interrupt a speaker (we'll discuss this more fully later on).

One of the most common, if somewhat sneaky, methods of grabbing the floor is to wait for a moment when the speaker hesitates to search for a word or decide what to say next. You quickly jump in, complete what you think he was trying to say, and then move on with your own comments.

Sarah:	So I marched straight into Bill's office even though I wasn't sure it was, um…
Sam:	Appropriate. Hey, I think it was entirely appropriate. I remember being in a similar situation once. I was about to start a new project and …

This method is sneaky because the speaker clearly had not finished her remarks. However, even though her turn was hijacked, it's hard for her to get too upset with the hijacker. He seized the conversation not by challenging her but by speaking on her behalf, even appearing to help her say what she wanted to say.

In fact, completing another's thought proves that the hijacker was interested and listening closely, and that fact softens the blow of the interruption. Usually, however, when people complete a speaker's thought, they don't go on to seize the floor.

Once you've gained the floor, how do you hold people's attention and discourage them from interrupting you? These two goals are not unrelated. If you are skilled at holding people's attention, they'll be less inclined to interrupt.

Capturing listeners' attention and interest is, of course, no simple matter. Still, there are some basic guidelines to keep in mind. The bottom line rule is to remember that when you have the floor, you are on stage. To varying degrees, you are giving a performance, and your listeners are your critics. If your performance is poor, they'll close down your show and move on to a new show. What does this mean? It means that you should never speak just to hear yourself fill the air. Keep the well being of your audience in mind. Always make an effort to be as interesting as possible.

Your first task is to pre-plan what you wish to say. Map out your approach rather than just blurting a rush of words and hoping it all comes out right. Ask yourself where you want to go with your words. What is the destination or goal of your comments? Knowing your goal will help you organize your comments and determine what is worth saying and what isn't.

Your listeners want to hear comments that are relevant to the current topic, logically organized, and no lengthier than necessary to make your point. They don't want to kill time while you hesitate, backtrack, overemphasize trivial points, omit critical points, and wander aimlessly all over the map talking about whatever pops into your mind. To speak without purpose is to invite interruption.

Look for the drama and human interest in whatever topic you choose to discuss. Ask yourself what you can emphasize that people will personally relate to. Look for a way to provide a little suspense or uncertainty as to how things will turn out.

Remember to use humor whenever appropriate. Cultivate an eye for the silliness or foolishness in even the most ordinary of situations. If the topic isn't a serious one, it doesn't hurt to exaggerate a little to improve your story. Most listeners are willing to tolerate a little stretching of the truth if they are entertained by the result.

When telling a story, many people will reveal the outcome or result first and then explain how it came about. Most stories would be more intriguing if the payoff were delayed as long as possible. For instance, don't begin a story by saying, "Did you hear about Alice losing her winning ticket at the horse races?" Instead, begin with "Did you hear about Alice's disaster at the horse races?" It's far more interesting to wonder what happened to Alice (the imagination runs wild with speculation) than to wonder about how it happened.

Look for the drama in a situation. For instance, you could begin a story with this limp intro—"What a terrible day. The copier broke down just when I needed it to copy a bunch of reports for a meeting." Or, you could begin the same story by building a dramatic scene—"I had the most incredible crisis at work today. I had spent two weeks putting together some reports that I was to present to the president of the company. He was flying in from Tulsa with a bunch of VP's just for this meeting. We worked all night on the reports and only finished writing them 30 minutes before the scheduled meeting. But then, just when we were all starting to relax, I saw smoke coming out of the copier and…"

See the difference. The second version of the story has more human drama. Listeners can get involved in it and relate to it. The first version of the story just sounds like someone getting ready to whine and complain. The point here is that to hold the floor and avoid interruption you have to make it worth your listeners' while to pay attention. It's a trade—you give listeners something interesting, they give you their time and attention.

Another rule for maintaining the interest of your listeners is to avoid losing their confidence. In this instance, confidence means their faith that you can effectively and accurately tell them something that's worth their time. Expect declining interest if you um and ahh, backtrack, hesitate excessively, speak chaotically, or assume listeners have information they don't have.

You're in trouble if you find yourself saying things like "Oops, wait a minute, that's wrong, now let's see, how exactly did it happen?" or "Oh, sorry, I forgot to tell you something important." You seem foolish and unprepared. It won't be long before your audience begins interrupting or daydreaming.

An easy trick for maintaining interest is to use phrases that refer to the listener and involve him or her in the process of telling the story. "Tell me what you think of this idea…," or "Let's suppose that you were…," or "What do you think I did next?" are all comments that invite the listener to actively work through the story or issue with you. These are comments that draw a person in and increase his investment in your comments. In addition, you might pause briefly after a comment like "Do you know what happened then?" Such a pause delays revelation and builds expectation.

Avoid focusing on unimportant trivia. Stories have a forward momentum that can be lost if you stop dead to figure out whether an event occurred on Monday or Tuesday, or whether it took place in Ma's Home Cooking Restaurant or Ma's Old Fashioned Restaurant. Skip over irrelevant facts and keep the story moving ahead. Focus only on information that is critical to understanding and interest.

Some verbal habits can be distracting to listeners and lessen the impact of your comments. Most of us um and ahh periodically to give ourselves a moment to consider our next comment. Often, without realizing it, these ums and ahhs become habitual and excessive. They slow down the speed of your speech and, if they are really overdone, can be downright annoying to others. Worst of all, they make you seem less intelligent. Make the effort to rid them from your speech, even if you have to enlist the help of your friends to do so. I know one person who instructed her friends to say "Ouch" every time she said um or ahh. It wasn't long before she was cured of her habit.

Similar to um and ahh is the habitual use of vague filler expressions, which we employ when we're too indifferent to think of more descriptive words and phrases. Expressions such as the following— *kind of, somehow, sort of, that sort of thing, like, all that stuff, almost every, things, kinds, you know what I'm saying,* and the infamous, *whatchamacallit.* These words and phrases are just crutches for the linguistically lazy. They add little or no meaning and aren't as interesting as more colorful and specific terms.

Okay, suppose you are following all the guidelines we've discussed. You're dramatic, concise, funny, and relevant, but lo and behold, people still try to interrupt you and seize the floor for themselves. Sorry, it happens, no matter how fascinating you are. Sometimes, if you really want to be heard, you have to play hardball to hold onto your turn. Let's look at some self-defense tactics.

The simplest and most direct way of holding the floor is to address the issue head on by insisting on adhering to accepted turn-taking rules. "Let me finish. I'll hear you out when I'm done, and I won't interrupt." Then keep your promise. This method is assertive, usually accepted by others, and makes for a more orderly exchange of ideas. Another direct method of stopping interruption is to quickly hold up a hand in a gesture that tells others you want to finish. Don't hold your hand way out at the end of a straight arm like a traffic cop. Just make a quick palm-out gesture, elbow bent, close to the body.

The best way to avoid interruption is to speak quickly and steadily. Slow speech and hesitation is an open invitation to interrupters. It gives them numerous opportunities to complete your sentences or to step in and take over.

People often interrupt slow speakers out of sheer impatience. Typical speech is about 140 words per minute (w.p.m.), and many people speak considerably slower. The brain, however, is capable of processing speech much faster than even 140 w.p.m., and it quickly gets bored at slower rates. Studies show that interest and comprehension improve greatly at speech rates from 190 w.p.m. all the way up to 280 w.p.m. Moreover, increasing the speed and volume of your speech is an effective way of eliminating gaps listeners can exploit to interrupt you.

Sometimes we allow an opportunity for interruption by pausing to briefly perform another activity—taking a sip of coffee, puffing a cigarette, pulling a cheese puff out of the bag, and so on. You can discourage takeover artists from exploiting these activities by holding up your hand or saying "Just a moment."

As mentioned earlier, avoiding eye contact is a subtle way of fending off interruption. Although you may not be conscious of it, eye contact is sometimes a signal to others that you are ready to give up your turn and that they should pick up the conversation. It is also a means by which others catch your attention and break in. By the same token, avoiding eye contact can signal others not to interrupt. Essentially, by refusing to establish eye contact, you indicate that you are mentally laboring to put your words together and should not be disturbed.

This is not to say that you should avoid eye contact as a general rule. It is quite natural and desirable for speaker and listener to share a good deal of eye contact, especially as they find agreement or common ground. Eye contact avoidance should be used only when you sense that a listener is about to jump in, and you are eager to complete your thought first.

You can also resist interruption with the manner in which you organize your comments. Lead up to the main point of your comments gradually or make your point toward the end of your statement. Once you have revealed your primary idea, and it is clear that your remaining comments will merely expand or explain, the temptation for others to jump in increases. Even if your listener doesn't immediately interrupt, he may allow his attention to wander once he thinks he has heard your main point.

Other methods for signaling your intent to hold the floor are a variety of linguistic forewarning devices indicating that your immediate comments are part of a larger unit. You can, for instance, give your audience some measure of the extent of your message with quick comments like "Three points I want to make...," or "There are two reasons why I disagree with you...," or "I have a couple of comments." Such devices act as notifications, telling listeners to hold their comments until you have completed your predefined statements.

You can also link your utterances together in a chain with words that essentially say to a listener, "Stop, don't interrupt yet, there's more." Examples of these linking words and phrases are *first of all, to begin with, then, next, that leads me to, also,* and *after that.* These are connecting phrases that join a series of comments and relate them to one another. For example, you can use the phrase *for example* to warn others that you intend to follow your previous statement with an illustration.

And if you're really selfish about hogging the floor, you can exhaust one topic and slide right into a new one with other linking devices such as *by the way, speaking of, that reminds me,* and worst of all, *changing the subject* (worst because you are openly admitting that your next comment has no relation to the current topic). These phrases can also be used by a new speaker to initiate his comments.

Occasionally, despite all your efforts, someone will interrupt you and get a word in edgewise. Fear not, there's no need to lose hope, you can still retake the floor. Act as if you've only been put on hold for a moment, and then at the first available opportunity, use one of the following re-openers—*Anyway, as I was saying, Where was I,* or *So anyway.* These work so well that you'll often get an apology from the interrupter, who will then listen even more attentively to make up for his transgression.

This is a good time to emphasize once again that if you are excessively prone to monopolize conversations and refuse others their turn, you are headed for trouble. We all talk too much now and then, but once people realize that someone is a habitual conversation bully, they start to run and hide when they see him or her coming. The goal of this chapter is to show you how to deal with a bully, not how to become one.

Related to turn holding methods are techniques that allow you to select whose turn will follow yours. Suppose you want Jane, and not John, to respond first to what you've just said because you think her input will be more relevant. One method is to settle your gaze on Jane as you wrap up your comments, while avoiding eye contact with John. Another method is to attach a short tag comment to the end of your statement and address it to Jane. "So that's the way I see it. (looking at Jane) I know you've dealt with this kind of problem yourself, Jane." Finally, you can terminate by asking Jane a specific question. "So that's why I get my teeth cleaned every four months instead of every six. Jane, how often do you go to the dentist?" None of these methods guarantee that your choice will be the next speaker, but they greatly increase the odds.

Now that we've considered techniques for ensuring that you get your say, let's look at how our verbal forms and styles are perceived by others. Whenever you meet someone, he or she will immediately begin to make judgments about you based on your style of speech. Does the way you speak present you as someone who is strong, confident, and intelligent, or does it communicate the opposite?

Below are some language forms that studies have shown communicate weakness and lack of intelligence to others.

Hedges — "I sort of liked it."— *I suppose, I guess, sort of, kind of, maybe, it's okay, it's all right.* Hedges are used to avoid expressing certainty, making a decision, or making a statement that can't be taken back. These phrases communicate indecisiveness, lack of enthusiasm, and general ineffectiveness.

Tag Questions — "That's the way it happened, wasn't it?" — *You know? Didn't it? You agree, don't you? Right?* Tag questions communicate the speaker's uncertainty and an unwillingness to commit without agreement and support from others.

Hesitations — "I...uh...liked it." — *uh, umm, ahh*. Hesitations communicate uncertainty, lack of fluency, slow thinking, and lack of preparation.

Avoiding these three speech forms will make you seem more intelligent, confident, and competent. You may actually be overflowing with brains and confidence, but if you um and ahh, hedge, and constantly ask others for support, you may be perceived as weak and unintelligent by others—and perception is often more potent than reality.

Studies have shown that negative impressions have a greater impact on others than positive impressions. This is probably a holdover from primeval times when negative information often meant the difference between life and death. Thus, low-power speech such as we have just described has an exaggerated effect on listeners' opinion of you.

People are attracted to power. Power is sexy. Speech patterns that communicate strength and credibility draw people to you. On the other hand, weakness, incompetence, and unreliability are turn offs and repel people. Train yourself to avoid low-power conversation styles and speak with fluency and confidence.

Sometimes even forms of speech that are desirable on the surface can prove to be a negative if overdone. Excessive politeness or excessive concern about the reactions of others can be an indicator of low status, even servility. Be polite, but hold on to your self-respect. Others owe you as much politeness as you owe them.

Vocabulary richness and versatility is another sign of personal power. Using the right word to accurately describe what's on your mind not only improves others' ability to determine your true meaning but also heightens their respect for you. Being lazy about your vocabulary, using a handful of words to communicate widely varied meanings, is going to adversely affect your social power—your ability to persuade and influence those around you.

If you say you're "in a bad mood" to describe everything from being angry to being tired, you are verbally lazy. If you use the phrase "in a good mood" for every positive feeling you experience, you are verbally lazy. To improve your verbal skills, you don't need to carry a dictionary or buy a vocabulary-building program. Nor do you need to start using a lot of five-syllable words understood only by English professors. You only need to make an effort to use the most precise word you know to describe what you are experiencing.

For example, if your feelings are being negatively affected, you can define that feeling with words like *discouraged, pessimistic, gloomy, hopeless,* or *furious*. These aren't fancy, exotic words. They are words we all know but often ignore in favor of a small number of habitual words such as *upset* or *depressed* that we use far too broadly.

In addition to preventing interruptions, a quick speech rate also makes what you say seem more interesting, intelligent, competent, and believable. The phrase fast-talking salesman has its origins in this effect. It means that a person who speaks quickly is just naturally more believable and more capable of persuading. Salespeople don't talk fast just for the fun of it. They know it is effective.

The above suggestions for power speech aren't carved in stone. People's opinion of you won't collapse in a heap if you occasionally hesitate, speak slowly, or use a nonspecific word. It's the pattern of use that's important. We all use these low power speech forms to one degree or another. If you use them as a habitual crutch though, rather than making an effort to speak more fluently, they can cause you trouble in both your social and business life.

Now that we've covered the basic skills of conversation, it's time to look at the specific categories of conversation.

Chapter 5:
Social Talk

If you read a lot of the available literature on effective conversation, you're bound to run into one particular piece of advice over and over—be yourself. It's advice that seems to make perfect sense, except for one thing—what the heck does it mean? We all behave differently depending on the situation. The self we present when we're with co-workers is not the same self we put forward when we're in a discussion with our boss. We certainly don't act the same with our parents as we do with our friends. We don't speak to our spouse the way we speak to our children.

In truth, each of us modifies our persona considerably to fit the social environment. Much of what we describe as "social skills" involves picking a role that is appropriate to a situation and then inhabiting that role. For example, few of us would choose to speak to a recent acquaintance as if we had known him for years.

The basic social truth here is that the times when we really get to be ourselves are rare. We're probably closest to "being ourselves" only when we are with old friends. Most of the time we're carefully picking and playing out a role in order to make the appropriate impression on others. That's almost a definition of the word social. We restrain our true selves in order to live harmoniously with other people. If everyone decided to literally be himself or herself, the result wouldn't be society, it would be anarchy.

This book is built on the premise that the successful conversationalist, far from being himself and doing what he wants, has to make a lot of sacrifices in order to flourish socially. We all want to talk, but the good conversationalist has to train himself to listen. We all want to focus on our own interests, but a successful conversationalist has to give others the chance to discuss their interests. We all find it much easier to vent our prejudices and personal desires, but a good conversationalist has to make an effort to empathize with others.

A good conversationalist makes others better speakers, storytellers, and humorists by the attention and interest he gives them. If you get anything from this book, understand the following—the world is full of selfish, egotistical people, and this fact offers a great opportunity for the person who is attentive to the needs of others. This is one of the true secrets of life.

Most successful people are successful conversationalists. Let's make the meaning even plainer—success in conversation contributes mightily to success in life. Studies have shown that a common trait of the wealthy is a wealth of friends and associates. This extensive web of contacts, advisors, and supporters is a valuable resource for successful individuals, an ever-available pool of ideas, information, assistance, advice, influence, and even investment money. And how are all these friends acquired? Through good social and conversational skills.

We all admire and even envy the person who seems to be able to strike up a conversation with anyone, anywhere. It's an ability we all wish we had because we know the benefits that come from it. We know that the skill, confidence, and energetic humor of these people are catching. These folks are human magnets who seem to have little trouble meeting people, making friends, and creating allies.

On the other hand, we also know that our own shyness or lack of social skill makes it harder for us to make friends and impress others. We may truly be warm and good-hearted, but our inability to communicate those characteristics can make us seem unapproachable or uninteresting. And with each failure to connect, there may be a loss. The person we couldn't charm or intrigue may have been the one who would have recommended us for a better job, helped us solve a problem, or introduced us to our future spouse (or become our future spouse). Concern about lost opportunities is one of the reasons you are reading this book.

Rewards go to the risk takers. Most people who have difficulty talking to strangers or handling the give and take of conversation understand this well enough. They see the confident person who can talk to anyone, anywhere, and admire his or her ability to think on his feet and to accept the risk of rejection. They know such capabilities bring rewards.

Let's look at shyness and fear of rejection. Good conversationalists don't really see themselves as taking risks or exercising great skill. If these people were being roundly rejected on a regular basis, even their powerful confidence would soon start to dwindle. Confident conversationalists know that real rejection is relatively rare. Most of the people you'll come into contact with are as interested in striking up a conversation as you are. The risks are not nearly as great as we imagine, but the rewards are as great as we imagine.

Shy people often believe that they'll have to hold up a new conversation single handedly. They forget that their conversational responsibility is only 50%. The other party in any conversation is, after all, a live and intelligent being who given the proper motivation should be happy to shoulder a good portion of the talk. Have faith not only in your own conversation making ability but in that of the other person as well.

The fear that one's mind will go blank is a common obstacle to initiating conversations. People are often so unwilling to trust their spontaneous ability to talk that they feverishly try to pre-plan the discussion several subjects and statements in advance. They become actors reciting their lines. This intense mental preparation and rigid follow-through blocks their spontaneous nature. It also cripples their ability to observe what is taking place in the moment, a rich source of subject matter.

Other major types of conversation fear are concerns about saying the wrong thing, or saying the right thing in the wrong way. Additionally, there is the "no one will be interested in what I have to say" fear, or the "they all know so much more than I do" fear. Then there's that great all-purpose fear of the shy at heart, the "I don't want to seem pushy" fear.

The consequence of these fears is that instead of jumping into a conversation to see what develops, a shy person waits, and waits, and waits. Often this waiting lasts a lifetime. Stop waiting and refuse to be intimidated by anyone. Every human on this planet has his own personal set of fears and inadequacies. No one is better than you, and no one is so formidable that you need to avoid him or her.

Many people accept their own self-description of "shy." They say it so often that it becomes true. Then they reinforce it with a lot of negative self-talk such as—"I really don't have anything interesting to say," or "They won't like me," or "I can't go talk to them with my hair looking this way," and so on. But, here is the good news— much of shyness and social awkwardness is a learned response, and as such, it can be unlearned.

Here are a few ways to cope with a fear of strangers. Suppose that after much fretting and stewing, you summon all your nerve and open a conversation with the woman across the aisle from you on an airplane. The two of you talk for a few minutes and then she turns back to reading her magazine.

Now, notice your internal mental response to her apparent termination of your discussion. Do you tell yourself that your comments to her were lame? That you are a boring person? That you can't make women laugh? Do you also mind-read what you assume her thoughts are? "She thinks my glasses are goofy looking," or "She probably only likes guys who are taller than I am."

What will be the likely result of this self-critical internal commentary? If you are already ill at ease about meeting new people, thoughts like these will only increase your feelings of inadequacy. This will in turn result in an even more nervous performance in the future. It's hard to avoid all self-criticism (and probably not a good idea), but don't get carried away. Analyze what you did or said with an eye toward improvement, not self-destruction.

Watch out for irrational extrapolations. For example, if you say something stupid, does that make you a stupid person? Clearly, it does not. We all say stupid things from now and then. In any conversation with a stranger, we are more likely than usual to make foolish comments because we are thinking on our feet and dealing with an unknown person, not because we lack intelligence.

Another self-critical habit to watch for is mind reading. Although most of us know logically that we can't read the mind of another, in practice, we often assume we can. In the situation above, many men would decide that the reason the woman turned back to her magazine was that she found them lacking in some way. As stated above, men often imagine a specific problem such as "She probably only likes guys who are taller than I am."

Is that what she really thinks? In fact, there is absolutely no evidence to support this assumption. This concern about tallness came from inside the gentleman's head, not the lady's. If you find yourself mind reading, you need to sit back and clearly tell yourself that this line of thought has no factual basis. Mind reading almost always results in negative, faultfinding personal judgments that further decrease your confidence. Catch and stop such notions as soon as you initiate them. Train yourself instead to distinguish clearly between real world facts and ideas your imagination has manufactured.

Another way to reduce the threat of meeting and talking with strangers is to reframe your expectations. The negative self-talk that many of us engage in ("Why would she be interested in me?") sets us up as a worthless person asking a worthy person for undeserved time and attention. Paradoxically, at the same time we are tearing ourselves down, we may also be setting the goals of the meeting sky high. The meeting may become an intimidating test of rigidly set expectations, any departure from which will be defined as failure. For example, you are not a failure, nor have you screwed up, if you speak to someone new and don't seem to find much in common.

To increase your comfort level and self-confidence, lower the hurdles. Stop the negative self-talk and minimize any particular goals when initiating a conversation. Tell yourself that by making contact with others you are merely exploring the potential opportunities that flow from communication. And, the other person can reject your offer and miss the opportunity without necessarily rejecting you.

And speaking of rejection, are you really being personally rejected if a stranger declines your offer of conversation or participates halfheartedly? Many of us believe that rejection means there is something inherently wrong with us. Others will rightly recognize that there are any number of reasons for someone to reject an invitation to talk, and the vast majority of those reasons are not personal.

Think about this—if someone doesn't know you is it really possible for him or her to reject you? If a close friend rejects you, maybe you have something to worry about. A friend knows you and knows what he or she is rejecting, but a stranger does not. The woman above who talked briefly and then returned to her magazine might be feeling airsick, depressed, extremely tired, or just anxious to finish a great article before the plane lands. Who knows what her frame of mind is or what her problems might be? She may have bigger fish to fry at this moment than small talk with a stranger.

Here are a few closing thoughts on surviving an attempt at conversation with a stranger. Keep track of the thoughts and feelings that pass through your head when you approach someone. Are they primarily negative and self-destructive? How did your internal expectations play out in reality? If things went better than you expected, good. If things didn't go well, ask yourself whether your negative prophecies are self-fulfilling. In other words, your expectations of failure are so strong that failure is just what you get.

Finally, keep your focus outward, not inward. An excess of self-analysis and self-criticism is the enemy of all novice conversationalists. The greatest source of information for satisfactorily propelling a conversation forward is not within, it is without. Listening to what is being said, observing your conversation partner, and observing your surroundings are a far better use of your mental resources than navel gazing (How do I look? Do they like me? Was that a stupid thing to say?).

Now let's look at the nuts and bolts of initiating a conversation.

Nothing gets a new conversation off to a better start than conveying enthusiasm and interest to the other party. We all like to be liked. If your goal is to make friends, it is done far more efficiently by showing interest in others than by attempting to coax others into being interested in you. When you show people respect, give them your full attention, respond to their ideas, and do so with energy and genuine enjoyment, everything else will be a heck of a lot easier. If you make meeting someone seem like a chore or even just a neutral event, all the other techniques you're about to read will fail.

Sometimes our own demeanor and habits discourage others from reaching out or opening up to us. Many people appear so solemn and unsociable that only the bravest of souls would risk approaching them or attempting any kind of familiarity. The first step in starting a new conversation, or encouraging others to start one with you, is to make yourself open and non-threatening

You may be the friendliest person in the world, but if you habitually avoid eye contact, cross your arms, stare at the floor, and refuse to smile, you are communicating antisocial messages to others—Stay away, I'm not friendly, I don't want to talk, I'm thinking, don't bother me. That may not be your intent, but it is the result. We all try to avoid risk, and few would be willing to chance approaching a person with the expression and defensive body language described above.

Use your body language to communicate that talking to you will be a low risk move. Make establishing eye contact easy, smile, and stand or sit with an open body posture (which generally means keeping your hands away from your face and your arms uncrossed). When someone approaches you, or vice versa, lean slightly forward rather than back (many of us do this without realizing it).

Put some enthusiasm or emotion into your voice; let others know they are making a positive impact on you. By the same token, use your face muscles; let your expression communicate interest, excitement, and feeling. An expressive face is another way to give people positive feedback. A blank expression tells others little, except that perhaps they are boring you.

One caution here, don't try too hard to please by laughing at everything that's even remotely humorous. If you overdo your laughter, a common nervous habit, it isn't long before people are thinking, "Hey, I wasn't that funny." Laugh when you genuinely find something humorous, smile and look interested the rest of the time (I'm assuming a light conversation here in which serious or depressing subjects are unlikely to come up).

Another way to ease the opening of a conversation is to initiate some kind of nonverbal communication prior to addressing any comments to another. The goal is to achieve a small, shared understanding that pre-establishes some common ground. For instance, you might catch another's eye and make a pained face when a waiter drops a stack of dishes in a quiet restaurant. Or, when someone comes indoors from a freezing, blustery night, you might look at him or her and pretend to shiver. This makes it much easier for the other person to acknowledge you with a smile or a brief comment, something that you can use to initiate conversation. If the person doesn't respond, it's a minor rejection that's easy to cope with.

A similar method, although not quite as suave, is to concoct some sort of attention-getting device that's hard to ignore, and use it as the starting point for a conversation. For example, you're reading a newspaper in a waiting room, and you suddenly exclaim, "Oh no!" It's very hard for others to ignore such a blurted comment. When someone turns toward you, you can explain what your excitement is about.

You: It says here that there was a carjacking just two blocks from here last night.

Other: Oh, I know. This neighborhood is changing for the worse.

You: No kidding. Did you hear about the...

The best, all-purpose way to begin a conversation is to key off of something that you observe in the surroundings or about the other person. The main requirement here is observation, so stop, look, and listen. Look for similarities to yourself or your situation ("Looks like your car has the same paint problem as mine."), or differences ("I wish I had hair as long as yours, but mine just grows too slowly."). Search for some characteristic of the other party or something he or she is wearing or carrying that you can comment on. And remember, it doesn't hurt to make a comment that's also a compliment.

> Excuse me, those look like Navajo earrings. Did you get them in Arizona?
>
> Wow, *War and Peace*. I'm impressed. Are you reading that for school or pleasure?
>
> You sure have a great tan for January in New York.

If you can't find anything about the person that's worthy of comment, then make some reference to the surroundings, preferably some aspect of the experience that you both share.

> Why is it that air conditioning always breaks down on the hottest day of the year?
>
> Excuse me, is that veal scaloppini good? I was thinking of ordering it myself.
>
> Are you here to sign up for the Windows computer class?

Generally, it's wise to start with a closed question that's easy to answer ("Is that veal scaloppini good?"). After the response, follow up with an open question that will draw the person out and give you more information to work with ("I'm new around here. How does this restaurant rate against other local Italian eating places?").

All too often we delay opening a conversation while we rack our minds for the perfect opening statement, the statement that will instantly convince the other person that we are brilliant, witty, and exciting. Not uncommonly the moment to speak passes into oblivion while we cogitate.

If you can't concoct something brilliant to say, it's better to say almost anything as opposed to saying nothing. "Hi," "Hello," and "Nice day, isn't it?" may not be showstoppers, but they are vastly superior to silence in their potential. There's probably a 50% chance that the other person will assume the burden of conversation and follow up your hello with some comment that will seed a longer discussion.

Most conversations begin with a search for common ground. This is true even when we are conversing with an old friend, but it's especially true when you meet a stranger.

Your primary goal when talking with an unknown or barely-known person is to find out who he or she is as rapidly as possible through the use of questions, reflections, self-disclosure, and so on. The more info you uncover the greater the chance that you'll stumble onto shared views or interests, coincidences, and common experiences that can fuel discussion and enjoyment.

To get the ball rolling, you might ask how the person came to be wherever you are—"How do you know Bob (the host)?" Occupational information is almost always a gold mine of material for further talk—"So, Jane, what do you do to make ends meet?" If you're in a lighter mood, you might ask how the person spends free time—"What do you do for fun, Jane?"

Carefully listen and watch for any information that might invigorate the conversation or anything you can comment on—"Oh really, I was in Miami last summer also." Look for things to inquire about—"Where did you get that ring? I love it." Look for general background information. Is the person a college or high school graduate? Single or a married? Grew up locally or born and raised out of state? When you find something worth discussing, urge the other person to expand on it with an open question—"Computer programming must be an intense job? Tell me about it."

A new conversation is like a recently started campfire. If you don't feed the conversational flame with new fuel in the form of thoughts, opinions, and stories, it will sputter and die out. In addition to collecting info about the other person, be sure to offer him or her plenty of info about yourself. Disclose a rich and detailed picture of who you are, what you do, your history, and anything else that might be pertinent. Observe reactions to what you say and clarify or offer additional facts if you think the person misunderstands or doesn't follow your meaning—"That was a joke," or "Let me rephrase that," or "I should explain further."

Keep in mind that the person you are speaking with may be more nervous about meeting a stranger than you are. Providing lots of fodder for palaver helps people relax and reduces their fears about what to say next. It gives others something to ask you about, allows them to assess who you are, and gets the conversation going both ways. The more others feel there is plenty to talk about, the more comfortable they'll be and the greater the role they'll play in the conversation. That in turn means less conversation maintenance work for you.

Guard against making premature judgments. Even when proved incorrect later, they're often hard to shake off once you've committed yourself to them. Periodically test your assumptions or your understanding to make sure you've correctly interpreted the other person's meaning. One way to do this is with questions, but another is to reflect or summarize what you believe the person means—"Sounds to me like you are...Is that what you mean?" or "Let me make sure I understand. Are you saying...?"

In addition to listening for facts and meaning, you must "read" peoples' personalities and adjust your approach to suit. Are they shy or outgoing? Do they seem more comfortable with facts or with emotions? Do they laugh easily? Are they conservative? Are they skeptical, positive, negative, cheerful, assertive, shy, unenthusiastic, funny, sarcastic, or generally outrageous?

For example, if you meet someone who is creative and artsy, don't force her to listen to a number-laden story of the trouble you had with your accountant. Talk about your visit to an art museum and how you felt about what you saw.

Often, introducing yourself will not be the first thing you do when approaching someone new. First you get a little small talk going as described above, and then at some later point, when the two of you have established some common ground, you will move to introduce yourself. Wait for a pause in the flow of discussion and say, "By the way, my name is _____. What's yours?"

After he or she responds, say, "Nice to meet you, _____." Note here that it is important to use the other party's name in your response. People enjoy hearing their name and using it as quickly as possible helps to burn it into your memory. Throughout the rest of your discussion, make a periodic effort to address the person by name (don't overdo it). This makes a good impression. It shows that unlike most people you didn't forget the name two seconds after you heard it. Your partner will be pleasantly surprised and, importantly, will be more likely to remember you and your name thereafter.

Few of us give much thought to introductions, which probably explains why so few of us perform them well. You may be thinking, "What's the big deal? You tell them your name, you listen to theirs, no big deal." Well, yes, but there's a little more to it than that.

In many situations, an introduction is more than just an exchange of names. It also incorporates a brief explanation of who you are. If you are at a wedding, you might introduce yourself by giving your name and your relationship to the marrying couple—"Hi, my name's Bill. I'm Jim's best friend, and today I'm also his best man."

Use your introduction to provide enough information to encourage a broader conversation. If you meet someone at a party, you might say, "Let me introduce myself. I'm Carol, I was Geena's best friend in high school back when we lived in Michigan." Or at a business convention—"My name's Jack. I'm here to promote our company's new 3-D graphic design products." The object is to provide the other party with some descriptive information that might point to an area of mutual interest or something in common.

Give some advance thought to your self-description. Be able to tell others who you are and what you do in a few concise sentences. Prior to any situation in which you will meet people, prepare answers for the ritual questions they are likely to ask so that you can respond smoothly. The most common questions will be about your occupation, so compose a good, brief description of what you do. In fact, occupational info is so important for telling people who you are and for giving them material to discuss that you should volunteer it early on, even if no one asks.

A related skill is the ability to confidently introduce others. This is a function that if properly done makes a very good impression, and if poorly done makes a terrible impression. If you have never given any thought to how to introduce one person to another, there's a good chance it will come out like this—"Uh...okay, uh, Jack, oops, sorry,

I mean Jim. Where did 'Jack' come from? Wow, uh, anyway, Jim this is, this is, uhh, what was your name? Vicki? Oh yeah. Vicki, this is Jack, NO! Jim! Jim! Geez, sorry." Believe me, if you're at a party, and you introduce your boss in this way, he's not exactly going to think you have leadership ability.

Two other guidelines for introducing. First, introduce the more important person to the less important person, not the other way around. For example when introducing your boss to the new office clerk, the boss comes first. "Mr. Jackson, this is our new clerk, Bill Smith." Second, as with introducing yourself, provide some additional information about the parties and what they might have in common. This provides some opening fuel for conversation between the two after your introduction. "Bob, this is Mike Smith. Mike founded the computer club I've been telling you about. Mike this is Bob Jones. Bob's trying to buy his first computer. Maybe you could help him out."

Keep in mind that the goal of an introduction is more than just tossing names around. You want to make it easy for the people introduced to begin a conversation.

Want to make a good impression on someone you've met only once before? Immediately call him or her by name when you meet again. The person is bound to be flattered because, as we all know, names from a first introduction are often quickly forgotten. Want to impress further? Remind the person of what the two of you spoke about at your first meeting. "So, did your daughter's dance recital go well?"

Of course, while remembering a name is great, the reverse is often the case. Suppose someone approaches you and cheerily calls out your name. He goes on to ask you about a few matters the two of you had chatted about at some previous time. Soon you're both having a nice little conversation. There's only one problem—you can't remember this person's name. And, your fear of being found out is growing. What do you do?

The first rule for situations like this—don't try to fake it. You'll be uncomfortable throughout the whole conversation, and sooner or later the other person will probably figure out that you don't know his name. The best solution is to come clean and confess, preferably softening the blow with a little self-deprecating humor—"I'm sorry, I really hate this, but I've just gone blank, please remind me of your name," or "I know I should remember your name. Maybe this smog is damaging my brain," or "It's been a crazy day. I'm not sure I could remember my own mother's name."

Be kind to others who may find themselves in the same fix. If you run into someone you've met only once or haven't seen in a while, there's a good chance he or she has forgotten your name. Don't make the person sweat. As a matter of course, in any situation where the other party might have forgotten your name, restate it or reintroduce yourself from scratch. Re-introducing yourself relieves the other person's embarrassment, allows him or her to relax, and makes the rest of the conversation go a lot easier.

Forgetting a name isn't as bad as it seems. We've all had the experience, and while everyone likes to be remembered, it's easy to understand how it can happen. In other words, people are usually pretty forgiving.

Now that you've gotten past the ice-breaking and introduction stages, how do you keep the conversation rolling and prevent it from dying?

Before the twentieth century, people took conversation much more seriously than we do today. They considered being a good conversationalist a vital skill for any successful, educated person. Given this view, they were more willing to invest time and effort in developing their abilities to a high level. While today our conversational skills are developed more or less by osmosis and random experience, in the past, people approached the development of their social powers in much the same way as we might devote ourselves to mastering a musical instrument. Next we will review techniques you can use to hone your conversational skills.

Here are some methods that will expand the supply of conversational material you can draw on whenever you find yourself in a social situation.

The first step is to pay attention to what is going on in the larger world. It's always discouraging to attempt to discuss a hot new movie or an event that's all over the news only to have the other party give you a blank stare and say, "Hmm, I guess haven't heard about that." What a letdown. Make sure you aren't the uninformed party.

Make an effort to keep up with what's likely to be on people's minds. Watch the news periodically, read the newspaper, subscribe to a health newsletter, go to movies that are making a big splash, and read some of the best selling novels or nonfiction books. Follow what's hot in popular culture such as music, TV shows, and clothes. Keep your ears open for the issues and events that people are talking about.

You can't be knowledgeable about everything, so try to focus on information that will interest the people you're most likely to associate with. For example, you might not be interested in sports, but if your friends or your superiors at work are sports fans, then it wouldn't hurt you to spend a little time on the sports page every morning. Information is power. Having it allows you to fit into the group more easily, impress the boss, ask intelligent questions, keep people entertained, and converse with greater ease. This is how you begin to build rapport with people.

Think about who you are. Sounds simple but most of us never really take a close look at ourselves. Once you have, it will be a lot easier to describe yourself and what's important to you. If you can clearly and easily tell people your hopes, dreams, values, loves, joys, goals, and struggles, they will be more able to identify with you and discover areas they have in common with you.

As discussed in the chapter on self-disclosure, expressing your thoughts and feelings makes it easier for others to discuss theirs with you. You don't need to "tell all," reveal the family secrets, get into the depressing parts of your life, or blurt out controversial ideas to total strangers. However, the more defining information you reveal, the faster you'll develop relationships and the greater the impression you'll make.

Consider starting a notebook in which you record virtually anything that might interest people. This can require some work, but the payoff of such a record in the richness, variety, humor, and interest of the topics you would be able to discuss is extraordinary.

We've all heard thousands of great tales, fascinating ideas, and truly funny jokes that we forget a few weeks after we've heard them. Wouldn't it be worthwhile to spend a little time every night briefly writing them down so that they would never be lost? Every once in a while you could refresh your memory by skimming through your notes so that the ideas and stories would remain fresh in your mind. Now this material is ready for use when you want to impress the boss, entertain your friends, or survive a party at which you know almost no one. What kind of information would you want to record in such a notebook?

Collect anecdotes as if they were gemstones. When you hear a good story or have something funny or interesting happen in your own life, write it down. Such stories don't necessarily have to be real. You might, for instance, note a good scene from a TV show or movie.

Anecdotes are great fuel for conversation. When you tell a humorous story and get everyone laughing, others will jump in with their own stories or reminiscences. Additionally, you can use anecdotes to illustrate a point or explain the consequence of some type of behavior. Stories are healthy for a conversation. They bring it to life because people almost always prefer a humanizing tale to dry facts.

Beyond preserving good material, writing anecdotes down also helps you tell them more smoothly. The effort and thought required to organize them on paper will increase your skill in relating them verbally.

Clip and collect humorous or interesting articles from newspapers and magazines. Keep track of clever remarks, sayings, new words, new slang, and so on. If you have an observation on life, work, or the opposite sex, make a note of it. Recently, for example, I took note of the word *T-boned* which in this particular context describes an auto accident in which one vehicle rams head on into the side of another. I thought it was a thoroughly descriptive term that perfectly evoked a mental picture of two cars colliding in this fashion. It wasn't a big deal, but it was interesting, and I made an effort to retain it. This kind of small effort, repeated often enough, is what makes a fascinating conversationalist.

There are people who have very sharp memories and a natural eye for human interest. These folks may not need to physically record as much information as the rest of us, and yet their conversational skills may be quite impressive. But, don't be mislead. These are people who instinctively put a lot of effort into noting what others find interesting and thinking about how best to tell their stories. Their quick replies and ready anecdotes are the result of minds that have filed away and worked through conversational material in advance. As a result, their performance seems effortless and spontaneous.

In the past, when the art of conversation was more highly valued, people who traveled in sophisticated social circles took great pains with their conversational training. They often developed their abilities to levels that would be marveled at today. By making an effort to train your spontaneous nature and build your personal library of anecdotes and general knowledge, you'll find you have powers you never suspected were in you.

The people who make conversations successful are the people who continually feed them with new facts, stories, and revelations. They aren't know-it-alls; they're just people who are fully engaged with the world around them.

Now that we've discussed building a stockpile of raw material for conversation, it's worth pausing to discuss habits that should be avoided in conversations with strangers, acquaintances, and even at times with good friends (although friends are considerably more tolerant than strangers).

First, there's an old saying that "to be interesting you have to be interested." Put another way, if you are bored, you are probably boring. The importance of enthusiasm as a listener and as a speaker can't be stressed too much.

I'm convinced that when a speaker has an audience that communicates enthusiasm, that speaker's mind works better. His jokes and stories will be told better. His observations will be more acute and confident. His own enthusiasm will rise. This in turn generates even stronger interest among other participants, and the conversation spirals upward.

Boredom or distraction among participants results in just the opposite. The speaker senses the lack of interest and becomes self-conscious, uncomfortable, and less energetic. This causes his conversational skills to spiral downward, resulting in even more boredom among listeners.

On the other hand, truly boring and disfunctional conversationalists are out there. These people have conversational flaws that can't be solved by enthusiasm. Here's a list of common habits that turn otherwise good people into bores.

Forgetting that common interest is one of the foundations of good talk—This is basically a violation of the cooperative nature of conversation. The speaker is determined to discuss something in which he is interested and is unconcerned or oblivious that others find the topic as dull as battleship paint. Don't try to force others to listen to something they could care less about. A successful speaker is attuned to the response of his audience and moves on to another topic if the current one isn't a box office hit. It's a waste of time to regale a sports car nut with tales about the joys of owning a new minivan. The rule—seek out interest.

Refusing to admit that you are not well informed about the current subject—If you are uninformed say so. At the very least, avoid pretending you know what you're talking about when you don't. You can deceive people for a while, but it isn't long before they realize what's happening and label you a pompous fool.

Overstaying your welcome—One renowned conversationalist made it a point never to speak longer than thirty seconds. You don't have to be that rigid but exercise some self-control. Do your listeners a favor, plan what you intend to say, speak concisely, be relevant to the discussion's current topic, and refrain from talking just to hear yourself talk.

Holding the false belief that small talk is irrelevant and unimportant—It has been said that a bore is someone who does not indulge in small talk. Some people are merciless in their insistence on analyzing the big, the serious, and the profound. Most of us enjoy conversation for its own sake. We want the simple pleasure of communicating in a relaxed, lighthearted manner with our fellow human beings. The aim of small talk is to put people at ease, to familiarize one person with another, to pass time pleasantly, and most importantly, to build relationships.

There are some, however, who feel this is a waste of time. They want to use conversation to lecture, educate, show off their knowledge, and wrestle with the big issues of the day. Sometimes that's okay; we all enjoy a good serious debate now and then. In social situations, though, people commonly want to take it easy and will run from anyone who insists on being overly serious.

Again, keep in mind that conversation is a cooperative venture. If everyone in a discussion is eager to debate federal budget deficit issues, by all means, fly at it. Otherwise, this is the rule—never stay serious for too long.

Being relentlessly humorous—This is the flip side of the previous rule. Some people simply cannot bring themselves to be serious about anything. I would guess that psychiatrists would claim these people use humor to avoid confrontation or troubling emotions. Or, perhaps they don't have any faith in the correctness of their opinions or ideas and use humor to avoid expressing them. Humor is a wonderful conversational skill, but it can be overdone. Take a chance, express yourself honestly and seriously when the conversation requires it.

Focusing interminably on yourself—People who talk about themselves to the exclusion of all else get old fast. No matter what the subject is, this type of person finds a way to bring it back home to good ol' number one—"Yep, nuclear war would be a real bummer. It all reminds me of the time I got lost in the woods. I remember thinking, geez, I wonder what it would be like if I was the last person on earth."

Bringing every topic around to your pet belief or interest—A corollary of the previous failing. "Yeah, the pollution down in the bay is bad. That's just one more reason why the government should release the information it has about UFOs. Alien technology could help us clean up the planet." Part of the pleasure of conversation is not knowing what's coming next. If you always return to the same subject, this pleasing feature is lost.

Using erudite, polymathic, and recondite language—Huh? Just because you happen to know a lot of obscure, scholarly words doesn't relieve you of the responsibility of speaking so that others can understand you. Generally, using a lot of big words falls into the category of showing off, not communication. The rule—if a simple, commonly understood word is available, use it in preference to a more obscure word. Find some way other than vocabulary to show people how smart you are.

Staying too long on the receiving end of the talk—Once again, conversation is a cooperative venture; everyone has to do his or her part. If you decide to take it easy, think about a problem at work, or remain silent because of shyness, you're in violation. In every conversation, you should make an effort to balance the giving and receiving of talk. Refusing to hold up your end is as bad as hogging the floor. If you are too passive, don't be surprised if others give you a bad review—"What an ordeal! I single-handedly kept that conversation going for twenty of the longest minutes of my life."

The above violations of the rules of order for good conversation apply to all kinds of talk. Below are some rules that apply specifically to conversations with strangers or acquaintances.

It's wise to avoid certain subjects until you have a feel for the other party's worldview and a certain level of comfort and familiarity. Politics, religion, shop talk (with people not in your industry), putdown humor, and complaining or negative talk are all wise to skip. During the initial feeling-out period, stick to reasonably safe subjects that allow safe disagreement (disagreement that won't be taken personally). If you say the traffic on the way to a party was terrible, it won't be a big deal if someone else says it wasn't any worse than usual.

Watch out for highly unusual or controversial subjects. It's not a good idea to bring up your unwavering belief in reincarnation with someone you've only known for ten minutes. The odd thing about discussing controversial beliefs with a stranger is that it can make a bad impression even if the other person agrees with you. There is an unwritten rule in our society that it is improper to discuss charged or unconventional subjects with someone you don't know well. People have tendency to label those who break this rule as weird and suspicious. It may be immaterial that they happen to agree with you. On the other hand, once you get to know someone, it then becomes okay to bring up and discuss non-mainstream ideas and beliefs.

Faultfinding and disagreeing with your new conversational partner is another no-no. Small talk is just that, small. When a speaker makes a minor mistake or indulges in an innocent exaggeration, it's unlikely that anything of real value is at risk. There's no need to feel duty bound to impose strict rules of accuracy on your fellows. If you like to call people on their errors, gleefully point out discrepancies or contradictions, and habitually play the devils advocate, you will be forcing the small talk to adhere to a harsher standard than is natural.

People engaging in a relaxed, comfortable conversation don't want confrontation and egotistical debate. Even less do they want to be proven wrong or made to look foolish in front of others. That is a blow to their ego for which you may never be forgiven. What are your priorities—accuracy and resentment or flexibility and friendship?

It's certainly okay to ask for clarification, and it won't kill anyone if you periodically express disagreement or offer a different perspective. Problems arise when your disagreements are so frequent that people notice a pattern and tag you as a habitual nitpicker or quarreler. If you must disagree, avoid telling the other party that he is wrong. Leave him a way to escape and save face. Offer him an excuse for his error.

For instance, here is a confrontational response that leaves the other party feeling attacked—"Oh come on, there's no way Jackson threw the fight. Montoya's knockout punch was right on target. I saw it! There's no way that punch missed." This statement basically communicates that the other party is a blind fool and forces him to defend his own point of view to the death, no compromise.

If the statement were rephrased as follows, there would be more room for concession—"You know it's hard to tell on TV, camera angle can make a bad punch look good, but my impression was that Montoya's punch was dead on." This statement isn't an attack on the other person's judgment, and the camera angle reference offers him a way to save face. In this case, the other person now has room to express uncertainty or even agree with you—"Well, it's true, the camera can fool you. Maybe that punch was heavier than I thought."

Another way to let the other person down easy is to fasten your opposing view onto something in the other's statement with which you agree—"I have the same opinion as you. There is a lot of funny business going on in the fight game these days, but in this case, I thought Montoya won honestly. That last punch looked pretty good to me."

Before you convince yourself that the other guy is wrong, make an effort to empathize. Try to understand his reasons for holding a particular view. You may find that what is wrong for you is reasonable and logical for another. And by the way, if you expect others to admit their errors, then you should be willing to do the same. If you admit error genuinely, not grudgingly, a spirit of fair play is engendered that makes it easier for others to admit their mistakes.

If you embarrass or oppose someone you just met, someone who is still forming an impression of you, there is a good chance he will decide that you are an unpleasant and difficult person. Once a first impression of this sort has been made, studies have shown that it is very difficult to alter later on, even in the face of contradicting evidence. First impressions, especially negative ones, can last forever.

Speaking of first impressions, here are a few other bad habits to avoid. Try not to come on too strong and/or talk too loud when you first meet someone. This is a trait frequently displayed by aggressive individuals, but it can also be overcompensation by someone who is shy or nervous. Whatever the cause, it can overwhelm people who don't know you or are shy themselves. This is not to say that you should curb your enthusiasm and energy. Just don't bowl the other person over.

As mentioned previously, make an effort to get rid of involuntary verbal tics such as the infamous *uh*—"So, uh, I uh, went to the, uh, park and, uh…" We've all heard that one, but verbal tics come in limitless variety. For example, *you know, basically, like, kind of, whatever,* and any other word or phrase that you use much too often. If you're trying to identify other verbal tics, one frequent characteristic of these words is that they add virtually no concrete meaning to what you are trying to say. They are simply empty filler words.

One final piece of advice for eliminating bad habits. Study the manner and method of those people who bore or annoy you. First, analyze what they are doing wrong. Then, ask yourself if you share any of their unfortunate peculiarities. Self-analysis isn't simple. It's all too easy for us to explain away our own weaknesses while despising the same in others.

Now that we've covered the don'ts of social conversation, lets look at the do's.

First off, we'll answer the question all aspiring conversationalists ask themselves—"How do I find topics that are interesting and appropriate?" The primary secret is to discover what the other party wants to talk about. Like a prospector, you need to dig here and dig there until you find the vein of gold. From then on, your job is to help the other person mine that vein of gold.

Interest is the foundation of all good conversation. No conversation will be a real success unless all participants have some interest or stake in what is being said. Many shy conversationalists try to plan what they will say in advance, but this advance planning almost always fails because it violates the principle of exploring the interests of the other parties.

Exploring and seeking is a flexible, turn-on-a-dime process. You need to be ready to instantly adapt what you are saying to the interests of others. Planning what you will say in advance is a static, head down, straight-line method that isn't much different than an actor delivering his lines. It appeals to the nervous conversationalist because it seems safer to have all your lines stored up in your head, but it is a formula for failure (such preplanning is not the same as building a stockpile of topics, stories and information to selectively draw on as needed).

If you are planning what you will say in advance, you will inevitably be focused inward, not outward where your attention should be. Instead of listening to and observing others for clues about who they are and what interests them, you will be concentrating on delivering your next pre-planned line. This can lead to disasters in which you miss important information and plow ahead blindly.

Jim: Did I tell you about the new computer I'm going to buy?
Jane: I'm sick of computers. I work on them all day. They drive me nuts.
Jim: Uh, yeah, well, anyway I'm getting this new Acme Pentium with a huge hard drive and…

See what's going on here? Jim is so determined to stick to his pre-planned script that he willfully ignores the fact that Jane has explicitly stated that she has no interest in this subject.

The other problem with a preplanned script is that you cease to explore. You become so preoccupied with remembering and delivering your lines that you fail to follow up on valuable information that others happen to reveal.

Jim: Did I tell you about the new Acme computer I'm going to buy?
Jack: No—by the way, I just got a report that assesses the quality of Acme computers.
Jim: Uh-huh…anyway, I'm going to get an Acme Pentium with…

Surely Jim would like to hear about this report, and just as surely, it is something Jack would like to tell him about, but Jim's tunnel vision is so severe he blows right past this nice piece of information.

Conversations are alive. They branch, twist, and turn, and you have to pay attention to stay with them. If you focus inwardly during a conversation, spending too much time trying to work out your next statement, you will miss critical information that you need to effectively converse.

Consider the cheetah pursuing an antelope over the open grassland. The antelope turns left and right in a flash, accelerates, feints this way and that, and leaps over rocks and streams. As the cheetah, your only hope of staying with the antelope is to focus totally on every move it makes. On a higher level, the cheetah must observe the antelope so closely that it is able to predict where the antelope will go before it goes there. In a conversation, think of your partner as the antelope. You must watch his or her every move, assess every comment, if you are to keep up and remain interesting and relevant.

For example, suppose that you mention a movie you've seen recently with the intention of discussing your reaction to the plot. However, as soon as you mention the movie, your conversation partner jumps in and enthusiastically tells you how amazed he was by the film's computer-generated monster. If you are observing and listening, it will be clear that he has revealed something important about himself—he is fascinated by movie special effects. Now you are home free. You no longer need to support the conversation single handedly. Allow the other person to focus on his interest, ask appropriate questions to draw him out, and any worry you had about keeping the talk flowing is over.

Just as the cheetah tries to anticipate the antelope's moves before they happen, a good conversationalist tries to get ahead of his conversational partner by looking deeper than most people. Try to respond not just to the words but also to the intent of those words and the feelings behind them.

For example, if you ask someone how he enjoys his job, and he says, "Interesting, it's always interesting," but he says it in an unenthusiastic voice, you may interpret the normally positive word interesting to be negative in this situation. Respond to the feelings, not the specific words. An undiscerning listener might reply, "Great, glad to hear it!" The discerning listener would note the underlying message and say, "Sounds like things could be better."

If your first choice for a topic of discussion arouses little interest, keep trying, move on to another topic. Whenever interest is shown, zero in on it. Probe any topic that receives a positive response. Explore it, dissect it, seek the maximum point of interest.

Perhaps a person shows moderate interest when you bring up the general subject of music. Good, you can safely assume that somewhere in this broad topic is buried a smaller topic that truly fascinates her. Start to narrow the subject down. Ask her what kind of music she likes best. When she answers, ask her which artist or group is her favorite. When she reveals that, ask her to tell you what it is about the group that makes them special to her. Ask her if she's seen them in concert, and what was it like. By now you've probably found the subject closest to her heart, and she is speaking eagerly.

Probe and ask questions, but allow others the freedom to talk about whatever interests them. Here's the procedure—find a general area of interest, home in on it, narrow it down, find the specific interests, and finally, show enthusiasm and interest to keep the person talking. Even if you've said very little, people will come away from such a discussion saying, "What an interesting person!" That's the strange thing about helping people talk about *their* interests; they always come away thinking *you* were an interesting person.

In addition to finding others' interests, try to stimulate their thoughts. Analyze what they're saying, and ask them if a new fact or a different way of looking at the issue affects their opinion. Share your perceptions, experiences and thoughts about the topic. Tell them any relevant information that you've heard or read. Ask them how they think this topic relates to some other topic. In other words, without arguing, challenge them to think or to look at the subject from new angles. As in the last example, people will come away from such a discussion thinking well of you—"I like him (or her). He makes you think."

The richest areas to explore with others are those that relate to their life experience. Encourage people to talk about themselves, their history, their challenges, and their accomplishments. Discover how they invest their time and energy. The things that are closest to a person will be the easiest for him or her to open up about. When you meet a parent, talk about the idiosyncrasies or abilities of kids. When you meet a local business owner, ask him or her about the challenges of running a successful business. When you meet an avid tennis player, ask about the latest developments in racquet design.

Don't be too concerned about prying or being too personal. Although openness varies somewhat from person to person and from region to region, people are generally more willing to reveal their lives than they once were (if you don't believe it, watch a few afternoon talk shows). Many of us are simply too concerned about "prying."

There are still questions that are too personal, but far fewer than in the past. It's very important in a new conversation to learn as much as possible as quickly as possible. The fastest way to do that is to ask questions and make your own disclosures. A new conversation, particularly between strangers, needs facts, feelings, and opinions to keep it going. So, ask questions liberally and use any other method that will bring out information such as disclosure and reflection.

Besides fishing for information, you need to get a feel for the mood of the person or group with whom you're speaking, and then stay in tune with that mood. A lighthearted group that's laughing and joking isn't going to want to discuss the high cost of childcare or hear about the tough time you had at work today. A serious group having a fairly intellectual discussion may not be the right forum for a story about the silly trick your five year old played on his brother yesterday. Give some thought to whether the story that just popped into your head is really appropriate for the particular conversation you are in.

And, as stated earlier, remember that conversation is a two-way street. Make it easy for others to find your hot buttons. Give them lots of information about what excites you and what's important to you. Initially, give them a broad general picture of your life and then reveal the details of any area in which you sense their interest. This is the way you discover common interests, and ultimately, make friends.

Previously, we've discussed the risks of interrupting speakers. While it's true that disruptive interruptions are a violation of good conversational etiquette, if you think about it, you'll realize that *brief* interruptions occur frequently in healthy discussions. In fact, quick interruptions probably increase as a conversation really begins to click. An enthusiastic, animated discussion is often characterized by listeners readily interjecting quick comments into the speaker's remarks.

Here are a few random, unrelated interruptions I've taken down from some recent conversations I've been a part of.

Wow, the same thing happened to me!
What did you do then?
What's Joe look like? Is he short and blond?
Oh, I know, isn't that a joke?
How did you know he was going to do that?
It's true, it's true. I hate that!
Man, talk about great timing. I can't believe it.
Yeah, that's happened to me too.
Don't get too excited. You don't have the check cashed yet.

These interruptions are all quick, they ask for clarification or express interest and editorial comment, and they're not at all unwelcome to the speaker. Such interruptions indicate to the speaker that the listener is involved and anxious to hear more. As long as these interruptions aren't an attempt to seize the floor or so frequent that the speaker loses his train of thought, they probably add to the richness and enjoyment of the exchange.

Interruptions are often used to communicate to speakers that their comments have zeroed in on a subject that the listener is interested in. Don't assume that speakers know you approve of their comments, tell them. A quick interruption such as "Hey, I loved that movie!" or "I'm going to Hawaii next month! What's it like?" signals the speaker that he has hit on a topic you want to discuss and encourages him to go on.

One of the most common functions of interruption is to request that the speaker clarify a comment you didn't understand. In this case, you quickly and concisely explain your confusion and return the floor—"Uh-oh, you lost me. How did you get to the airport if your car had broken down?" Unless you are nitpicking or clarifying trivial, nonessential facts, speakers usually welcome such interruptions. After all, you are only trying to help him get his point across.

Interruptions often come in the form of questions. Questions are tools that can track down the core of people's fascinations and draw them out. Good questions clear up confusion, encourage the speaker to provide greater exactness, reconcile one fact with another, gather information to support a claim, and correct errors. Ask your questions with care. Guard against questions that are frivolous, requestinging unnecessary information and distracting the speaker.

Frequently, you can bamboozle others into believing you are far more knowledgeable than you are simply by asking intelligent, well-timed questions. Good follow up questions, those that stimulate the speaker or make him look at his topic in a new way, make you seem not only interested but discerning and intelligent as well.

Once a conversation has moved past the opening stage, questions such as "What do you think?" and "Why?" (the simplest but most effective question of all) keep the information flowing. If someone says she thinks the smog is getting worse, ask her why. If you say that you think the local economy is getting better, pause and ask the other person what she thinks. Another great question is "Can you give me an example?" After someone states that the local mall isn't as safe from crime as it once was, ask him to give you examples of what's been going on.

Questions can be used to generate talk in other ways. "What if...?" is a great way to get people talking, thinking, and having fun—"What would you do if you found out your girlfriend's father was a Mafia boss?" or "What would you do if you won $10,000,000 in the lottery?" Such questions get debate going and make people explore their preferences and priorities in new ways. Good what-if questions are almost guaranteed to stir up interest and fun.

Now let's confront another of the great conversational challenges of people everywhere—How exactly do I figure out what to say? Generally speaking, once you've learned to listen well and to encourage others to reveal themselves, you will find that topics come easily in the regular course of the discussion. Still, it's worth going over some methods for generating the exact words that will pop out of your mouth.

The biggest obstacle to finding something to say is the fear that you won't be able to come up with anything. The mind only has so much capacity. If you divert a big chunk of its resources to deal with worry, fear, and self-consciousness, there's not much left over to work on formulating your comments. Furthermore, your imagination will work best if you aren't in a state of psychological turmoil. Fortunately, with practice and training of the imagination, most of us can learn to come up with topics of discussion in even the most arid and bleak social situation. In other words, being tongue-tied is a problem of nervousness, not genetics.

The majority of conversation is organized as a chain, each comment linked to the one before. Unskilled conversationalists tend to break that chain with comments that either don't link up with or fail to expand on what's been said previously. If someone says, "We just got back from a vacation to Disney World in Florida," and your reply is, "Oh, really," or "That must have been nice," you have just broken the chain. Bad, bad, bad. Such responses leave the other party with nothing to respond to and talk dries up.

The proper response is to link your comment to the *topic nodes* of the original statement. A topic node is any word or phrase in a message that contains substance for discussion. What are the nodes in the above statement? They are *we, vacation, Disney World,* and *Florida.*

Your next comment should expand on one (or several) of these topic nodes. A response keying off the *we*-node might be—"Just you and your wife, or did you take the kids too?" Now the other party has something to respond to; he can describe his decision to take or not take the kids. Or, you could key off of the *vacation*-node—"I can't tell you how long it's been since I've had a vacation. Did you really get to relax or was it pretty hectic?" Let's say you decide to key off the *Florida*-node—"I've heard Florida is miserably hot this time of year. How was it for you?"

Suppose you choose to make the comment about Florida, and the other person responds, "Oh, it was hot during the day. We got pretty worn out standing in the sun, waiting to get on the rides." The topic nodes in this statement are *day, worn out, sun, waiting,* and *rides.* Take your pick, you can comment on any of these nodes without too much imagination. Choose *worn out* and you might comment as follows—"Yes, vacations are fun, but sometimes they can actually be more tiring than being at work." Or you might say something about the *day*-node—"You say it was hot during the day. Was it comfortable at night?"

Such chained comments allow a lot of flexibility in conversational direction. Clearly, the main thrust of the above comments is vacation and Disney World, but if these topics don't interest you, it's quite easy to steer the conversation in the direction of one of the peripheral nodes such as your reaction to Florida's heat and humidity. If you allow your mind to identify topic nodes and wander without restriction, you'll find that it is quite capable of providing you with numerous avenues of response. Very likely you'll find more than you'll ever have time to discuss. The problem will be an excess of topics, not too few.

Another way to formulate comments is to link new information with old information. For example, suppose that Mary had told you five minutes ago that she hoped to move to Idaho someday and live in the mountains. Later on, however, she casually mentions that she thinks she has poor circulation because when the weather gets chilly she can never seem to get her hands and feet warm. Linking these two statements provides you with a perfect topic of discussion. "Mary, if you have such a hard time with cold weather, how are you ever going to survive an Idaho winter?" This is sure to be something Mary has thought about and should keep the conversation rolling for some time. From here, you can then branch out to discuss whatever is said about Idaho or living with weather extremes.

The situation or surroundings you and your conversational partner are in is another great source of topics. Look around. Where are you? Why are you here? What is unusual about the place? What's good about it, or bad? How do you feel about being here? What prior experiences have you had here? How has it changed? What common influence does this environment have on you and others? All of these questions are loaded with conversational possibilities.

For example, at a party, you might comment, "Bill and Shannon have really fixed this place up since they moved in, haven't they?" At the grocery store, you could say to someone in the checkout line, "The last time I was here all the scanners went down and I had to wait half an hour while they entered everything by hand." In a college class, ask the person next to you why he or she is there. "Are you taking this class for a degree or just personal interest?" The rule here is to get in the habit of observing your surroundings with an eye for possible topics.

A periodic change of topic is necessary to maintain the health and well being of a conversation. Topics don't last forever. Eventually they all run out of steam. Dying topics need to be allowed a quick and painless death, and yet people often keep them on life support due to uncertainty about how to replace them. Watch carefully for growing disinterest and restlessness as a topic grows old and then take prompt action. As discussed previously, you can key off of something that's been said that isn't really in the mainstream of the current topic, or you can link old and new information to create a fresh topic.

Changing topics can also involve a sudden jump to a new subject that is completely unrelated to what is currently being discussed— "Changing the subject, I heard that…" You will find that people are usually quite supportive of such seemingly illogical transitions. Why? Because clean breaks add variety and spontaneity that is refreshing and energizing. Additionally, you aren't the only one who's concerned about the talk drying up. Conversational dead spots are abhorred by almost everyone, and people are generally grateful when someone provides a new subject to replace a topic that's going nowhere. "By the way, before I forget, did I tell you about…"

The only caution about abrupt subject changes is to make sure the current topic really is dying before you leap to a new one. If the present topic isn't fully talked out, people may resent your surprise course change and consider it an unwarranted interruption.

Now that we've discussed some methods for finding topics and formulating comments, let's discuss how to deliver them in a way that interests and involves your listeners. Finding a topic is only half the struggle. One person can hold forth on a certain topic and bore everyone to tears while another can relate the same ideas and have listeners hanging on his every word. Good conversation requires more than just words; it also requires a certain amount of drama and showmanship.

When you speak, stir people up by putting a little P. T. Barnum into everything you say. Be enthusiastic about your message, gesture with your hands, move in toward your listener, let your face express your feelings, speak up (no mumbling), use humor, and present your comments smoothly and efficiently. And, in addition to all the above, you must always, always, always look for the drama and human interest in whatever you are saying.

Finding drama and human interest almost always means telling a story in a way that moves the listener to feel what is said personally. Once a listener connects what you are saying with his or her own feelings and experience, that listener's interest will greatly increase. Always seek out the elements that can engage the feelings of the listener. The difference between a dry telling of facts and a tale of human interest is the difference between tide and tidal wave. For example, consider the following two versions of the same story.

Did you hear about Mike's auto accident? Well, he'd been working quite a lot, and I guess he was pretty tired. Anyway, he fell asleep at the wheel and hit someone from behind. He didn't really get hurt, just a sore neck. The real problem was that he didn't have insurance, and I guess the damage to the other guy's car is going to cost a fair bit. So anyway, now he's got to come up with the money somehow.

This is a fairly dry description of the facts. Very little indication of how Mike feels or how it affected his life. In other words, very little drama. After such a telling, the listener is likely to react with a bland "Too bad" or "Tough break." Now let's consider another version.

Did you hear about Mike's disaster? Well, you know he's been slaving at two jobs so he and his wife could finally go on a long postponed honeymoon. They didn't have the money for a real honeymoon trip when they got married, so they've been saving up for it. Anyway, Mike said he was so exhausted from overwork that he nodded off for a moment while driving and plowed right into the back of a Mercedes. No one was really hurt but he knew it was going to cost a fortune to repair that Mercedes. Of course, insurance would cover it. But when he called his insurance company, they told him he isn't insured. He was stunned. Turns out his last insurance bill had fallen down behind his desk. He was so busy he didn't miss it, and the bill was never paid. Now all that hard-earned money he and his wife struggled to set aside for their trip is going to Mercedes repair. The honeymoon trip is dead, again.

This version would involve all but the most hardened listener. The story begins by building sympathy for Mike. Here is a guy who is working at two jobs to take his wife on a belated honeymoon. You want things to work out well for him. He deserves it. And that feeling creates the drama, because you know from the first sentence ("Did you hear about Mike's disaster?") that he is headed for trouble—and you want to know what is going to happen.

In this telling, it's easy to put yourself in Mike's shoes and imagine how you would be affected by such a disaster. And once you do that, the story has you hooked. Instead of an unemotional "Gee, that's too bad," the listener is likely to react with real emotion and want to hear everything the speaker knows. "Wow, what incredible bad luck! It's unbelievable. He and his wife must be miserable. What are they going to do? Are they going to try and do the trip next year or have they just given up?"

When comparing the two versions of Mike's accident, notice the difference in vocabulary. The second version uses more powerful, evocative, and descriptive words than the first—*slaving* versus *working*, *exhausted* versus *pretty tired*, *nodded off* versus *fell asleep*, *plowed into* versus *hit*, *a fortune* versus *pretty expensive*. Then there are other expressive words such as *hard-earned, struggled, stunned,* and *dead*.

Also, the first version omits the make of the car that was hit, while the second version reveals that it was a Mercedes. When the listener hears it was a Mercedes, the feeling of disaster is heightened because we all instantly assume the repair is going to be more expensive for a luxury car.

The words and style of the second version evoke stronger images and emotions and as a result make it a more absorbing tale than the first version. The lesson here—relating the big picture is fine for getting basic facts across, but human interest requires drama. Drama is usually built by good story design and attention to key details.

When you tell a story or anecdote, decide what the main dramatic theme is and then eliminate anything that doesn't further that theme. In the story above, the main theme is how Mike's incredible bad luck tragically ruins his and his wife's honeymoon plans. That is what will hook the listener, and that is what you should focus on.

A common fault in story telling is breaking the flow of the tale in order to discuss something irrelevant that distracts from the primary theme—"So anyway, Mike calls his insurance company on, uh, Wednesday, and they tell him…no wait, I think he actually called on Thursday. Yeah, yeah, it was Thursday because that was the day I had my dental appointment, and uh…hmm, where was I?"

Keep your stories lean and mean. Don't overdo the minor facts, and don't short the important facts. Tell what has to be told to create drama and no more. Some studies have shown that listeners start to lose interest when narrations run over 200 words. This isn't certain. A good story, well told, can capture attention longer, but the risk of losing your audience increases with story length.

Put some planning into your stories. Think about what needs to be included and how the various elements should be ordered. How often have you had a speaker stop in the middle of his tale and say, "Oh, wait a minute, I forgot something…"? We all make mistakes like this occasionally, but be aware that they are very destructive to the spell you are casting on your listeners.

Don't necessarily tell an anecdote the minute it pops into your head—wait for the proper moment. Pay attention to timing and mood. If the group you are conversing with is discussing the funeral of someone's father, it's not a good moment to relate the funny thing that happened in the office the other day. If the group is laughing and joking, it's not the right time to bring up your recent bout with migraines. Just hold off for a while, wait for the mood of the talk to change, and then tell the story.

Certain elements of story narration can only be learned by observation and experience. The internal timing of a story—when to slow the pace, when to speed up, and when to pop the punch line—is not something I can show you. Some people are naturally better at these skills than others, but with observation and practice, we can all substantially improve our storytelling skills.

Even those who seem to have been born witty and interesting have to work at it. Professional comics, for instance, don't just think up new jokes and then go out that night and spring them on an audience. They write them out, practice them alone, test them on friends, wring out the non-essentials, rewrite them, and then do even more practice. Only after going through this long process do they present their latest attempts at humor to the public.

I'm not recommending that you go through such an ordeal before you tell the story of how you dropped a plate of spaghetti on your mother-in-law. The point here is that storytellers who seem naturally adept have probably given a fair bit of thought to what they say before they say it. Most other people don't, and it shows.

Another caution, avoid had-to-be-there stories that depend on intangibles such as the expression on someone's face, the tone of a voice, or a subtle personality quirk. These are things that usually can't be properly described with words and thus can't be appreciated by your audience. When such stories don't work, you end up giving a nervous and somewhat lame apology that starts with "Well, I guess you had to be there, but I'm telling you, no kidding, oh man, it was reeeally funny!" Yeah, right.

And while you're at it, you might as well skip the stories that depend on information or experience the listener doesn't have. The classic example of this is the shoptalk joke that only people familiar with your work or industry have the background to comprehend.

Most narrations profit from the listener's desire to hear what happens next. So, if you want to grab someone's interest, hold back the punch line or payoff until the conclusion. Many people begin their tales by removing all suspense—"Did you hear that Mike got into an auto accident without insurance and now he can't afford to go to on his honeymoon?" Hey, that's the whole story! What does the listener have to look forward to now? Instead, start the story in a way that builds tension and draws the listener into the tale—"Did you hear about Mike's disaster?" Now the listener is interested. He wants you to relieve his curiosity by explaining the details of Mike's "disaster."

Relate your story in such a way that important elements have maximum dramatic impact. Try to give the listener a surprise. Construct your story in such a way that there is an unexpected ending, or even multiple shockers during the course of the telling. For example, don't just casually reveal that Mike had no insurance; build up to it. Give the listener a feeling that something big is coming.

> Mike knew that fixing the Mercedes was going to be hideously expensive, but he wasn't worried, he had insurance, and it was a good company, one that had always paid promptly in the past. He was so confident that he didn't even call them that day. But when he finally did call the next morning, he was stunned to hear that…

When telling a story, don't be overly afraid of exaggeration. There are certainly areas where exaggeration would be undesirably misleading, and it's generally wise to avoid it in any conversation of substance. However, when telling light anecdotes and stories, unwavering adherence to what actually happened may not make a very fascinating tale. A little exaggeration or reordering of the facts can turn a mildly entertaining story into a hilarious one. Don't get carried away, but remember, in casual conversation, the goal of everyone involved is to enjoy themselves. People tend to be pretty tolerant of a little massaging of the facts if the result is a good time for all.

Here's an example. After Christmas this last year, I told friends a story about how I was forced to decorate the tree single-handedly, even though it's a job I go to great lengths to escape. The way I told the story, the whole family had started to decorate the tree together. Within minutes though, everyone except me became obsessed with finding a bad bulb that was preventing all the other lights from working on a tremendous string of old Christmas lights. I ended up performing the entire, tedious tree-decorating job alone while the rest of the family focused on tracking down the inoperative light bulb.

It was a good story, but only loosely related to the facts. I don't really dislike decorating Christmas trees as much as I declared in the story, and the rest of the family didn't actually struggle with the light bulb as long as I claimed. But, these exaggerations seemed forgivable because they improved the story and gave listeners a good laugh.

If you want to improve your story- or joke-telling skills, watch how your funny and interesting friends capture attention and make people laugh. Analyze their efforts and learn. Think about the jokes that fail as well. Ask yourself what went wrong. You might also pay closer attention to how the jokes in sitcoms or other comic shows are delivered. Additionally, you can go to the library and check out books on humor. As you get a feeling for what works and what doesn't, you can start to incorporate these new skills in your own drollery.

While everyone enjoys a well told story, the skill we often admire the most in a conversationalist is repartee, the ability to make quick and witty replies. We've all had the experience of coming away from a discussion thinking to ourselves I wish I'd said this or I wish I'd said that. When you kick yourself about a lost opportunity, you are wishing you had better repartee skills. Repartee, like humor, can't really be easily summed up in a series of rules. You learn it through observation, experience, and practice. However, there are a few basics that will give you some ground to stand on while you develop your abilities.

Repartee is the ability to verbally duel with others. It is often characterized by an ingenious contrast or an unexpected combining of the content of previous remarks. Successful repartee surprises or even shocks by looking at something from a new angle.

For example, I was with a group of friends not long ago, and one of the guys happened to mention that his wife was in London on business. Now this woman was well known to the group. She is somewhat abrasive in personality, highly opinionated, and tends to speak in a loud voice at a high rate of speed. My friend went on to say that his wife had informed him that she was going to use some vacation time to extend her stay in London. He then said, "So I made an airline reservation last night." At this point one of the guys called out, "To London, or away from London?"

Everyone in the group, including the husband, exploded in laughter. Why? By reversing everyone's expectation that he would fly toward London to join his wife, the speaker made a devilish comment about her widely known difficult personality. This is classic repartee, which uses contrast and a surprise twist to entertain.

Winston Churchill was a master of repartee. Those who matched wits with him did so at their own risk. Once, at a dinner party,

Churchill found himself seated next to Lady Astor, a woman whose dislike for him had begun with his politics and in time became personal. At one point during the dinner, Churchill made a comment that irritated her and she looked him in the eye and said, "If I were your wife, I believe I would put poison in your tea and be done with you." Without missing a beat, Churchill replied, "Madam, if you were my wife, I would drink it."

This famous rejoinder worked because it is at odds with what we expected. Obviously, no one wants to be poisoned, so Churchill's declaration that he would gladly kill himself to get away from Lady Astor catches us off guard. The surprise and the wit of his returned insult make us laugh.

Don't be tempted to believe that you're either born with the ability to pull off clever repartee or you're not. As with story telling, if you begin to analyze and focus on the repartee successes and failures of the people around you, read some books on the subject to increase your awareness of the basics, and then begin to use what you've learned in the real world, you'll find that your skills can be sharpened considerably.

Now that we've discussed how to start and maintain a conversation, it's only reasonable that we discuss how to get out of one. Whether you are short on time or desperate to escape a dull discussion, it's always best to depart in a way that doesn't offend. Some departure methods are more successful than others in maintaining goodwill. Here are some general guidelines to follow.

When you decide to break off a discussion, do it as decisively as possible. If you delay, more than likely you'll communicate your impatience or boredom to the other person in a multitude of subtle ways—fidgeting, a wandering gaze, resistant body language, desperate facial expressions, and so on. Also, don't make it a big deal and don't get so carried away with apologies that you appear guilty.

On the other hand, don't cut off the discussion so abruptly that the other person is left wondering what the heck happened. Breaking off a discussion requires that you lay some groundwork to prepare the other person for termination. A hasty departure without groundwork is socially comparable to hanging up on someone during a phone conversation.

Groundwork usually begins with subtle signals that the conversation is approaching an end. This may be somewhat reduced eye contact, a change in body posture (moving forward in one's chair as if to stand up), a quick glance at the clock, etc. Put out your signal and then move rapidly to more direct closing behavior. Most people are quite alert to even exceedingly subtle closing signals. They will often jump ahead of you and initiate their own closing dance.

An intermediate closing technique is to summarize what has been said. This shows the other party that you've heard what he or she has said (which leaves a warm feeling) and also communicates that you believe the conversation is wrapping up.

Direct closing behavior generally begins by serving notice that you have to end the discussion. Whatever you say by way of escape, try to leave the impression you would much prefer to continue talking but circumstances force you to depart. Wait for a pause in the conversation or for the floor to be passed to you and then make your move—"Well, I don't want to take up any more of your time," or "I hate to go but I've got to get this report in by two o'clock," or "It's been great talking, but I have to go pick up my husband." Smile and use your body language and tone of voice to communicate friendly warmth.

You can also plan your escape in advance. If you inform your partner at the beginning of the conversation that you only have a certain amount of time, this forewarning will usually reduce the possibility of insult when you terminate. It also increases the cooperation you're likely to receive when you break off.

Once you've served notice of departure, soften the blow with some manner of conciliatory statement or compliment—"Hey, John, it's been great talking to you, let's do it again soon," or "Bill, I'm glad we talked. You've given me some great advice."

Note that in the previous paragraph's examples, the person departing uses the other party's name. It's a small thing, but it adds warmth and a feeling of closeness that has added importance when breaking off from someone. It's another element that softens the blow of departure and works to repair any damage done to the other's ego.

A party is a situation where you may find yourself cornered by someone from whom they would like to be liberated. Here are a few lines you can use to make your escape—"You know, I'm so hungry, I think I'm going to have to go for seconds," or "I'm sorry, I need to go thank our host," or "Excuse me, but I see my friend waving to me," or (and this one rarely fails) "I have to use the bathroom." Once you've broken off, move to another part of the room, making it difficult for the person to re-engage you in further talk.

Of course, some people are totally oblivious to even the most direct signals that you want to end the conversation. You may desire to end the talk, but they don't. Furthermore, it's often impossible to get a closing comment in edgewise. What can you do? Sadly, there's only one solution. You have to be brave, cut into their flow of words, and announce nicely but firmly that you must go. Then do so. Don't give them a chance to get their engines going again.

If you use the above methods when ending a conversation, you're less likely to give inadvertent offense. A little extra effort is what maintains trust and friendships.

All right, now you know how to get into a conversation, how to hang in there, and how to bail out. What more could you ask? Magic. Divine intervention. The main goal of this chapter is to convince you that good conversation is a skill anyone can develop. It's not something passed down to you in your DNA. Of course, simply reading this chapter won't transform you instantly. You do have to get out there and make the effort. Familiarize yourself with the basic guidelines, practice them until they become second nature, and then sit back and glory in your newfound self-confidence and easy fluency.

Chapter 6:
Meeting the Opposite Sex

Although today there are far fewer limitations on what women in our society can and cannot do, the task of approaching the opposite sex still falls largely to men. As such, this chapter focuses primarily on men. However, almost all of the methods discussed below would apply equally to a woman who wished to approach a man.

This chapter addresses that most troubling of conundrums—when you see an attractive woman on the other side of the room, how do you get from where you are to where she is, and what do you say when (and if) you get there? She may be only ten feet away, but shyness and fear of rejection can make the distance seem like miles. In the following pages, we'll show you how to get your apprehensions under control, break bad habits, and say the right thing once you are face to face.

If you don't look like a male model, you probably assume that looks are the key to success with the opposite sex. Okay, looks can't hurt, but that's not the secret. Most of us know good-looking guys whose luck with women is nothing to write home about. Still, lots of guys persist in blaming their appearance for whatever poor luck they've had with the opposite sex.

Many guys let their self-doubts poison their confidence, and this is where the trouble really starts. Women are more likely to reject men because they are nervous, clumsy, and boring rather than because of looks. The most attractive feature a human being can possess is confidence and strength of personality. And because conversation is the most obvious outward manifestation of this self-assurance, what you say and how you say it is more important than how you look.

Can confidence be learned? Yes, but it takes practice and experience, the very things our fear of rejection discourages us from doing. Taking command of a social interaction requires a sort of gut instinct that can only be acquired through experience—and experience is only acquired by having experiences.

To make sure you get the practice you need to become comfortable meeting and talking to strangers of the opposite sex, always set out with a goal when you are going to any social gathering such as a party, wedding, or night on the town. For example, you might say to yourself, "I'm not coming home until I speak to at least ten women." You don't have to marry them or ask them out, just talk to them. This is how you learn to handle yourself and ultimately overcome shyness and clumsiness.

All right, there you are, walking across the room toward that unknown female. What are you going to say when you reach her? First of all, forget trying to come up with a clever, foolproof opening line. Most such lines are verbal suicide. To the woman, these lines usually say that you are there to scam her, pick her up, and generally put her on the spot. Whether it's an aggressive line—"Hello there, sweetheart, has anyone ever told you that your big blue eyes are hard to resist?" or a humble line—"Uh, hi, look I'm not really good at striking up a conversation, but would you mind talking for a while?" these approaches just aren't spontaneous or natural. Even with the humble line, the woman knows she's being hit on and feels the pressure.

Pressure is a key concept here. You don't want your approach to cause the woman stress or discomfort. If she does, she may try to escape. Forget the obvious lines and go with an approach that barely seems like an approach at all. Position yourself near her and then wait for something to happen that you can comment on, preferably something the two of you have in common. If you are observant, you won't have to wait long.

For example, if the room is hot and you notice she's fanning her face, you can lean forward and say, "It gets pretty hot in here when the room fills up, doesn't it?" It's also okay to comment on something you overhear in her conversation with friends. "That was a good movie, wasn't it? I saw it last weekend and loved it." These are natural ways to open a conversation. She won't have any trouble responding, and your opener communicates that the two of you have something in common.

If you can't use the above techniques and have to start a conversation cold, remember that the most successful opening lines are the ones that are positive, casual, easy to respond to, and not blatant pick-up lines—"You look like you're enjoying yourself." or "Hi, are you girls having a good time tonight?" That's all you need. You're a nice guy, not a cocky jerk. You're glad to see she's having fun. It's a good first impression.

Okay, you've opened the conversation, now what? The first thing to keep in mind is that you don't need to prove that you're a brilliant comedian or conversationalist with every comment. No one expects that so don't weigh yourself down with all that pressure.

Here is another key rule of conversation with a female stranger—Don't say stupid stuff. This may sound self-evident, but it's a rule that's violated all the time. The pressure and nervousness of a first meeting can make it easy for you to blurt out something foolish. There you are, trying to talk to an unfamiliar woman, and suddenly an uncomfortably long gap in the conversation occurs. She's staring at you, waiting. Your brain races, struggling to come up with something to say, but nothing comes. Here, right here, is where that fatal comment is likely to take wing from your lips—"Boy, you sure do have big eyebrows," or "Gee, my grandmother does her hair just like yours."

What's the solution to this inevitable situation? For one thing, don't live in fear of a pause in the flow of conversation. Better a pause than to utter a killer-filler comment. The real solution is to learn how to jump-start a flagging discussion. In any given setting there are probably hundreds of things you could use to prime the conversational pump. Be observant about her and the surroundings, and you'll never run out of things to say. For instance, in a bar or dance club, you could say the following—"So, who gave you those blue eyes, your mom or your dad?" or "Do you like the artwork here?" or "Your watch is unique. Can I see it?" or "What do you think of the way that woman is dressed? Thumbs up or down?"

Remember to sell yourself. You aren't just a man when you meet someone you're attracted to—you are a salesman. You have to put your best foot forward, you have to win her over. Just because you were able to strike up a conversation doesn't mean you can now go to sleep. Talk and act with a purpose. Here are a few tips.

Don't put yourself down.—This may seem like an obvious no-no, but it's amazing how common it is. Here's how it sounds—"Uh, hi, uh, I was just wondering if you'd, uh, like to dance. I know I'm not the best looking guy here, and I wouldn't be surprised if you said no, but, uh, would you?…like to dance, that is." What's she going to think? "You're right, you gibbering fool, you aren't the best looking guy here. Take a hike." If you are confident, you don't put yourself down. You may have faults, but there's no advantage in pointing them out to her.

Don't be negative in general.—Remember this poor female is out to have a good time. She may have had a tough week at the office. She may be worried about money. Who knows? The point is that she wants to forget her problems, and you aren't going to go over very big if everything that comes out of your mouth is a downer. A few negative comments in the course of a conversation are no big deal, but remember, a little goes a long way.

Avoid the commonplace.—Try not to say what everyone else is saying. The classic examples of this are—"Do you come here often?" and "What's your (astrological) sign?" Keep an ear peeled for overused statements and then avoid them. The best way to sell yourself is to distinguish yourself from the pack. Show her that you are different and therefore worthy of her attention.

Make your compliments count.—Compliments are a great idea, but if you don't give them some thought, they can fall flat or backfire. Suppose you approach a woman with beautiful, long, shiny, black hair. Should you compliment her on her hair? Probably not. It's almost a certainty that every other man she meets says something like the following—"I don't know if anyone has ever told you this, but you have great hair." She'll be polite, but she's probably thinking, "Yeah, enough guys to fill Yankee Stadium."

Instead, study her closely and find something attractive about her that isn't immediately apparent. The best compliment of all is one that focuses on a feature she herself may not have been aware of. "I love the way you walk. The way you move is so graceful."

Look her in the eye and smile.—Selling yourself to a stranger can be stressful. Uneasiness can cause you to avoid eye contact and forget to smile. You end up looking like your dog just got run over. Such behavior not only communicates that you aren't much fun but also makes you look like what you probably are—nervous and shy. This is not an impression you want to make. Nervousness is catching. If you seem uncomfortable, she'll feel uncomfortable. If you make her feel too uncomfortable, she'll leave or ask you to leave.

Watch those jokes—When you use humor, there is great potential for saying "stupid stuff." We all want to be funny, we all want to be the life of the party, but a common way to turn a woman against you is to get carried away with a joke that goes bad. By this I don't necessarily mean a joke that isn't funny. I mean a joke that makes you look bad, insults the woman, or makes fun of something she believes in.

Get a feel for who she is before you start throwing around the heavy-duty humor. Stick to the safe stuff until you know whom you are dealing with. For instance, perhaps in your haste to keep the conversation rolling, you make a joke about that cat you unintentionally ran over with your truck that night. "Ho, boy, you should'a seen that sucker. It looked like a pancake with legs." Har, har, har. You're laughing so hard you don't even notice that your female companion is fried. She's an animal activist. She eats, sleeps, and breathes the welfare of animals. Three strikes and you're out, pal.

Don't just kill time, show her a good time—Initially, the best impression you can make is to show her that you are a fun guy, so keep the conversation light. You can talk about world hunger, your uncle who died of a brain tumor, or your recent divorce some other time. If you are angry about something, keep it to yourself. If you are depressed or tired, don't show it. She's not going to be attracted to an angry, depressed, tired guy. Remember, his woman just met you; she doesn't know anything about you. Now is not the time to be in a bad mood. Everything you say and do should tell her "I'm having a great time and I love being with you."

Don't sprain something trying to show off—Few of us have the skill to blatantly puff ourselves up without looking like egotistical boasters. Sure you want to impress her, but too much swagger may impress her in a way you never intended.

Find out her name—This seems like simple enough advice, but it's often ignored. When you meet a woman, tell her your name and ask for hers. Do this early on. A name is a very powerful tool in relationship building. Using each other's names in conversation builds intimacy. It creates the illusion that the two of you aren't strangers, even though at this point you really are. You will both feel more comfortable if you can call the other by name. And anything that makes her more comfortable is a good thing. One other point, once you have asked for her name, remember it. No woman is going to feel good about you if you have to ask for her name twice.

Now let's inspect talk that falls under the general heading of flirtation. Flirtation is a game, but it's not totally about having fun. When men and women flirt with each other, they are having a good time and there is usually a lot of laughing, but this only masks the fact that they are testing each other. Flirtation involves applying mild pressure to another and then observing how that person handles it.

For example, suppose you are talking to a woman who is complaining about her long work hours. "I haven't slept more than five hours a night in the last three weeks," she says. Not realizing that you are stepping into a trap, you innocently respond, "You do look tired." Now comes the flirtatious test. She puts on an insulted expression and says, "Oh, you don't like the way I look, do you?" She is applying a little stress to see how you handle it.

In this situation, most guys will react as if her mostly put on resentment is real and fall into the spineless apology trap, the Oh-gee-that's-not-what-I-meant response. Generally speaking, this isn't what she wants to hear. Flirting test grade: F.

What she wants to hear is a confident, cool-under-fire male who doesn't lose it when a little pressure is applied. She wants to hear a smooth reply with a little sex appeal to it. Something like this—"On the contrary, a little sleepiness gives your eyes a very appealing sensual quality." Not bad. This answers her challenge and throws in a sexy compliment as well. Flirting test grade: A.

Boredom is your worst enemy when meeting the opposite sex. Aside from testing, one of the key functions of flirtation is to keep boredom at bay. When you flirt, you create a little conversational friction. You avoid dull, lifeless talk by throwing a bit of pressure and challenge into the mix. This doesn't mean getting into an insult-trading match. Nor does it mean that you should be unpleasant, aggressive, or generally hard to live with. It does mean that you should be alert for chances to stir things up.

For example, let's say you've been talking for about fifteen minutes to a woman you just met. She tells you a story in which she mentions "this guy I know." Shortly after this, she tells another story in which she mentions "this other guy I know." Here is your chance to create a little flirtatious friction. You stop her in mid-story and say, "Hey, wait a minute, I don't think I should be talking to you." Her eyes fly open and she asks, "Why?" You grin and say, "Because you have too many boyfriends. I should go find a woman who isn't so popular." She'll probably laugh and say something like, "Oh, no, they're just friends!" (or "Well, I am engaged to one of them.") This stirs things up in a good-natured way, and you may get some valuable information about her relationship status.

Used correctly, embarrassment can be a pretty stimulating flirtation tool. Eye contact held a little too long can be pleasantly uncomfortable. A compliment given the right way can be a face reddener. A joke skillfully phrased can make the hands cover the face. All these things can stir up the blood and make a woman who felt calm and bored suddenly feel excited and vulnerable. Pretty sexy stuff. It takes a light touch though. It's easy to cross the line from amusing embarrassment to terminal insult. Don't link these kinds of comments to anything serious or potentially painful (such as weight, nose size, job failures, etc.).

As an example of pleasantly stimulating embarrassment, let's say you are walking past a group at a party when a woman telling a story gestures with her arm and almost hits you as you pass by. "Whoa! Watch out there," you say, taking hold of her hand. "You're a wild one, aren't you?" you add, still grasping her hand. By now the combination of almost hitting you, being called a "wild one," and having her hand held has the woman quite embarrassed, but not unpleasantly. You have taken charge of the situation, shown a certain unflappable confidence, and gotten the woman and her friends laughing. Certainly, if you want to stay and talk, you'll probably be welcome.

Another lesson to be learned from the previous example is that opportunity has to be seized whenever it knocks. Most guys would have dodged when the woman swung her arm and kept on going, leaving a great opening for conversation unexplored. If you want to get the most out of what this world offers up, you have to be ready to grab opportunity on a moment's notice. In many instances, if you pause even for a second, the moment evaporates. Analyzing, plotting, and planning are the death of spontaneity. Don't think so much, just start talking and see where it goes.

Now let's look at a concept we've already touched on briefly—focusing the conversation. If you want to make a positive impression on a woman you've just met, there are topics to avoid and topics to encourage. When speaking with a female stranger, many guys are satisfied just to keep the talk flowing. If they avoid any long silences, they figure they're doing well. Unfortunately, such thinking often results in talk the woman has no interest in, or worse, turns her off.

Go for the subjects that will make her feel good. Talk about the vacation she took to Hawaii, the great old Victorian house you drove by the other day, the new car she's thinking of buying, or the romantic movie she saw recently, and so on. Keep the tone of the conversation lively and spontaneous; it should feel like a game. There should be an animated give and take, humor, exaggeration, compliments, flirtation, mild challenges, and an element of unpredictability. These are topics and practices that make conversation fun and entertaining. They will make her feel good and, more specifically, feel good about you.

On the other hand, try to guide the conversation away from her troubles at work, her ex-boyfriend, your ex-girlfriend, her oil-burning car, etc. Also try to stay away from the standard, boring topics that people too often fall back on such as the weather, local traffic, or anything else that lacks life and energy. If you are attracted to her, these topics are romance killers. Is she suddenly going to feel amorous while telling an angry story about how she was ripped off by a plumber hired to fix a leaky toilet? She'll have a hard time making that transition.

Also, ask yourself if the topic you have chosen to discuss is likely to interest her. Your need to keep the talk going may lead you to bring up subjects you are comfortable with but which are otherwise poor choices. They may assure that you won't be at a loss for words but do nothing to sell the woman on you. If you drone on and on about football or stock car racing to a woman whose eyes are glazing over, you may have kept the words flowing, but you've hardly made a positive impression. If you are a mortician who likes to talk shop, don't be surprised if the girls don't go for you. Find the topics she is interested in and focus the conversation on those areas.

Guys who are skilled at guiding conversation in the direction they want it to go are always on the lookout for opportunities. They watch the woman's reactions to what is being said, they probe for information and interest, and they deflect the talk away from depressing subjects. Conversation is a tool you use to influence the woman of your choice. Keep your eye on the ball.

As stated many times in this book, the best way to discover what will interest and please another person is to listen. When meeting a woman for the first time, especially if you find her attractive, it is very easy to focus your attention internally. Your mind races with questions about how you look, what you will say next, whether your last comment sounded stupid, and so on. It is critical to push these thoughts aside and focus externally, in other words, focus on her. Listen to her, watch her reactions, observe her body language, and then use the knowledge you collect to direct your comments to the most fruitful areas.

Aside from gathering information, listening makes a good impression. Men often unconsciously communicate disinterest in what women have to say by interrupting. If you listen well, it sets you apart from others and indicates that you find her thoughts worth hearing. It's a better compliment than the usual "Has anyone ever told you that you have great eyes?"

Another topic that we've discussed previously, one that is especially important when interacting with women, is focusing on feelings. More so than men, women see the world through emotion tinted glasses. They define their experiences less by the facts than by the emotional impact. Consequently, if you, a fact and solution oriented male, want to have maximum impact on a woman, you need to focus on the feelings behind what she is saying. All too often, when a woman relates an incident or problem to a man, his focus is on fact collecting—who, what, when, where, why—not emotions.

For example, a woman tells a man that her car has been in the shop for two weeks and she has to get friends and family to take her everywhere. The man will probably respond by asking what's wrong with the car. However, if he were smart and looked at the situation from the standpoint of emotions, he would probably say something like this—"You seem like an independent person. It must be frustrating and uncomfortable to have to depend on others to take you everywhere." At this point, she may think to herself, "Hey, this guy is different from most guys. I feel like he really understands me."

Finally, it's important not to be in too big of a hurry when you meet a woman that appeals to you. Not uncommonly, guys rush a woman to say yes to a date, give up her phone number, or accept an invitation to dance. Women have different priorities than men. For them, every aspect of relationship building proceeds at a pace slower than most men find reasonable.

If a man is wise, he will take the time to get to know her before he tries to push her into a commitment, large or small. This doesn't have to mean days or months. It may be little more than talking for five or ten minutes before saying, "Would you like to dance?" Even five minutes of talk before asking her to dance would probably greatly increase the odds of getting a yes answer, but many guys can't wait that long.

So, what's the rush? Probably male insecurity. Men often have little confidence in their ability to entertain or charm a woman, so they leap ahead in the relationship process and try to nail down a commitment before she gets away. "Come on, go out with me this Saturday. I'll pick you up at 6:00, okay? Come on, say yes." The man's goal is to get a commitment as quickly as possible so that he can relax and free himself of the fear that she will reject him.

Unfortunately, hurrying a woman is often counterproductive. The more the man pushes, the more the woman pulls back. Paradoxically, she will read these seemingly gutsy, high-pressure male tactics as weakness, not strength. She knows he doesn't have the self-confidence to let her take the time to get to know him. She also knows he may not respect her enough to try. Women respond best to a confident, natural relationship building process that makes them feel like a person, not a hunted animal.

This ends our chapter on meeting the opposite sex. The most important point to remember is that developing social skill with women requires you to seek out contact with them as frequently as possible. This is true regardless of whether any particular woman is "your type" or not. Regular and repeated contact with many different women inevitably leads to confidence. And confidence is catching. The more confident you are in your ability to interact with women, the more confident they will be in you. To women, confidence (not arrogance) communicates intelligence, strength, and character. All very attractive qualities.

Chapter 7:
Assertive Talk

Suppose that a fellow employee comes to you and says, "Would you mind taking my phone calls? I have to leave early to pick up my kid." You agree, happy to do a favor, but before long this person is making the same request two or three times a week, and the extra calls consume so much time that your own work is being adversely affected. What would you do?

Very likely, your response would be either submissive, suffering in silence, or aggressive, making angry demands and personal attacks ("This foolishness has to stop. I can't put my work on hold because you can't manage your life properly.") Submissiveness means silently enduring the problem. Aggressiveness often means terminating the problem but making an enemy. Is there a way to have your cake and eat it too? Yes, it's called assertiveness, and once you understand the techniques, it is an astonishingly effective way to bring about positive change.

Assertiveness can be defined as standing up for your legitimate needs without trampling on the legitimate needs of others. An assertive person makes clear and direct statements that express his or her needs, feelings, and thoughts. Sound like a great idea? It is, and yet studies show that less than 5% of the population communicate assertively. Let's look at the common alternatives to assertion—*submission* and *aggression*.

Submissive people find it very hard to ask for what they want, communicate their views, or say no to the requests of others. Their need for acceptance and approval, and their fear of rejection, makes it hard for them to stand up for themselves. As a result, they feel ignored, used, and powerless to control their lives. These people often seethe with internal anger and frustration. Periodically, this results in volcanic emotional eruptions followed by guilt, profuse apologies, and a return to their submissive ways.

Most of us are submissive some of the time. We may, for example, stand up to our spouse but cave in when we deal with mother. The question is really a relative one—how often is our behavior submissive? We all have a personal space, and that space needs to be defended. It's a defend it or lose it situation. If you are submissive too often, others will begin to encroach on your space and ultimately take it over.

Submissiveness boils down to a lack of respect for your own needs. It often manifests in expressions such as *It doesn't matter to me, I don't care, Do what you want, What do you want to do?* and *That's okay, I don't mind.* All these statements communicate the submissive person's belief that others' needs are more important than his or her own.

Submissiveness is commonly a holdover of rules we learned in childhood. As adults we may over-adhere to rules that were used to train us as children—*Don't be selfish, Listen and learn, Never interrupt, Keep it to yourself, Don't be a showoff, Don't take others' valuable time,* and *Always help others.*

These rules aren't necessarily wrong for adults but taken as a whole, the message they communicate is to put the needs of others before your own. The new rule, the adult rule, is that you often have the right to put your own needs first. You have the right to deal assertively with manipulation, insults, unwanted advice, controlling affection, intrusive behavior, and the attempts of others to impose their values on you.

If submissive, passive behavior is so bad, why is it so common? Well, as it turns out, such behavior does have advantages. Submissive behavior allows people to avoid conflict, harsh emotions, rejection, argument, defiance, and defeat. It's a great way to gain the approval of others—why wouldn't others approve, they're getting their way. It's also an escape from the risks of taking responsibility—for instance, if you let others decide what movie to see, and the movie is a dud, no one can blame you.

But there's a flip side to these advantages. A submissive person doesn't pilot his own ship. Someone else is always at the rudder. Relationships are weakened because the self evaporates; no one knows for sure who a submissive person really is, what he wants, or what he stands for. In short, there's very little to have a relationship with. Finally, people simply don't respect a person who won't stand up for himself or herself.

The above discussion of submissive behavior might convince you to charge out into that big, bad world and deal out a little rough justice. Take that you so and so. Hey, aggressive action works for Rambo, right? Actually, no, it doesn't. Rambo is a loner with no family, few friends, lots of enemies, no steady job, and no likelihood of ever finding a life insurance company that will insure him. His aggressive ways have resulted in a lifestyle few of us would willingly tolerate.

Aggressive does not equal assertive. While assertive behavior means disclosing your feelings and needs, aggressive behavior means trampling on the feelings and needs of others. An aggressive person grabs what he or she wants through abuse and domination of others. The aggressor's gain is your loss. And although he certainly has no difficulty expressing his requirements, this expression often comes in a loud, sarcastic, abusive, and domineering form.

In the short term, aggressive behavior can seem rewarding. Aggressors frequently get what they demand. They have the apparent security that results from being a person no one wants to mess with. And, on the surface, they seem to be very much in control, not only of their own life but also of the lives of others.

Viewed from a larger perspective, however, many of these seeming advantages collapse. When you go through life bulldozing other people, you find that your world is full of vengeful people who oppose and betray you at every turn. You can pressure others to do your bidding, but you rarely persuade them. Everyone has to be watched, and no one can be trusted. In response, you may redouble your aggressive ways, but as your enemies multiply so does your anxiety, insecurity, and yes, even guilt.

Then there's the seeming paradox of the aggressor's lost freedom. He appears to be in control, but control is not freedom. So much of the aggressor's time and energy is consumed in bending others to his will that he can hardly be described as free.

In addition, good relationships and friendships are strained or impossible. It's difficult for aggressive people to love or respect those they dominate. If you treat others not as people but as means to your ends, warmth and closeness will be as scarce as calculus in kindergarten.

So now we come back to assertion. Given that submission and aggression have been shown to be ineffective means for achieving your life's goals, what is the alternative like? What is assertion?

Assertion is about getting your needs met by taking responsibility for the direction of your life. It is the ability to communicate your feelings, thoughts, and requirements clearly and confidently without abusing the rights of others.

Instead of being assertive, most of us are indirect about our feelings and needs. We come at others from an angle rather than head on when we want something. Very often our wishes are so roundabout that others don't even realize a request has been made. A wife might say to her husband, "Honey, Susan told me that she and Jim went to that new restaurant on Main Street. They sure do get out a lot." Now unless this husband is particularly alert (few are), he may not recognize that his wife is asking him to take her out on the town.

On the other hand, if the wife had said, "Honey, this is the third weekend in a row we've stayed home. I'm bored and stir-crazy. Let's go to that new restaurant on Main Street, tonight," even the slowest of husbands would understand her. Assertion is skipping the hints and leaving nothing to chance. You say what you want and why you want it. Assertiveness falls into three main categories—

1. Asking for what you want or for a change of behavior— "When you have people over late, I feel disrespected, because I don't get enough sleep and I'm tired at work the next day."

2. Differing with the opinions or ideas of others—"I understand your reasoning, but I don't think business is going to pick up enough to justify leasing a larger office."

3. Saying no—"I'd be glad to take you to pick up your car, but I can't. I have plans I don't want to cancel."

Assertion doesn't always work, but it works surprisingly often. Nor is it risk free; people sometimes respond disagreeably to independent expressions. But, the risks are far lower than with submission or aggression. Assertive people feel good about themselves. They are living their own lives, not submissively ceding control and not aggressively expending energy to dominate others.

Many problems can be resolved immediately by the clear and complete expression of one's feelings and needs to the concerned parties.

Disputes are frequently based on an incomplete understanding of the other's point of view. Open expression of feelings often results in comments like—"I had no idea you felt this way," or "Why didn't you tell me sooner? I didn't realize the situation you were in."

Failure to clearly express feelings is commonly justified by the belief that others "know how I feel." Sometimes our lack of real communication causes us to put a very negative spin on another's behavior—"He does this just to bug me." We assume that the offending behavior is premeditated and done with malice. No one can deny that such things occur, but they occur with much less frequency than most of us believe.

Generally speaking, people aren't as devious as we think. It is far more likely that poor behavior is the result of inattention to others rather than planned disruption. Think about it—do you go through life looking for ways to make people miserable? Don't you feel you have good reasons for your behavior? Few of us purposely behave in ways that set us up for confrontation. It takes too much energy to deal with angry people.

Most people are busy focusing on their own lives and unwittingly miss the effect of their acts on others. Because they feel justified in their acts and are often totally unaware of the negative impact on you, your subtle hints won't be understood. Sudden accusations will result in surprise and angry, defensive reactions. Assertive methods are designed to increase others' awareness of your needs and avoid angry disputes.

Now that we've defined assertion and explained some of its benefits, let's work through the nuts and bolts of incorporating it into your life. We'll start with the most basic and flexible assertion technique for changing the undesirable behavior of others—*the three-part statement*.

It's shocking but true—the three-part assertion statement has three parts. Taken together, these parts attempt to describe all aspects of your experience to the person whose behavior you want to change. The goal is to leave nothing implied or unsaid. You make a detailed, direct statement of the situation as you see it so that others don't have to guess about your feelings or intent. The three parts of the statement are—

1. An objective, nonjudgmental description of the behavior you want changed.

2. A declaration of your emotional response to the behavior or situation. In other words, how you feel about it.

3. A statement of the concrete, practical effect of the behavior or situation on your life.

The general form of the statement loosely fits the following formula.

When you (state behavior to be changed), I feel (state emotions) because (explain the concrete effects on your life).

Here's an example of a statement designed to bring about a change of behavior.

When you are late coming home and don't call (behavior to be changed), I feel worried and ignored (emotions) because I'm here alone, eating by myself (concrete effect).

Without assertion training, our requests for behavior change are often designed to hurt the offender. We're in an emotional state and our message reflects that emotion. Unfortunately, these attacking statements are far more effective at inflicting damage on the other person than they are at persuading him to change his ways.

I'm sick of you strolling in here at all hours. What is it with you? Are you really so lazy you can't pick up a phone for sixty seconds to tell me some lie about why you're late? Oh, by the way, I've cleaned the house by myself, again.

The first rule of assertion is to plan your statement with an eye toward influencing the other party rather than injuring him. The goal of assertion is to meet your needs, to alter the other's objectionable behavior in the way you desire. If your true goal is to judge, threaten, or dominate, then assertion isn't for you. Attacking and judging others simply isn't a good way to effect real change—this approach will almost always be vigorously resisted. People are most likely to change if they are treated with respect and given a clear picture of your situation.

In a moment we'll discuss using the three-part assertion statement, but first let's go over some general rules for assertion.

Successful assertion begins by minimizing the other person's inclination to resist. The best overall way to achieve this is to be consistently respectful of the other person's sensibilities. And the best technique for maintaining respect is to remember to focus on the behavior or situation, not the person. If you address the behavior

("When you arrive late…"), you may get a cooperative response, but if you attack the person ("When you are too lazy and careless to get here on time…"), you'll get instant resistance. By allowing the other party to save face, he or she will be able to listen to your request for change with much less disruptive emotion.

Presenting your own view objectively isn't as simple as it sounds. There's quicksand all around, and if you're not extremely careful, you'll get sucked into a totally counterproductive emotional exchange. Here is a list of the most common troublemakers.

Belittling or degrading—"I don't know why I thought you could remember to be on time."

Making demands—"Get your butt off that couch and mow the lawn now."

Attacking or indulging in name-calling—"What an idiot you are."

Playing the guilt card—"After all I've done for you…"

Blaming—"This never would have happened if you had just…"

Being sarcastic—"Oh, right, this from a guy who needed four tries to get a driver's license."

Making negative comparisons (especially with family members or friends)—"Your brother seems to be able to get by on his salary. Why can't you?"

Criticizing in front of others—"So, Bill, do you have any idea why Ted here would do such a stupid thing?"

Using judgmental "you" criticisms—"You never stick to anything. You're just a quitter."

Making once-and-for-all declarations—"I'll never listen to you again."

Flinging around threats and ultimatums—"If you don't shape up, you're going to come home and find all your stuff out in the street."

Another mistake is delving into the past for ammo in the current dispute. "Ho boy, this is the way it always is with you. This is just like the time you forgot about Grandma's funeral. I don't know why I expected today to be any different." Focus on the here and now, not the missteps of the past. Using the past as a weapon only convinces everyone concerned that change is impossible, which is often untrue. Treat people as if they can change and it becomes more likely that they will.

Generally speaking, abusive methods of presenting your views bring effective communication to a screeching halt. Instead of working to understand and solve the problem, all of the other person's energy goes to self-defense, rationalizing, sabotage, and retaliation. While this may make for very exciting arguments, it destroys working relationships and virtually ensures failure to achieve change or resolution of differences.

Here are some techniques that will increase your chances of success when using assertion to effect a change in behavior.

After stating your views, give the other person a chance to tell his side. Listen as objectively as you can. Who knows, you might find he has reasons for his behavior that you never understood. On the other hand, if you approach the person with an I'm-right-you're-wrong attitude, you may win the battle but lose the war (or, you may lose the battle and the war).

Of course, being respectful to a person who is offending you is easier said than done. When you are tense and upset, it's easy to allow yourself to slip into the attack mode. A nicely crafted cutting remark feels good when you're angry—but, it won't achieve your goal of altered behavior.

If you feel yourself losing control, call a time out and take a breather—"I'm getting too angry to talk calmly right now. Let's finish this conversation after lunch. I need time to cool down." Note that it's important to assure the other party that you fully intend to complete the discussion later. Then leave the scene, take a walk, and when your blood pressure has returned to normal, try again.

If you wish to discuss a problem with someone, watch out for poor timing. Insisting on confronting emotionally charged problems when you and/or the other person are tired, irritable, tense, hungry, or occupied with other matters, greatly reduces the chance of success. Wait for a quiet time when both of you can focus on the problem and cope better with the emotional stress.

It's often a good idea to make an appointment to discuss a problem with someone (even if it's a family member). Making an appointment not only prepares the other party for the discussion but stresses that this issue is important to you and should be taken seriously. Some people will object to making an appointment. "No, no, let's talk about this now!" If the timing is good, go ahead and talk, but if the timing is bad or if the person is emotionally stressed, insist on waiting until a specific later time.

It is important, however, to set a time in the near future. "Let's discuss this after lunch, when things have slowed down and we'll have more time." Don't make an appointment for a week from next Thursday. Problems need to be addressed with a minimum of delay. When offensive behavior drags on, your resentment increases and you ability to discuss it rationally decreases.

Work at solving one problem at a time. You can't change the whole person in one sweeping, monumental conversation. Change isn't easy. If someone is going to make a change in his behavior, it will have to come one small piece at a time. Bringing up more than one issue only makes the other person feel attacked, and that will bring out resistance. The more complaints you bring up, the less cooperation you are likely to receive.

It's always hard to resist bringing up additional failings that occur to you during the give and take of discussion. "That reminds me, I also don't like it when you…" Before you meet with the offender, ask yourself what you specifically intend to accomplish and then refuse to allow yourself to be sidetracked. Focus on that one issue like a laser beam. Persist until both you and the other person understand each other's positions clearly, and then call it quits. Save other issues for other times.

Make your communications about problem behavior as brief and precise as possible. Because of the emotional element, it's already difficult for people to hear and understand criticism, even under the best of circumstances. If your message is further clouded by a rambling, fuzzy description of the situation, the odds that your meaning will be fully appreciated drop dramatically.

For example, if you say, "When you come home late and don't call…," the message is clear because it is specific and describes concrete behavior. But if you say, "When you are thoughtless and disrespectful…," the message is unclear because it fails to describe actual behavior. Making matters worse, words like *thoughtless* and *disrespectful* heighten the listener's emotional response and bring out resistance.

Brevity is crucial. The more you elaborate, justify, and explain, the greater the likelihood that you will veer off into unimportant side issues or confuse your main point. To ensure a concise presentation of your message, think it through before you discuss it with the other person. If the message is really important, you might even consider writing it out beforehand. Advance preparation allows you to eliminate irrelevancies and speak more precisely.

Finally, make sure that your stated complaint is the real complaint. Do a little self-analysis before you speak up. What are your true needs? You can't clarify your needs to others until you are clear about them yourself. For instance, suppose that you are at a party and your spouse drifts away, talking to the other party-goers and leaving you alone most of the night. By the time the party is over, you're upset.

On the way home, you say, "How could you leave me alone like that? You know I have nothing in common with those people. I've never been more bored in my life." Sounds like a straightforward description of the problem, but it isn't. The real problem wasn't boredom. You should have said (Note—three-part statement format), "When you go off and leave me like that, I feel neglected, because it seems like you'd rather be with them than me." True feelings are often hard to reveal, so we paper them over with phony statements. However, problems can't be dealt with until they're accurately identified.

Now that we've looked at some general rules for assertion, let's analyze the three parts of the assertion statement designed to change troublesome behavior. Here is the format of the three-part statement again.

When you (state behavior to be changed), I feel (state emotions) because (explain the concrete effects on your life).

Part One—"When you (state behavior to be changed)…"

As noted previously, it's very common to assume that others know that their behavior is objectionable. While such assumptions may sometimes be true, much of the time they aren't. The problem with assumptions is that because we feel the other party knows the behavior is driving us nuts, we never actually verbalize our disapproval. If undesirable behavior and its consequences are never specifically stated, the offender may never fully realize that you are being injured. Keep this rule in mind—Don't just think it, say it.

No one will make an effort to change unless they understand exactly how their behavior is troublesome. As stated earlier, behavior and its consequences have to be described as clearly and specifically as possible. Whenever possible, try to describe observable behavior. Avoid fuzzy accusations that can't easily be traced to specific actions.

"When you don't take care of our tools..." is a nonspecific behavior description that may leave the offender wondering what exactly you are referring to. "When you leave the tools outside overnight..." is hard to misunderstand. The exact nature of the undesirable behavior is clearly described.

Don't mix what you observe or hear with opinions about the offender's motives and morals. What you see and hear is fair game. Making guesses about what is going on inside another person's head is not.

> Whenever you have a bad day at work, you have to come home and take it out on me.

This statement makes the assumption that the bad treatment is directly related to stress from work. Maybe it is, maybe it isn't. In any case, the accused person is almost certain to claim that "work has nothing to do with this." Any discussion of the objectionable behavior will be lost in a pointless argument about whether the work experience is responsible. Making matters worse, the specific behavior is not described. It is only obliquely referred to in the loaded phrase "take it out on me." The offender can only guess what it was that he or she did, and believe it or not, that guess will often be wrong.

> When you raise your voice, slam doors, and demand that I pick up the kids...

This is a clear, easy to understand description of behavior that doesn't make judgments, attack motives, or indulge in mind reading. It is a simple description of what has taken place, and if the description is accurate, the other person has little room for disagreement. Even if the other person does raise objections, the discussion is more likely to revolve around the actual problem behavior rather than side issues.

Sometimes you may think you are making an objective, straightforward description of the facts when you are actually stacking the deck to make the other person look bad. It's very important to make a distinction between observations and opinions. Opinions often leak into behavior descriptions and contaminate the message.

"When you are over twenty minutes late" is a nonjudgmental description of what happened. There is no analysis of the behavior here. It's pure observation. Here's an attack version of the same statement—"When you come dragging in here half an hour late without a care in the world..." This statement describes the situation but is liberally contaminated with opinion, judgment, and exaggeration.

The person didn't just arrive, he came "dragging in," a loaded phrase that's sure to raise the hackles of the listener. Also, the statement is not factually accurate. The degree of lateness has been exaggerated from twenty to thirty minutes to increase the potency of the accusation. And finally, the phrase "without a care in the world" is not really an observation at all. It's speculation about the offender's frame of mind. All these contaminations are sure to be interpreted as attacks by the listener, and the problem of lateness will be lost in the ensuing argument over peripheral details.

Omit absolutes from your descriptions. Absolutes are words, which imply that a certain behavior occurs or fails to occur 100% of the time. Words and phrases such as *always, never, no one, everyone,* and *all the time* are rarely accurate. If you tell someone he is always late, it is unlikely to be a true statement. If you accuse someone of never cleaning up after himself, it's probably false, and that person is sure to tell you so—"Get out of here, I spent two hours cleaning out the garage and washing the car just last week." Absolutes only bring out the combativeness in people. They're good for starting emotional disagreements and little else.

Before closing this section, it is worth stating again that loaded words can destroy the effectiveness of an otherwise good behavior description. For example, "When you forget to go to the store..." will get a far more cooperative response than, "When you *kiss off* going to the store..."

Part Two— "...I feel (state emotions)..."

Once you've described the behavior you find troublesome, you need to describe your emotional response to that behavior in specific terms. The three-part formula uses the phrase *I feel* to introduce the words that identify your exact emotions. For example—"When you raise your voice, I feel resentful and humiliated because..."

It is crucial to use the most accurate words you can find to describe your internal experience. Don't settle for the first all-purpose word that pops into your head. We often fall back on a handful of habitual words that are used to describe a wide range of emotions. You can be certain that "I feel upset" will not have as much impact on the other person as "I feel resentful and humiliated."

Picking the right word to describe an emotion can be an unexpected challenge. Those who aren't writers don't really spend much time identifying the perfect word to express nuances of emotion. In fact, when you get right down to it, not many of us spend much time thinking about our emotions at all. We feel our feelings, we don't analyze them. The first time you really try to accurately describe an emotion you are experiencing, you may be surprised at how difficult it is. If your actual feeling is vulnerability, you may not recognize it immediately and in the pressure of the moment find yourself saying you feel "irritated." This is a skill that improves with practice, so work at it.

Being able to accurately identify the emotions you are experiencing greatly increases the effectiveness of assertion statements. Making the other person understand your emotional response to his or her behavior is a big motivator for change. Most people don't want to hurt others, and when they are truly aware of another's feelings, it does move them. Studies have shown that people are far more willing to change if they are provided with a reason. Providing a clear, accurate picture of your emotional state is a powerfully motivating reason.

The *I* in *I feel* is an important element of the three-part statement. It is crucial to stress that the feelings you describe are yours. A workable variation is to say, "It makes me feel angry," instead of, "I feel angry." However, other phrasings can weaken the potency of the message. "*It's* upsetting" lacks impact. Some people even use *you* when they mean I—"When something like this happens, *you* feel crummy." If the feelings are yours, claim them. Use *I*, not weaker substitutes.

Accuracy in the description of feeling, not magnitude, is what you are seeking. Don't exaggerate your emotions on the theory that twice the emotion will generate twice the impetus for change. This may work for a while, but people are good at sensing baloney. Pretty soon they're saying, "What a phony," or "He deserves an academy award for that performance." Soon they dismiss your requests as simple theatrics that don't deserve much attention.

By the same token, don't understate your emotion for fear of "making too big a deal" or "getting everyone all upset." Let your emotions fall where they may, describe them as they are. If you understate your reactions, you weaken the motivation of the offender to change.

As with describing behavior, when you describe your feelings, avoid loaded words and phrases such as *fed up, sick and tired,* or *pissed off.* These are the types of words that are often used to hurt and attack others. Even if accurate, you might do well to search for a less provocative word that still gets your feeling across. "When you don't keep your promise to visit me, I feel discouraged " might not stir up as much defensive behavior as "I feel fed up."

One last precaution. The statement of feelings describes your own feelings, your personal emotions, and not your feelings about the other person. "I feel you are stubborn" and "I feel you are rude" aren't descriptions of your feelings. These are judgments or criticisms of another. In fact, there are no true feelings at all in these two statements; *rude* and *stubborn* do not describe emotions. In this context "I feel" actually means "I think" or "I believe." A true feeling statement includes an actual emotion that you are experiencing, for instance—"I feel sad."

Part Three— "...because (explain the concrete effects on your life)."

This is where you relate the tangible, non-feeling consequences of the other person's behavior. In the three-part assertion statement, the last two parts deal with the consequences of the behavior described in the first part. The middle part deals with feelings, the internal emotional consequences, while the last part deals with the exterior, real-world consequences.

When you...I feel...because I can't get to work by 8:00.
                    ...because the boss blames me for the backlog.
                    ...because we don't have time to be alone.

As with the statement of feelings, the purpose of stating real-world consequences is to motivate the offender to change. The more specific and tangible the description of the consequence the greater the motivation to alter behavior. "...because it causes me a lot of inconvenience" is far too vague to really motivate a change in behavior. "...because I have to drive twice as far and have no time to relax when I get home" is more specific, concrete, and easier to sympathize and identify with.

Sometimes you may find that it's hard to put your finger on a concrete, real-world consequence of another's troubling behavior. This can be due to a lack of awareness. In other words, you aren't used to analyzing situations with an eye for actual consequences. You tend to register the emotional aspects of the behavior more readily. When a husband fails to help with household chores, it may be easier for the wife to feel the resentment and frustration than it is for her to note that she has less time and patience for the kids. If you are certain that behavior is affecting you adversely, search carefully for the tangible consequences, and you will probably find them.

Suppose you search with great care for a tangible consequence and simply can't find one. Suppose that your three-part statement comes out like this—"When you wear that dress, I am embarrassed, because it makes you look overweight." What's wrong with this statement? "...it makes you look overweight" is not a tangible consequence for you. Nothing is being done to you in a tangible way. If you alter the statement to end with, "...because people look at you funny," there's still no real concrete effect on you.

If your assertion statement defines your emotional reaction but lacks a personal tangible effect, it probably means that you are attempting to control someone in a way you have no right to do. In the above example, although the statement is phrased assertively, it is actually a bullying attempt to control the way another person dresses.

There's certainly nothing wrong with expressing your opinion— "I've never liked that dress. I think it makes you look heavier than you are." But, an assertion message in these circumstances is improper. You cannot demand that others respect your rights and then turn around and trample on theirs. So remember, no concrete effect on you, no right to assert for change.

Now let's look at some methods for delivering your completed three-part statement and handling the offender's reaction.

You may have noted that the three-part assertion statement has no provision for suggesting a solution to the objectionable behavior. Nowhere in the statement do you offer a plan for solving the problem. This is not an oversight. Discovering a way out of the difficulty is *initially* left up to the other person.

It can be difficult for a novice asserter to refrain from proposing solutions, but that's just what you should do. One of the primary tenets of assertion is to avoid anything that backs the other person into a corner and results in emotional resistance.

Assertion is often perceived, at least at first, as criticism, which can make the other party tense and defensive. At this point, any suggestion for changing behavior will likely be received as a demand,

and resisted. By not offering a solution, you allow the person to come up with his own solution—and do so of his own free will. An effective assertion message, given properly and persistently, guides others toward a solution of their own without making them feel their rights and dignity are being trampled on.

As you might imagine, a single assertion message doesn't always induce others to immediately cave in and change their ways. People don't like change. It's a pain. They resist it. They don't like the implied criticism. They may feel their rights are being infringed. And worst of all, what they hear may not be what you said. For instance, if you tell your girlfriend that you are disturbed by her unwillingness to discuss relationship problems, she may hear that you think she's a bad person. Most people resist or fail to understand initial assertion messages. They may argue or verbally counterattack. If that's the case, what do you do?

After calmly and rationally delivering your assertion statement, you need to shut up. Give the person time and room to think and to give you his or her perspective on the situation. Resist the urge to argue, assert again, or defend your point of view.

It is crucial at this point to allow the other party to talk without constraint. Talking is a great way to use up defensive, emotional energy and also gives you a lot of information about the person's situation and needs. You may discover that the offending behavior is the result of circumstances you never imagined. In any case, listen carefully, gather in whatever info is volunteered, and then adapt your response accordingly. Don't move forward until you are convinced that you understand the other party's position.

Don't allow yourself to be distracted or sidetracked if the person brings up an extraneous issue ("Oh yeah, well what about that time you…"). Keep your original goal front and center in your mind, directing all your effort to its achievement. Other issues can be dealt with on another day. This is a remarkably effective tactic. The other person will probably lack focus and a plan. Your organization and single-mindedness can overwhelm his disorganized reaction.

The response of the other person may be downright hostile. Some people will perceive even the most neutrally phrased assertion as an attack. Their first reaction won't be to analyze your claim for validity or rationally discuss the issue. Their first response will be to inflict as much damage on you as they feel you have inflicted on them.

In this situation, your best tactic is to refuse to get involved in an attack and counterattack exchange. Continue to treat the other person with respect even if he won't do the same for you. The great thing about being calmly respectful with angry people is that eventually they begin to feel guilty about the way they're treating you. Once again, patiently listen and allow the offender to blow off steam without hindrance until he exhausts himself.

If the other person's statement convinces you that there were circumstances unknown to you that justify his behavior, you can stop the assertion process here. Don't resist apologizing or backing off—"Sorry, I didn't realize the situation you were dealing with. Forget I mentioned it."

The next step is to reflect what the offender has said and then restate your assertion if necessary. Reflecting the other person's statement primarily serves to show respect. You are demonstrating that you have made the effort to hear him out and have tried to understand not only what he said but his feelings as well. Reflecting what's been said in no way indicates that you are in agreement. You are merely mirroring back your understanding of the meaning of the other's statement.

If the other person tries to sidetrack you, reflection can be used as an all-purpose tool for returning to the original issue. For instance, if you tell a friend that it makes you nervous when he eats messy food in your new car, the offender might respond by saying, "Oh, excuse me, what about the time you spilled your coke on my new CD player?" Reflecting as follows brings the discussion right back to your concern—"You think that my spilling coke on your CD player excuses eating messy food in my new car?" Take care not to lose control and answer argumentatively—"Hey, just because I had an accident with a coke two years ago doesn't mean it's okay for you to turn my new car into a piece of junk."

If the person agrees that you have a valid complaint and offers you a satisfactory deal or solution, your work is done. But if, after listening, reflecting, and receiving a suggested solution, you think the person still hasn't resolved the problem properly, it's time to repeat your assertion. What do you gain by doing that?

When people receive an assertion statement, they often jump so rapidly to their own defense or to a counterattack that they never really hear or consider what you've said. There is no pause to do any soul searching or to come up with a solution. You may have to reassert numerous times before the real meaning of your message finally sinks in.

This is another reason why maintaining a respectful attitude throughout the discussion is so important. Asserting until you are heard and understood can be a long process. Consistent respect is the glue that keeps the dialogue from flying apart before the other person has had time to get his rational mind working. If you are disrespectful, the conversation will degenerate into a pointless argument long before any meaningful understanding occurs.

Aside from a respectful attitude, persistence is the other key to successful assertion. Many people fail to recognize how thoroughly emotions can block the reception of an assertive message in the early stages of the process. Their words seem to be falling on deaf ears and so they give up in dismay. Don't do it. Continue to alternate listening and reflecting on the one hand and restating your assertion message on the other hand.

By the way, you don't need to restate the assertion statement in the exact same words. Rephrase it and fine-tune it based on what you have learned in your discussion with the other party.

It's always possible that after one or two assertions the offender will offer a complete surrender—"Geez, I had no idea I was being such a thoughtless fool, I'm sorry and I'll never do it again." It's possible, so is winning the lottery, but don't count on it.

Admitting error or bad judgment is extraordinarily difficult for the average person. Even when the truth of his misdeeds begins to sink in, the person may still resist an open admission of fault in order to save face. And that's okay. Your goal is not to get an admission of fault. Your goal is to get a change of behavior. A person who doubts his position or secretly knows he is wrong, may be willing to change his ways, even though he won't openly admit error. In most cases, this should be sufficient. Allow him to maintain his dignity. A wrong word at this point can drive him back into his shell of defensiveness and eliminate any chance of a solution or compromise.

For example, the person might begin to weaken with a statement like this—"Well, I'm not saying you're right. You've been late a few times yourself you know, but I guess I could try harder to be on time."

This is actually a pretty solid apology combined with a promise to improve. Of course, in order to save face, the speaker has also thrown in a shot at the asserter ("You've been late a few times yourself..."). Don't react to this jab. See the statement for what it is—an admission of guilt. Offer thanks (always thank someone who is willing to make the effort to change) and, if appropriate, offer some kind of quid pro quo to further reduce the pain of submitting to your request ("I'll try harder to be on time too.").

If you are offered a solution that doesn't satisfy your needs, say so and say why. Then press for a solution that works by asserting further. Watch out though. There's a danger here of being too rigid—having your mind fixed on only one solution or being too determined to bend the offender to your will. Even if the solution offered differs greatly from your expectations, keep an open mind and ask yourself whether the proposed idea will resolve the problem.

If the person doesn't volunteer a solution, you might push him to do so with questions such as this—"What do you think would resolve this situation?" or "Do you have any ideas of how we might settle this problem?" Now the ball is in his court. If he says, "Uhhh, nope," and it appears he probably isn't going to come up with a solution on his own, then it may be time to present your ideas for solving the problem.

There are a number of factors to consider before offering a solution of your own. Managing them properly will increase your likelihood of success.

The first rule is to maintain your composure. The other person has resisted all your attempts to find a solution, and you may now be angry. It would be easy to lose your patience and fall back on threats and demands. "That does it! If you bring one more greasy burger into my car, you'll never ride in it again." Such emotional statements usually close down communication and often make you look weak when you aren't capable of carrying them out. If the person being threatened with the above statement is a family member or anyone the asserter spends a lot of time with, then the threat may be an empty one.

The next step is to carefully examine yourself and determine what it is you really need. Make sure that your suggested solution will actually solve your basic problem. It's not uncommon for people to address secondary problems, leaving their more important primary problem untouched.

For instance, a wife feels that her husband doesn't pay enough attention to her, but her suggested solution is that he spend less time watching football. Unfortunately, her primary problem (lack of attention) won't be solved even if the husband agrees to give up football entirely (highly unlikely). After altering his behavior, the husband feels he has made a major concession. However, because he now spends all of his time in the garage restoring his '57 Chevy, the wife is still unhappy. Always identify your real need and then ask if your plan for change will in fact meet that need.

Don't target attitudes, seek instead to alter behavior. Sure, attitudes are the root of behavior problems, but attitudes are almost impossible to alter no matter how assertive, or even aggressive, you are. Attitudes are almost as much a part of us as our arms and legs. They are formed by our total life experience, they define who we believe we are, and as a result they are extraordinarily resistant to change.

If you think about it, attitudes, no matter how objectionable, don't affect you. It's always behavior that does the actual harm. Remember this rule, if you can detect it with your senses (sight, hearing, touch, etc.), it's behavior; if you can't detect it with your senses, it's probably an attitude. Aim your assertion at the behavior. It's an easier target to hit, and it's the change that will most positively affect your life.

If your son has an attitude that it's a waste of time to clean his room, that's okay, as long as he does in fact clean the room. And, remarkably, many studies have shown that altered behavior will in time alter attitudes. It is very difficult for humans to do one thing and think another. We like to bring what we do and think into agreement. If the new behavior continues long enough, it's common for the attitude to change to fit the behavior. The kid who hated cleaning his room, but did it anyway, grows up to be an adult who believes that orderliness is a good thing.

As with all other aspects of assertion, your suggested solution should be specific and phrased in behavioral terms. "You need to get with it," or "Lighten up, stop being so cheap," or "Don't be so messy," are all broad generalities that fail the specificity test. They require the other person to make too many judgments about whether a certain behavior violates your request or not. And frankly, since these requests for change are so broad, they're very close to demanding an attitude change, which as we've seen has a very low probability of success.

Your suggested solutions need to be much more precise and leave little need for interpretation—"I'd feel a lot better if you would agree to spend at least four nights a week at home with me," or "Would you be willing to give me twenty-four hours notice whenever you decide to hold a staff meeting?" or "I want you to mow the lawn every second Monday without my having to tell you."

Now, let's return to the three-part assertion statement before we wrap up our discussion.

When you (state behavior to be changed), I feel (state emotions) because (explain the concrete effects on your life).

The statement is somewhat foreign to the way most people address problems with others. It is a skill that requires practice to master. Keeping one's emotions under control, evading side issues, staying consistently respectful, and being persistent are not abilities you acquire overnight. But, with practice they can be learned and will reward you generously.

You may be uncomfortable with the three-part statement's rigid format. If you are, it is important to recognize that you can change the wording of the statement to better suit the way you speak, as long as you retain the three major elements—description of behavior, feelings, and concrete effects. For example, you could rephrase the statement like this—"You left me alone almost all night at the party (behavior), and I felt neglected and bored (feelings). I was stuck talking to that gossip Carol all night (concrete effects)."

Now let's look at some other assertion methods. With each of these methods, the object is to let others know what you need or want, and where your limits are. In general, it's important that your actions and statements communicate what you will tolerate and what you won't. If you set out clear "No Trespassing" signs, many potential problems will never come up because the people in your life will understand in advance that certain behavior will never fly.

Another method of assertion is to simply tell people straight out what you want from them—"I'm going to have to work late on that project I told you about, so I'd appreciate it if you would pick up a pizza on your way home," or "Mike and Carol might ask us to go to dinner with them on Saturday. I'd prefer to go out with you alone though, so I'd appreciate it if you would tell them we're busy."

There's nothing complicated here, nevertheless, it's very common for people to fail to inform others of their needs. Forget about dropping hints or assuming others already know what you want. Just tell them.

To further the effectiveness of your assertions, include specific and tangible reasons for your request. Studies have shown that people are far more likely to comply with a request if it is accompanied by an easily understood reason. "Please don't make plans to use the van tonight, because I have to use it to pick up the couch."

In addition to providing reasons to buttress your requests, explaining the positive consequences of complying is also very effective. Rather than focusing on rewards, many of us habitually threaten people with the negative consequences of refusing our requests. "If you don't wash the car by noon, I'm going to take it to the car wash and put the $12 tab on your credit card." This might work, but more than likely the person receiving the threat will get annoyed and resist—"Fine, you do what you have to do. I could care less."

Pointing out the positive consequences of complying is more motivating and avoids stirring up face-saving resistance. You should explain not only the tangible positive results but also the beneficial effect on your feelings. "If you wash the car today, I can stop worrying about whether those bird droppings will hurt the paint job, and you won't have to listen to Bill's dirty-car wisecracks when we see him and Tina tonight."

One of the biggest difficulties in assertion is coping with people who respond by deflecting the discussion down a path that is easier for them to cope with or allows them to go on the attack. When this happens, one way to keep the talk focused on your original concern is to comment on what is happening to the discussion itself versus the subject matter of the discussion.

For example, suppose the other person skips past your assertion about lateness and begins to dwell on a minor detail. "I was not twenty-five minutes late. I know I got here at 10:20 because I looked at my watch when I got out of the car, so I was only twenty minutes late." If you respond directly to this claim by saying, "Yes, but it takes a few minutes to get into the building, so you really were twenty-five minutes late," you've fallen into his trap and are now arguing about details.

It's far easier for the other person to argue about whether he was twenty versus twenty-five minutes late than to discuss his general inability to be on time. To avoid this, you can respond by noting the nature of the other person's response rather than fighting over his claim. "You're talking about degrees of lateness now. Let's discuss being on time."

Another distraction tactic used by people confronted with an assertion is to change the subject from the present to the past. "Okay, you want to talk about being embarrassed. What about that time last year when you told Jim that I accidentally locked myself in the tool shed for six hours? I never heard the end of that." Once again, you can respond directly to the statement and get sidetracked, or you can note the course of the conversation and ask for a return to your original assertion. "We're talking about the past now. Can we please work on fixing our current problem?"

Successfully using this technique requires that you keep tabs on what is actually being discussed. The talk can veer away from your subject very quickly and subtly. Before you know it, you're talking about the other guy's issues, not yours. Stay alert for attempts to side-track your message, point them out as soon as they occur, and then persistently return the discussion to your assertion. Staying focused is a crucial element of assertion.

Our next assertion method is for some people the most challenging of all—saying no. One of the best ways to protect your rights is to learn to refuse others. Many of us, however, are plagued by the consequences of being unable to say no. We don't want to disappoint, to cause an argument, or to lose the approval of others, so we consistently say yes when it would be wiser to say no. The result is that much of our time is spent satisfying the needs of others, while our own needs get short-changed.

A person who can't say no is like a country that doesn't defend its borders, allowing anyone and anything to come and go. Obviously, such a country will soon degenerate into chaos. So will your life if you don't defend it with reasonable no's.

Most of us have difficulty saying no because of the disappointment or negative reactions of others. Here are some ways to soften the blow.

Combine your no with some empathetic recognition for the feelings of the person being turned down—"I wish I could go but it isn't possible. I know you've been looking forward to this party for a month, and I'm sure it won't be as much fun going by yourself. I'm so sorry."

Combine your no with a compliment or other positive observation—"This is excellent work, fine detail work and beautiful craftsmanship, however, I just can't use it. The design doesn't fit the theme we've agreed on for our offices."

Combine your no with a concise and specific explanation—Watch out here. Avoid the guilty, nervous explanation that rambles on too long. Keep it short and sweet. "I'm sorry, I have a midterm in my Thursday class and I can't miss it."

Combine your no with an offer of compromise or a rain check—Use this option only if you feel a compromise or rain check will work for you. Don't allow compromise to drag you into things you want to avoid. "Look, I don't have time to help you fix your car, but I can introduce you to a friend who's a great mechanic," or "I can't go this week, but I'm free next Tuesday if you'd like to get together then."

Combine your no with a statement that spells out your costs of complying—"I can't get involved with this. I have two reports due on Tuesday, and taking on this project would make it impossible to complete them by the deadline."

There are also different kinds of no's. There is "No, not right now," and then there is "No, not ever." Make sure you communicate the difference to whoever has made the request being refused. "No, not right now" tells people that circumstances won't permit you to say yes today, but a yes might be forthcoming in the future. "No, not ever" tells people that your personality, values, or personal preferences rule out a yes now and forever. "No, not ever" spells out your personal limits.

These examples illustrate the difference. "No, I'm not in the mood for liver tonight" versus "No, I despise liver! Just the smell of it makes me want to throw up." Both of these "no" statements clearly reveal what kind of no is being given. On the other hand, a statement like "No, let's not have liver tonight. I prefer chicken" doesn't allow the listener to really determine the depth of the speaker's no. Much of our trouble in communicating with others arises from wishy-washy no's that don't reveal our true feelings or boundaries.

Now let's look at a method for dealing with persistent or aggressive attempts to cross your boundaries—*the broken-record method*. The broken-record method involves responding to insistent, unwanted requests by stubbornly repeating an unchanging concise message until the other person gives up.

Salesperson:	Hi, I want to tell you about a great new product that will—
You:	I'm sorry, I don't have time to discuss this.
Salesperson:	That's exactly my point, our new product will save you time.
You:	I'm sorry, I don't have time to discuss this.
Salesperson:	I understand, but this product will change the way you think of dirty dishes.
You:	I'm sorry, I don't have time to discuss this.

Some people are so fixated on what they want that they ignore or fail to recognize that they are encroaching on your right to decide what you want. The broken-record method is designed to deal with the person who doggedly refuses to recognize your preferences.

The key to success with broken-record responses is to avoid the temptation to be drawn into a defense or explanation of your refusal. For instance, the salesperson above might have reacted to the broken-record statement by asking, "Oh really, why are you so pressed for time?" This type of response is a favorite not only of salespeople, but also, although they might not know what they are doing, of persuasive people in general. The object is to open people up, get them talking about themselves, and prevent them from escaping.

Broken-record answers also help you avoid the temptation to refute or argue with a false statement made by the other person. The whole point of the broken-record method is to prevent you from being swept up in a distracting and involving discussion that will allow the other person a greater opportunity to pummel you into submission.

Many of the assertion techniques presented in this chapter require practice to perfect. They may feel awkward at first, but with regular use and some adaptation to your own way of speaking, you'll find that they become second nature. Make the effort. Assertion has been proven to be a very successful way to influence others and get more of what you want out of life.

Chapter 8:
Persuasive Talk

Assertion and persuasion bear some similarity to each other. Both are often an attempt to induce another to make a change you desire. Assertion seeks to influence by request or resistance and has an air of self-defense about it. Persuasion, on the other hand, seeks to influence by convincing another with reason and salesmanship. Persuasion sells the rightness of your point of view. Your goal is to make the other person want to take the action you desire. Whether you are trying to convince your boss to give you a raise, talk a spouse into going to the ballet, or cajole a friend into making a beer run to the store, it's all persuasion.

A good persuader is able to influence others to act or believe as he or she wishes. While there are a few born persuaders in this world, individuals who could convince Tahitians to buy tanning beds, most of us can use some improvement in our persuasion skills.

The concept of persuasion assumes that there will be resistance. If there is no resistance, there is no need for persuasion. A man who loves barbecue doesn't have to be persuaded to go to the local rib house for dinner. However, if his wife dislikes barbecue, she will have to be persuaded to go because she will resist. The first rule of persuasion is to develop a plan for minimizing that resistance.

Whenever you attempt to persuade, you have to deal with the inevitable emotional response of the other person. Resistance to an idea or request always has an emotional element. If you stir up resentment or humiliation with an ill-designed persuasive approach, it becomes almost impossible to convince with logic or reason. Your initial goal is to keep the person in a calm, rational state and avoid any tactic that will stir up negative emotions.

The best way to avoid emotional resistance is to treat people with respect. Give them the opportunity to agree with you without seeming to be the loser in a contest of wills. Approaching people with demands, verbal abuse, criticism, condescension, or even an insulting tone or expression will cause them to stop listening, shut down their receptiveness to logic, and become inflexibly resistant. How can they do otherwise? To agree with you after such ill treatment would be to admit they deserved it or that they are too weak to fight back.

Never insult the person you are persuading by ignoring questions or taking a superior "you wouldn't understand" attitude. Such responses indicate that you feel the questions aren't worthy of an answer or that the person is too feebleminded to comprehend the points you see so clearly. It's enough to cause most people to seethe with resentment and to resist your persuasive efforts to the death.

Criticizing and arguing easily find their way into persuasion. For example, "Tim, you always waste money buying things on the spur of the moment. This time let's do some research before we buy our refrigerator." What do you suppose Tim is going to focus on in this statement? All he's going to hear is the criticism of his impulsive shopping habits. The attempt to persuade him to do research before buying will be lost. There is little room for reasoned thought once the vanity and self-respect of the other person have been threatened.

A persuasive person rarely communicates by word, deed, tone, or expression that he thinks the other person is wrong. A corollary to this is that persuasive people rarely communicate in any fashion that they are certain they are right. Violating either of these rules says to others, "I am a smarter, more discerning person than you." How many people are going to let you get away with that? Not many.

Instead of expressing certainty, respect the sensibilities of others by putting some flexibility and self-deprecation into your pronouncements. "I may be wrong about this, I've been wrong before, but…" Express some humility. "That's an interesting point. I could be off base here, but let me tell you how I see it." Ask people for their view rather than hogging the floor with your own. "So, Bill, what do you think about this?" The object here is to make agreeing with you easy by removing any emotional obstacles.

All these statements tell the other person that his or her thoughts are worthwhile and respected. And once a person knows that you not only respect his views but also admit your own fallibility, it becomes a comfortable environment for him to adopt your view without a loss of face. Your fair-mindedness evokes a similar spirit in others.

Admitting that you are wrong is a very powerful method of disarming an opponent. Paradoxically, it paves the way for the other person to ultimately agree with you. An admission of error, far from being seen as weakness, is usually perceived as a sign of confidence and fairness. Others will likely say to themselves, "If he is big enough to say he is wrong, so am I." It's just one more method that encourages people to spend their energy listening to your ideas rather than defending their ego.

Suppose that while attempting to persuade, you misjudge the other person and stir up a negative emotional response. What do you do? If you respond in kind, you can probably kiss goodbye whatever it was you wanted from this person. Instead, stay in control and keep your mind focused on your original goal. People who are truly effective at influencing others start with a goal, formulate a plan for achieving it, and then refuse to be shaken from it. Arguing or doing battle almost certainly was not part of your original purpose, so don't do it.

Stay calm, weather any abuse, maintain an open, friendly expression, and most important of all, show empathy for the other person's situation. Show concern, identify with his problems, and look for ways to show him that you understand his feelings. "Let me see if I understand your position. You're having trouble with this because…" Do all these things no matter how you feel inside. Self-control is critical when influencing others.

Empathy is particularly effective at disarming tension. Why? Because it is the clearest and most efficient means available for showing others that you respect them. Meet an angry response with "I'm sorry, I hadn't looked at it that way. If I had, I'm sure I'd feel just as you do," and the person will have a hard time maintaining his resentment. Empathy quickly moderates unproductive emotion and returns people to a logical frame of mind in which they can hear and consider your points.

Empathy also generates a spirit of fair play. How can someone stay angry or attack you when you are working so hard to understand his problems and feelings? It will be a lot easier for a person to be open minded and cooperative when your generous attitude makes it difficult to demonize you.

A smile is a deceptively powerful tool for preventing others from falling into a defensive or offensive response. If you consistently present a smiling, friendly countenance, people will respond to it. The effect of a smile is potent—our positive response to it is programmed into our DNA. A simple and genuine smile takes the threat out of your appearance and induces others to lower their defenses and be more receptive to your message. A sour or flat expression, on the other hand, will put others on their guard and prepare them to do battle.

Always ask yourself how others see you. Watch how they respond to you. You may feel that your approach is a model of reason and fair-mindedness, but others may not perceive you that way. Remember, your ability to influence is tied to how others see you rather than how you see yourself. A statement from a person who is perceived as even-handed will have far more success than an identical statement from a person perceived as biased and egotistical. If others find your manner demanding or troublesome, back off, apologize if you must, and adopt a gentler, friendlier, more respectful approach.

Now that you know how to keep people happy and cooperative, let's discuss persuasion itself, the working methods you can use to influence what others do and believe.

"What's in it for the other guy?" This question is the foundation of all good persuasion. The fatal flaw of most persuasive efforts is that the persuader focuses on a different question—"What's in it for me?" People are unlikely to be greatly motivated by what you want. The art of persuasion is the ability to induce others to comply voluntarily. In other words, to convince them that what you want should also be what they want.

To do this, it's essential to discover what another's needs are and then show how your idea will satisfy those needs. An even higher level of persuasion is to create a want or need in another, one that didn't exist until planted and nurtured by you, and then demonstrate how your ideas will meet it. Advertising, for example, often builds a specific need among consumers and then persuades them to spend money on a product that answers that need.

As with assertion, the first step in persuasion is to decide exactly what it is you want. This may seem simple, but it can be trickier than it sounds. We all engage in a lot of self-delusion to protect ourselves from unpleasant truths, and this can warp our perception of our true needs. It's also possible, without careful self-analysis, to become confused about what it would take to meet that need. Make sure you know what you want, and then be as specific and concrete as possible about what is needed to provide it.

Next, plan what you will say and how your presentation will unfold. Your approach should be uniquely designed to appeal to the specific person you are trying to influence. Forget about yourself and your needs; focus instead on who the other person is and what his needs are. Actually, this isn't quite accurate. You should focus not only on who the person is but also on who he believes he is. You may see the person as socially inept, but he may see himself as James Bond. If that's the case, and you want to have influence with him, you better treat him like 007. If you slight him or inadvertently undermine his self-image, you will have little persuasive impact.

What are the other person's interests, beliefs, values, fears, potential objections, personality attributes, and situational pressures? Only by thinking through these factors can you hope to predict his responses to your proposals and prepare methods for handling or answering objections, emotions, questions, abuse, or counter offers.

Knowing your opponent is the best way to prepare a presentation and maintain control of it. By being more prepared than the other person, you can control the encounter and probably the outcome. For example, if a person is financially oriented, don't appeal to his emotions. Show him how your idea will save or make him money. If the person has a big workload, demonstrate how your idea will make him more efficient. If your girlfriend might object to seeing a certain movie because it's violent, appeal to her romantic side by emphasizing that it also has a good love story.

Never assume that others think as you do or see the world as you do. Assumptions frequently cripple effective persuasion. To really understand the needs of another, you have to set your own ego aside and put yourself in that person's shoes. Failing to do this usually yields an approach that would work fine on you but fails miserably on another. Don't attempt to persuade someone until you've fully considered this question—"Why would this person want to agree with me?"

You can always ask a person to identify his needs, but you can't always count on the answer being accurate or honest. However, there is always a reason for the way people behave, that you can count on. You may have to play detective (or psychologist) to find it. For example, a man might claim that the reason he can't be convinced to go to an amusement park is his dislike of crowds. His real reason, which he's too ashamed to admit, is a fear of heights. Until you address his fear that he might end up on one of those towering thrill rides, he will stubbornly resist all your persuasive efforts.

If you try to persuade this person to go to the park by telling him that the crowds won't be so bad this time of year, you'll fail because you will have missed his true need (to avoid heights). Incorrectly understanding the needs of others is one of the most common reasons that persuasion fails. A good persuader is also a good detective, skilled at ferreting out people's true objections.

In the above example, you now find yourself confused as to why your persuasion is failing. Perhaps, as you are considering this failure, you recall some instances in the past when this individual displayed a fear of heights. If some questions and careful observation seem to confirm your theory, you might try a different persuasive approach.

You: Okay, Gary, just in case you change your mind about going, I want to warn you that you're not going to get me up in any of those sky-high rides that fly all around. They're just too hard on my stomach.

Gary: Really, well I'm not that big on rides like that either. You know, I've been working too much lately. Maybe I should get out. I think I'll go after all.

Bingo! Once you find the right buttons to punch, apparently unmovable resistance collapses. When a seemingly logical and fair-minded presentation fails to influence someone, it is probably because there is an undetected fear and/or need that is undermining your persuasion. Our emotions, particularly fear, drive us far more than logic. If you develop your skills in finding and resolving the hidden fears and worries of others, your persuasive success rate will skyrocket.

Here's another example. A boy who has just moved to a new neighborhood loves to play baseball. His father, seeing some boys his son's age playing baseball, says, "Why don't you go on over there and join the game?" The boy refuses even though the logic of the suggestion is clear—he is lonely, he is bored, and he loves baseball.

However, the father's persuasion is ineffective because the boy's shyness and fear of rejection by the other boys are overriding his desire to play ball. These are the issues that the father has to discover and resolve in order to successfully persuade his son.

In addition to seeking out fears and worries, another powerful persuasive tool is understanding what feeds a particular person's self-esteem. What is it that makes him or her feel important, influential, needed, unique, and so on? Because we all crave admiring attention, anything that draws positive interest from others will be a powerful motivator. Start by asking yourself what the person feels he is good at or what he considers his best characteristics, and then decide how you can appeal to those qualities.

For example, if a person is vain about his looks, you might be able to convince him to make a speech before a large group by saying, "I think you have the commanding presence and image that will give our message more credibility than the other speakers I've considered." Or, suppose you are trying to convince a person who considers herself an expert on classical music to go to a party with you. "The hosts of the party, Brenda and John, are big fans of classical music. They'd love to hear you explain the history behind some of their favorite pieces." By appealing to the factors that feed people's egos, you make it very easy for them to see the benefits of complying with your wishes.

So how do you discover the hidden fears, needs, and self-esteem factors that motivate individuals from behind the scenes?

The primary way is to be observant. In most cases, the people you will try to influence will be those with whom you have regular contact such as friends, family, and co-workers. Use the time you have with these people to learn as much as you can about them. What are their histories, their likes and dislikes, their motivators, their pressures, their fears, their current situations, and so on? You'd be surprised how much you can learn about the people around you, even about family members, if you pay closer attention to them than you're accustomed to doing.

Observe, learn, and remember. Then when you need to persuade, draw on this knowledge to help you formulate the best approach. Wisely used, this knowledge will also yield better, deeper, more satisfying relationships

Obviously, you could also use such knowledge of others to be unfairly manipulative. And it would probably work, for a while. In the long run, though, it's a loser. Exploitive manipulation eventually degrades relationships resulting in a personal loss that greatly exceeds the benefits one may have been gained from some persuasive victories.

The best tool for obtaining the information you need to effectively persuade is the ability to listen well. This is particularly true if the person you want to influence is someone you don't know well.

Listening well necessarily means giving others plenty of room to talk. Since your goal is to persuade, the natural urge is to do most of the talking yourself. Don't do it. A wise persuader let's others freely reveal the valuable information that will help him design the most potent persuasive approaches.

Unrestricted talk is also a great way for people to expend emotions that would otherwise prevent them from concentrating on your message. Also, any unexpressed thoughts would only rattle around in their heads, distracting them from really hearing what you are saying.

You can also use questions, disclosures, and reflections to encourage people to open up and fully reveal their thoughts and feelings.

The most effective questions are usually open-ended, general information questions that allow others to say what they want without direction from you—"How are you affected when you have to do these extra projects?" Also ask questions that request an opinion or sentiment—"What do you think of this?" or "How do you feel about this?"

You should also use reflection periodically to test your theories about what makes a person tick—"Let me make sure I understand what you're saying. You think that..." Putting the other person's ideas, meaning, and feeling into your own words gives him a chance to correct or expand on your interpretation and invariably gives you valuable additional information. These techniques speed disclosure of the pressure points that will be most susceptible to persuasion.

As stated before, the primary reason for listening is to uncover the needs you will have to satisfy in order to get the other person to comply with your wishes. Listen as if you were a detective seeking out the evidence and finding the clues. Listen carefully for hidden motivators. Try to hear not just the words but the underlying and possibly disguised meaning or feeling. Overall, your goal is to empathize so completely that you experience what the other person is experiencing. Once you've done that (it's not easy, you won't always be successful), your odds of designing a successful persuasive approach will increase greatly.

Persuasive presentations, whether you're trying to get your roommate to take out the trash or convince your boss to give you an important account, usually go astray because we act without a plan and focus primarily on our own needs. Unless luck is on your side, this is normally a formula for failure.

Before we discuss the design of a successful persuasive presentation, let's look at some general cautionary guidelines.

Approach the problem of persuasion from the correct angle—How will complying with your wishes benefit the other person? Because you want something and because you have an unsatisfied need, it's easy to attempt to persuade another by describing how his compliance will be a good thing for you. "Look, Jim, if you pick up Mom at the airport, I'll have more time to study for my final exam tomorrow."

Sometimes this will work. The person may feel sorry for you and grudgingly do what you want. But, it creates a debt. You owe him. He didn't act voluntarily, he was pushed. Always design your approach by focusing on the needs of the other person. Ask yourself what he has to gain and lose by complying and then prepare a presentation that answers those needs and objections. "Look, Jim, if you pick up Mom at the airport, she'll be so surprised and pleased that I'm sure she'll give you the car on Saturday night."

Speak with fluency and confidence—Many people have trouble making decisions and sit on the fence waiting to be pushed one way or another. If you speak with confidence and sound like you know what you're talking about, people will often accept your leadership. Practice your delivery, make sure that you are better informed than others, and your opinion will probably carry the day. This is especially true for complex and serious matters (as opposed to talking someone into going to the store for a quart of milk).

Put some drama into your persuasive efforts—A little showmanship makes people sit up and pay attention. It can also be used to focus their attention on a key point that might otherwise get lost in the general ebb and flow of the conversation. Physical demonstrations are a great way to make an idea stick in someone's head. For example, after his teenage son got a speeding ticket, a father throws a watermelon at a wall to emphasize what can happen to the human body in a car wreck. You can bet that this had more persuasive effect on the boy than any purely verbal discussion would have had.

Ask yourself if your expectations are out of line—Will the other person have to make a major sacrifice to provide you with a relatively minor benefit? Are you persuading to get something you really need or are you inappropriately attempting to control or interfere in the life of another?

Now let's analyze the factors that make a presentation effective and persuasive.

As noted previously, in persuasion the spine on which all else hangs is self-interest—not yours, the other guy's. This is pretty easy to understand when someone is trying to persuade you. You will immediately analyze a request in terms of "what's in it for me." But, somehow most of us forget this basic truth when we try to persuade others.

The result is that we never really make an effort to discover the needs of others or to demonstrate how our idea will satisfy those needs. Instead, we may fall back on demands, belittlement, guilt trips, insults, threats, and other inappropriate tactics. For a while this works. People will comply to get you off their backs or to avoid trouble. Over time, however, these tactics weaken the bonds that make relationships work. People cease to care what you think, get tired of being bullied, and start to resist and fight back. In other words, the real needs and interests of others, temporarily deferred, return with a vengeance.

Another method of successful persuasion is to convince others of the unqualified correctness of your position. If they truly believe, they will want to comply (usually, but not always). This can't be done with negative tactics like threats or guilt. It can only be done by clearly demonstrating a solid, well-reasoned logic. However, many of us have relied on and experienced the negative methods of persuasion so pervasively that we aren't really sure how to go about persuading on the merits.

In this case, the personal benefit to the other person is less easily defined. The person will agree simply because you have made your idea the most attractive in terms of practicality, effectiveness, or general emotional appeal. Sometimes people will agree to something not so much because of direct personal benefit but because they simply want to be right.

Of course, sometimes people will oppose even the best and most reasonable idea if it happens to impose a penalty on them personally. For instance, a certain site may be ideal for an airport, but if your house backs to it, you'll likely oppose such a plan no matter how many good reasons are given for it.

Next we look at some of the basics of benefit-based persuasion.

We often steamroll over the needs of others, assuming that their requirements are trivial, irrational, or stupid—They may be, but from a persuasion standpoint that's irrelevant. Good or bad, needs must be dealt with. You may find a person's particular need bone-headed in the extreme, but that doesn't make it any less potent as a motivator. If you can demonstrate to that individual how your idea or plan will fill his need, you greatly enhance your persuasive power.

Remember that while people's behavior often appears random, purposeless, and illogical to the casual observer, there actually is motivating rhyme and reason—The underlying rationale is simply hidden or unnoticed. Suppose that your girlfriend consistently refuses to go with you to the best and most expensive restaurant in town. The food is marvelous, but she always claims it's second rate. Her opposition to the restaurant seems irrational until she finally reveals that this is the place where her former husband told her he wanted a divorce. If you assume someone's resistance to your wishes is unreasonable and don't bother to look for the hidden causes, your persuasion will be unsuccessful.

Never assume that everyone responds to life in the same way, or with the same priorities as you—For instance, we all need to feel important, but an insecure person's need for attention and praise may be far greater than a self-confident person whose primary need is for freedom and decision making power. Plan your persuasive appeal accordingly.

When your persuasion is met with resistance, ask yourself what the person is gaining by refusing to comply—Suppose you have a teenage son who won't take out the trash without being hounded unmercifully. Instead of just assuming he's a lazy, ungrateful son, try to look deeper and find the benefit he derives from noncompliance. Perhaps your tone is so demanding that he feels resistance demonstrates the adult status he thinks he deserves. Or, maybe he's in love with the beautiful girl that lives across the street and fears he would be irreparably degraded if she were to see him toting garbage around. Once you've discovered the reason for his obstinacy, you can probably find a better way to move him.

Even if you can't find a personal need to fill, always give the other party some kind of reason for complying with your desires—We have all been trained from childhood to respond positively to reasons. Studies show that people are far more likely to agree to a request when it is accompanied by a reason, even when that reason isn't very good. Why? Having a reason as a justification for obeying someone's request allows us to save face. If no reason is provided, we feel like we're being used and pushed around.

Suppose you're in a pastry shop and have just asked the counter-person for the last chocolate-covered donut. Suddenly, the person behind you says, "Excuse me, I was hoping I could have that chocolate donut." Your response would probably be "So what." But, you would probably react more positively if that person had said, "Excuse me, I was hoping I could have that last chocolate donut because today is our chocolate-loving manager's birthday and I wanted to give it to her." Now, because you have a reason for altering your behavior, you would be more likely to cooperate. "Sure, go ahead, I'll get a sweet roll instead."

Now let's go over the basic structure of a persuasive appeal.

Begin with a straightforward request or description of your need as you see it. Keep your request simple, specific, and as concrete as possible. For example, "Jim, I know that on our vacation you expect to visit your parents, but this year I'd like to go someplace different, by ourselves. Your parents are wonderful, but I think our relationship will be strengthened by having some time together, just you and me."

Note the effort in this statement to avoid getting the other party's back up. If your object is to injure and argue, you might phrase the same request like this—"Look, Jim, I'm sick of spending every summer with your parents. Why don't you cut the umbilical cord and take me on a real vacation like normal people?" All righty, that's sticking it to him. Not very persuasive though. Have a good time at Mom and Dad's.

Now that your request has been defined, what do you do? Your first job is to handle any emotions brought up by your request. Persuasion is often a request for change, and people can interpret change as an attack or as something troubling, even when that isn't your intent.

No rational, generous, open-minded discussion is going to take place until you've doused the emotional flames that even the most evenhanded request can ignite. As stated previously, the best way to calm and reassure a defensive human is to listen and empathize. Before you go any further, make sure that the other party feels he has had every opportunity to express himself fully.

Even after he's made his case, and you have reassumed the floor, watch for signs of anger or agitation. If you sense that emotions are on the rise, back off immediately and resume listening and empathizing until he feels heard and calms down again. Repeat this procedure whenever the other person shows signs of becoming upset. By continually taking time out to listen and empathize, you prevent the other person from getting into an unproductive emotional state in which persuasion will be impotent.

In the early stages of your presentation, focus on areas of agreement or issues that will be easiest to settle. This establishes an atmosphere of cooperation before moving on to the more contentious issues.

Before we discuss the core of a persuasive appeal, let's mention an alternative method of opening the discussion, one that delays the stating of your request until some groundwork has been laid. This method uses an old sales trick to foster a cooperative attitude—guiding the other person into a pattern of saying yes.

To do this, you begin your presentation with a series of questions that the other party will almost certainly answer positively. This sets a psychological tone of openness, teamwork, and cooperation. By the same token, you want to avoid questions or statements that will elicit a no or any sort of disagreement. All this requires putting some thought into what you will say. Here's an example using the situation above.

Sarah: You know, Jim, I always try to avoid taking our relationship for granted. That would be dangerous, don't you agree?

Jim: Yes, of course I do.

Sarah: I think it's important to have time alone, just you and me.

Jim: Sure it is. Our lives are so busy it's hard for us to find five minutes to be together.

Sarah: Do you worry that our busy lives always seem to focus on other people, kids, work, our friends, and never just us?

Jim: Yeah, it does worry me.

At this point Sarah has Jim right where she wants him. It's not going to be hard for her to transition smoothly into a discussion about changing their traditional vacation plans. The two of them are sharing the same opinions, coming to the same conclusions. There's nothing adversarial or confrontational going on between them. They're working as a team.

In addition, Sarah has gotten a commitment from Jim. He has agreed openly that the two of them need some quality time together. We'll discuss the power of obtaining a commitment later on, but for now just understand that people find it very difficult to break a commitment openly made.

Now let's look at the core of a persuasive appeal—fulfilling and answering the needs and objections of the other person. For this we'll return to the first example above in which Sarah spelled out the general nature of her request.

What does Sarah need to consider before she gets down to the business of convincing her husband that they should vacation alone and skip seeing his parents? She needs to ask herself what his objections are likely to be. What constraints or pressures will he have to deal with? What personal stake does he have in seeing his parents? And, how might he benefit by vacationing elsewhere?

Let's assume the following scenario. Jim's parents look forward to seeing Jim, Sarah, and the grandkids with great anticipation. They'll be very disappointed and won't mind saying so if Jim tells them that the family won't be coming to visit. And, truth be told, Jim loves to vacation in his hometown. He and his parents are very close, and he enjoys seeing his childhood friends and his old stomping grounds. Complicating matters further, his parents are old and a little frail, and Jim feels guilty whenever he passes up a chance to see them. These are the factors that Sarah has to address if her persuasion is to prove successful.

Now that she's stated her plan and gotten Jim into a cooperative mood, Sarah needs to allow him to talk. She knows her husband pretty well, but it's possible that by listening she may find there are additional factors affecting him that she hadn't considered. She starts him talking with a fairly non-partisan, open-minded statement of her position and a request for his opinion.

Sarah: I've been thinking for a long time that we're overdue for a vacation by ourselves. It seems like a good way for us renew our relationship, but I'd like to hear what you think.

Jim: Honey, you're right, we do need some time together, but we haven't seen my parents for almost a year. It'll be pretty hard to tell them we aren't coming. You know how they look forward to seeing the kids. I'd feel kind of bad disappointing them like that. Besides, Dad says he needs me to help cut back that big tree out front before a storm blows it down on the porch. He can't do it by himself.

Now it's Sarah's turn. She's presented her basic case, gotten Jim into a cooperative, non-antagonistic mood, and listened to his side of the situation. While hearing Jim out, she learned of a previously unconsidered factor, the tree, which she also has to handle in her response.

There are a number of tactics she can use to persuade Jim. She can help him see things from an angle he hadn't previously considered. She can find solutions for the constraints that make it difficult for him to agree with her. She can use praise in advance to motivate him to do what she has praised him for. She can approach him in such a way that he feels he came up with a solution himself. She can appeal to his nobler motives. She can change his focus from one personal principle to another. And she can do some plain old horse-trading. Watch for some of these techniques in Sarah's presentation.

Sarah: Jim, I know your parents will be disappointed. You love them and it's hard to bring them bad news, but we need time to ourselves. Sometimes we have to say no to others and work on our relationship. Everyone depends on you and I being a strong team, the kids especially, but also your parents. (Here Sarah has changed the focus of Jim's values from loyalty to parents to loyalty to the extended family. She's asking Jim to look at the problem from a new angle, the needs of the extended family vs. the needs of his parents).

Jim: That's true (smiles). The kids deserve parents who have time to talk to each other at least once a year. Still, (frowns) it'll be a real mess telling Mom and Dad we aren't coming.

Sarah: Oh, I don't think it will be as bad as you think. You've always been a good son. You and your parents are able to talk honestly and openly. Give Mom and Dad some credit. I think they respect you a lot and will understand when you explain the situation. (Here Sarah is using praise to give

Jim an image to live up to. She's telling him that everyone
concerned knows he is a good man with good motives and
that his reputation will protect him from criticism.)

Jim: I suppose that's true, but it's still not something I'd look for
          ward to.

Sarah: Maybe there's a way to soften the blow. What can we do to
          assure them that they aren't being deserted if we decide not
          to come? (Note that Sarah is not suggesting a solution, but
          she is guiding Jim toward one. If Jim comes up with his
          own solution, he'll be far happier with it and more likely
          to support and act on it.)

Jim: Hmmm, well, what if we suggest coming to see them over
          the three-day Fourth of July weekend? That'd give us time
          to see everyone and I could still help Dad with the tree.

Sara: Perfect, you're a genius.

There, that wasn't so hard. Of course, in real life this conversation
would have gone on longer, there would have been more give and
take, and possibly more resistance, but the basic tactics used by Sarah
do work.

You might be thinking that it all seems pretty manipulative, but it
really isn't, at least not in a bad way. Everything Sarah said was honest
and heartfelt, she just arranged her presentation for maximum effect.

Also note what Sarah did not do. She never allowed herself to get
angry, insulting, sarcastic, or a hundred other negative tactics that
we've all used to browbeat people into conforming to our will. Would
her persuasion have been as effective if she had said, "Your parents
expect too much," or "They've got money. Let 'em hire a tree trim-
mer for crying out loud," or "You're just too much of a coward to
tell them you've got your own life to lead," or "You don't care about
me or the kids"? If she had taken any one of these paths, Jim would
have become angry and defensive. Defending his parents, defending
himself, Jim never would have agreed to change the vacation plans.

Let's take a closer look at some of the methods that can be used to
overcome resistance to persuasion.

People often view a problem or situation from one angle. All their
reasons for behaving or believing as they do are based on that perspective. You may be able to change their position by allowing them
to see the situation from a new angle. Once you've shaken them from

their old point of view, you have a good chance of altering all the assumptions that flowed from that perspective. In other words, you make it easier for them to change.

For instance, Shannon likes to buy expensive furniture on the assumption that "good furniture is a better money's worth because it lasts forever." This may be true, but right now the family needs to tighten its budget, and her husband Bill wants to persuade her to buy less expensive furniture. One way of doing this is to challenge her underlying assumption, namely, that it is good to have furniture that lasts forever.

Bill might present the new perspective like this—"Yes, but who wants the same old furniture forever? Wouldn't it be more interesting to buy less expensive furniture and replace it more often with new furniture that's up to date?" This new way of looking at things pulls the rug out from under the logic of buying expensive furniture.

Here's another variation on the same theme of redirection. People often resist an idea because it offends one of their personal values or principles. You can get around resistance like this by changing the person's focus from a principle that generates opposition to another principle that generates support.

For example, suppose you want to put together a company newsletter but believe your boss will resist the plan because he has often stated that "this company has to start cutting expenses." You can avoid this objection by presenting the newsletter as a solution to another of the boss's pet concerns, namely, that the company has grown so fast that the employees have lost the feeling of family and team effort.

The boss has two values here, the need for thriftiness and the need for a connected employee team. You can be pretty sure that if you say, "I'd like to put out a company newsletter for the employees," the boss will refer to the first principle and reply, "Too expensive, forget it."

But, if you appeal directly to his other value, the need for closer working relationships, he might buy the idea. "Boss, I know you've been concerned that as the company grows we're all drifting apart and loosing touch with our common goals. I think a monthly newsletter would help pull us back together." The boss may be so distracted by the idea of nurturing the bonds of workplace community that he will forget or ignore the expense of producing the newsletter.

Before beginning any persuasive appeal, always ask yourself what difficulties the other person will have to overcome in order to comply. Assume, for instance, that you would like Eric to go to the baseball game with you on Sunday afternoon. What would prevent him from doing that?

You know that Eric usually takes his wife to brunch on Sunday afternoon. You also know that he and his wife don't have much time together because he works long hours. If you are to have any hope of getting Eric to the game, you have to use an approach that resolves these problems.

> Eric, let's go to the baseball game on Sunday. I know you usually have brunch with your wife, but this weekend I've got a better idea. The stadium is down by the beach. Ask your wife to meet you at the restaurant down by the pier after the game. You'll be there just in time to eat dinner as the sun goes down. It will be very romantic, your wife will love you for it, and you'll be able to see the game too. What do you say?

This persuasive approach is likely to work because you've built a solution to Eric's concerns into it.

Because we all love positive attention, appropriately worded praise can induce a person to do the thing for which he has been praised. Why? To get more praise, that's why. Most of us quickly learn to repeat behavior that brings us admiration, applause, compliments, and smiles.

Suppose you want your kid, a devoted TV watcher, to get out of the house and join a baseball team. Try this approach. At lunchtime, ask him to open a can of soup and toss him the can. When he catches it, even if he fumbles it, comment on his skill—"Wow, son, you've got great hands. I didn't have that kind of hand-to-eye coordination when I was your age." Later on, when one of your friends drops by, you make this comment—"Hey, check out this kid's shoulders. With a little training he'd be knocking baseballs out of the park."

For maximum effectiveness and credibility, praise should be specific. And, really top-notch specific praise points out positive features that the person being complimented may not have been aware of. General praise is often ineffective because it is so all encompassing that people don't know what it means or how to behave to get more.

As a result, general praise is not a good motivator—"Johnny, you seem like you'd be good at sports. Why don't you sign up for Little League this summer?" This statement doesn't tell Johnny precisely why he'd be good at baseball, nor does it give him enough information to evoke a mental picture of himself succeeding. Specific praise clearly explains why he would be good—"With those big arms, you'd knock the cover off the baseball."

Finally, praise is far more effective than demanding or nagging. Comments such as the following are counterproductive—"Johnny, I'm sick of you and that TV. This summer you're going to play baseball, and if you don't, I'm throwing the TV into the trash," or "What's wrong with you anyway? I just don't understand why you want to sit on the couch all day. Why don't you go outside and play baseball or something?" Do you think either of these comments is going to persuade Johnny to leap up and run outside for a little batting practice? Not a chance.

A variation on motivating by praise is motivating by an appeal to a person's ideals or principles. If you tell someone that you believe he has certain good qualities or that he adheres to certain principles, chances are that the person will do whatever is necessary to live up to your expectations. For example—"I know I can trust you to be there on time because you are one of my most dependable people," or "This could be a touchy job. I need someone who can control his temper and stay neutral, and that's why I've chosen you," or "You've always helped me out when I needed it, so I know you'll help your father by keeping your room and the house clean while I'm gone. I know I can count on you."

Being highly regarded is something we all value. By telling people your good opinion of them, you give them a strong motivation to behave in ways that won't weaken or destroy that opinion. Negative approaches, on the other hand, tell people that they have nothing to lose by behaving badly—"Your Dad needs help while I'm gone. I know you've never understood the concept of neatness, but do you think that for just three short days you could keep that pig sty you call a room clean?" Ahh, there's nothing like heaping on insults and low expectations to convince people to shape up.

As noted earlier, people are far more likely to support ideas they consider their own than the ideas of others (especially if those external ideas are being forced down their throats). If you can guide a person toward an idea or solution without actually spelling it out, allowing him to discover it on his own, he will like it better and be more willing to act on it.

The best way to guide another person's thought is by asking carefully planned questions and by seeking commitments about his beliefs or goals. Suppose you want one of your co-workers, Jack, to support you when you present your newsletter plan to the boss. If it's approved, you also want him to help you put the newsletter together, but you fear he may object to the extra work.

You: Have you noticed how worried the boss is about the loss of communication between employees as the company grows?

Jack: Yeah, he's said some things about it to me.

You: No kidding. Did you know production wasn't even aware of the new purchasing system until last week? Lack of communication is a real problem, don't you think?

Jack: Yes, it definitely is.

You: The boss would love anyone who came up with a way to keep people more informed.

Jack: Yeah, he would, wouldn't he.

You: Good career booster, but what could be done?

Jack: More memos?

You: Nah, too boring, half the ones that come out now aren't read. We need something that's not so dry, something with more human interest.

Jack: How about a monthly newsletter?

You: Hey, Jack, great idea! A newsletter, that's brilliant!

This is a little oversimplified, but you get the idea. Jack's support for the newsletter idea will now be unwavering because he believes it was his idea. If you had simply presented the idea to him whole, his involvement and enthusiasm would never have been so strong.

When persuading, don't forget plain old horse-trading. If you'll do this for me, I'll do that for you. Horse-trading has power that goes beyond the simple fact that the other person is getting something in return for complying with you. A quid pro quo goes a long way toward relieving the other party of the feeling that he is being used or taken.

When you want something but aren't willing to give anything in return, people can become resistant simply to save face. No one wants to be thought of as a pushover. The interesting thing here is that you don't necessarily have to offer something equal in value to what you are requesting. Something small, even trivial, can often be enough to quell the other party's fear that he's being a softie.

Now let's look at a few characteristics of human nature that are understood and manipulated by the professional persuaders of this world—sales and marketing people.

A large contrast can be used to make something seem better or worse than it would have without the contrast—For example, a car salesperson might decide that although a customer could afford a $25,000 car, he might nevertheless object to paying that much. To induce the customer to psychologically accept a $25,000 price tag, the salesperson takes him around the lot, showing him fully loaded vehicles of the same model that cost over $30,000. When he finally shows the customer the $25,000 car, the contrast with the $30,000 cars makes $25,000 seem cheap. On the other hand, if the salesperson had shown the $25,000 car first, without the effect of contrast, it would have struck the customer as very expensive. You too can find ways to use contrast to make your ideas seem more palatable.

Our social training teaches us that if we receive a gift, we are indebted—We are also taught that indebtedness and obligation are undesirable states. The natural reaction to a gift is to find a way to repay it and thus relieve oneself of the burden. Thus, if you want something from someone in the future, do a favor for him today. When in time, you ask for a favor, the person will see it as an opportunity to unload the debt that was created when he accepted your favor or gift.

For instance, if you want to persuade a computer expert to help you set up your new computer when it's delivered, offer to pick him up after work when he tells you his car is in the shop. After you've done him this favor, he can hardly turn you down when you call the following week and ask him to help you with your new computer.

In any kind of give and take, a concession can be interpreted as a kind of gift. As we've just seen, gifts have to be repaid to settle the debt. If you concede something, the other person will frequently feel strong pressure to soften his position as well.

You've probably experienced this effect yourself. Someone angrily accuses you of doing something objectionable and instead of arguing or denying, you answer, "Yeah, you're right, I really screwed up, what a jerk I was." You've made a concession, and in so doing you put pressure on the other person to do the same. Usually the other person will back off almost immediately. "Oh, well, I wouldn't say you were a jerk. It wasn't that big of a deal. I might have done the same as you." Remember, if you want a concession from another, make a concession of your own. Of course, there are hard bargainers out there who will take a concession and give nothing in return.

Previous commitments often play a powerful role in determining what our behavior will be in a particular situation—Once we make a commitment, either by making a statement or performing a decisive act, we use that commitment to tell us what kind of person we are and how we will act in similar circumstances in the future.

Commitments, especially public ones, are not taken lightly. There is always a strong inclination for our behavior to be in accord with our previous commitments. This peculiar characteristic of humans is driven by a desire for order and consistency, and a fear of appearing erratic or unreliable.

Because commitments are such potent motivators, they can be used to influence behavior. The trick is to get a person to make the commitment without realizing that he is being set up for some specific request. The persuader gets the persuadee to make or agree to some general, safe-sounding statement. He then uses that commitment to induce the other party to accept something specific that flows logically from it.

For example, you want to convince a friend to take you to the airport on her day off. The day before your departure, you pave the way for your request with a casual, innocent discussion of how hard it is to find good friends. "Most people these days just aren't willing to make the kind of sacrifices that good friendship is built on," you declare with a sigh. Your poor unwitting friend agrees wholeheartedly. "Oh, that's so true, sometimes friendship requires effort, sharing the load." The next day you call and ask her to take you to the airport the next day. She has to agree. Her previous commitment would make her look hypocritical if she were to decline.

Scarcity is a powerful motivator—Imagine that you are normally equally fond of two ice cream flavors, chocolate mint and rocky road. Both are delicious as far as you are concerned. One hot evening, you go to the local ice cream parlor and find it jammed with customers. You take a number and start checking out the freezers as you wait to be called. You soon notice that there is a full tub of chocolate mint but the rocky road tub has only one scoop remaining. Although you love chocolate mint, your whole attention is now focused on the rocky road. There are six parties ahead of you, and you begin to listen closely as each party orders, praying that they won't request that last scoop of rocky road. You have no further interest in the chocolate mint, which you usually love.

What's going on here? What's going on is that the scarcity of rocky road has made it seem more valuable. If it hadn't been in short supply, you might have happily ordered chocolate mint. From diamonds to the first issue Superman comic book, scarcity increases value, and you can use this principle to boost the power of your persuasion.

All you have to do is convince the other party that his ability to do something (the thing you want done) might be taken away or become impossible if he doesn't act now. If you want a friend to go to a concert with you, it will increase his or her desire to do so if you mention that the concert could sell out at any moment. The possibility of missing out raises the value of attending, even if the group playing isn't a particular favorite. Alas, such is human nature.

This ends our exploration of successful persuasion. Keep in mind that no matter what technique you use to persuade or influence another, the key is to keep your ego out of sight. Train yourself to stay in control of your feelings and to focus not on your needs but on the needs of the other person. If your ego gets out of the barn, it won't be long before you are telling people what you need, why they are wrong, why they are thickheaded, what they ought to do, and so on. Once that happens, your persuasive effectiveness plummets.

Also, don't be discouraged if none of the above methods work in a given situation. Persuasion techniques won't make people your slaves. There will always be times when others simply won't do what you want, no matter what you say. The methods discussed above increase the odds that you will be successful, but they don't guarantee it.

Chapter 9:
Negotiatory Talk

Most of us recognize negotiation only within limited confines. We know we're negotiating when we try to hammer out a deal on a new car at the local auto dealership. We know we're negotiating when we go on vacation and haggle over the cost of a sombrero in a Mexican marketplace. But in our other more mundane interactions such as discussing what movie to see or what time the teenage son will come home on a Saturday night, we may never really understand that we are in fact negotiating.

If you can't identify a negotiation when you're in one, your personal power and ability to influence are crippled. In this chapter, you'll learn not just powerful negotiation techniques but also an expanded appreciation of what negotiation is.

Any time you interact with people whose interests differ from your own, there is potential for negotiation. I use the word potential because actual negotiation won't occur if you choose to forgo attempting to improve your position or if you fail to recognize that your position can be improved.

For example, you might believe that your restaurant meal was improperly cooked and should be taken off your bill, but you choose not to negotiate the problem because you don't want to embarrass your companion. Or, you probably wouldn't negotiate for a reduction in the price of a tank of gas at a service station because you don't think you would have any success.

In the first example, you purposely limit you own power for reasons outside the negotiation process, and in the second example, you don't believe you have any power. Power is at the heart of negotiation.

A goal of this chapter is to show you that you have more power than you think and to urge you to use it more often to get what you want. The best negotiator in the world, possessed of a dominant bargaining position, will gain nothing if he chooses not to negotiate.

A good part of negotiation is using your creativity and analytical skills to find where your power lies and then applying it. For instance, you might decide that you can negotiate the price of the improperly cooked meal if you wait until your companion has gone to the restroom. Or, you find you can negotiate a free tank of gas if you agree to buy a set of new tires from the service station.

A good negotiator is something of a rebel; someone who says, "I don't accept these rules, traditions, customs, prerequisites, or precedents. I'm not going to accept restrictions on my ability to negotiate a better deal for myself." A skilled negotiator looks at every situation and asks, "Can I do better than what I'm being offered?"

It is very easy to be intimidated by the knowledge that certain things are done a certain way. In many cases, the demands of others have legitimacy only because we ourselves give them legitimacy. We happily allow our needs to go unmet because we never stop to consider whether asking for more is even possible.

For example, not too long ago the newspapers told the story of a man who had gotten a speeding ticket on a local thoroughfare. In the past, thousands of people had gotten speeding tickets on this same stretch of road. Most had paid their fines without argument. Some of them had fought their tickets on the grounds that they had been falsely accused. This particular gentleman, however, agreed that the speed he was charged with was correct. Still, this didn't mean that he was going to accept his ticket without attempting to get a better deal.

Of all those thousands of people who had gotten speeding tickets on this stretch of road, none had ever negotiated the speed limit itself. Speed limits have a legitimacy that people assume is indisputable, but this particular motorist was a rebellious fellow. He was not intimidated by the seemingly unassailable authority of that speed limit sign on the side of the road.

The motorist did some legal research and then attempted to negotiate a dismissal of the charge with a representative of the DAs office. He told the DA that in his opinion the vast majority of drivers exceeded the posted speed limit on this particular roadway. The current limit, therefore, represented a speed trap according to state law and was thus illegal. The DA refused to accept this, so the motorist went before a judge with the same argument.

The judge listened and then directed the city to do a traffic-speed study on the road in question. Some time later the city reported that the motorist was correct. The speed limit in this area was almost universally ignored because it was set too low for a primary access artery with few side streets. The judge dismissed the motorist's ticket and ordered the city to raise the speed limit by ten miles an hour.

Even the most dedicated negotiator doesn't challenge every rule or tradition he encounters. Often the potential gain isn't worth the trouble. But, a good negotiator keeps his eyes open for opportunity. He thinks creatively, looking at situations from a fresh angle. When the time is right, he steps forward and says, "I see this differently. I would like to negotiate a different arrangement."

Now we're going to discuss the methods and mentality of good negotiation. First we'll look at traditional competitive negotiation, the type that usually comes to mind when we think of negotiation. After that, we'll consider collaborative negotiation, which attempts to minimize competition and one-sided victories.

Despite the name, competitive negotiation should not involve intimidation, gouging, putting one over, or taking unreasonable advantage. The goal is always to meet your own needs but to do so within a fair agreement that doesn't damage the relationship you have with the other party. Of course, there are times, such as a negotiation over the price of a new car, when there is no ongoing relationship to protect. However, most of the negotiation you do in life is with friends, family, and business associates. People you have to live with. People you'd do well not to abuse.

Still, even in competitive negotiations in which you are trying to be fair, you may still have to work hard to protect your own interests. Being fair doesn't mean that you shouldn't use the power available to you to achieve your reasonable ends.

In negotiation, as in persuasion, information is power. The first task in any negotiation is to gather as much information about your opponent as possible. Good information gathering is critical, but because negotiation is a contest, concealment rather than openness is the rule. You and your opponent would both be wise to conceal your true needs, limits, deadlines, and weaknesses. However, if you actively seek out information about your opponent, something most people fail to do, you'll probably discover more than you thought possible.

To further complicate the information gathering process, many negotiations are not strictly about the declared issues. In some cases, this may mean misrepresentation and trickery, in others your opponent may be unaware of his true needs. You neglect these hidden needs at your peril. If you misread the needs of the other person, you may find yourself in a surreal circumstance—your opponent won't be satisfied even if you fully meet his or her declared demands.

Suppose, for example, that a wife goes to her husband and says, "Honey, we haven't been out for a while. Why don't you take me to that new French restaurant downtown?" The husband answers, "No way, too expensive." An argument (read, negotiation) ensues, and after a while the husband gives in. "Okay, okay, we'll go this Saturday." Instead of smiling gratefully, as he expects, the wife yells, "Forget it!" and storms out of the room.

The husband is mystified. He gave her what she asked for, right? Wrong! He misunderstood his wife's true needs. They weren't negotiating over a meal at a restaurant, as he had assumed, they were actually negotiating over his willingness to give her some romantic quality time—and give it cheerfully. By forcing her to bargain hard for these things, he rendered his concession worthless.

Negotiation is a give and take process in which all parties strive to achieve their goals, stated or unstated, and consciously or unconsciously understood. It may appear that you and a salesperson are dickering over the price of a new dishwasher, but other factors are just below the surface. Things like ego and competitiveness may be just as important as the number of dollars to be exchanged. Therefore, negotiation success requires you to take a wider view than simply to focus on the primary issue.

What kind of person are you negotiating with? Quick paced and straight-forward or leisurely and indirect? Big-picture oriented or focused on details? Logical or emotional? Suppose your opponent is mild-mannered, and prone to ponder and decide issues slowly. If you come on like a Mack truck, pushing hard, rolling your eyes, letting your disapproval of delay show, you are ignoring his needs. He may refuse to make concessions simply because his pride won't allow him to concede when he feels bullied and rushed

Aside from identifying your opponent's style and personality traits, attempt to determine his attitude toward negotiation. Some people hate the confrontation of negotiation and will make large concessions to avoid prolonging it. Others feel just the opposite; they love both the competition and the verbal sparring. To them negotiation is an enjoyable game that they very much want to win. Still others feel that negotiation is a big waste of time. To cut to the chase, they begin discussions with their bottom-line, unalterable position.

If you are aware in advance of these negotiation attitudes, you can plan your tactics accordingly. The competitive negotiator has to be allowed the feeling of victory even if you get everything you want. On the other hand, the person who opens with his rock-bottom, no-retreat position has to be sidetracked before he commits himself, giving you time to lower his expectations.

In addition to gathering intelligence about personality and attitude, you also need to discover as much concrete info as possible about your opponent's circumstances, opening bid, general bargaining position, deadlines, and other limitations. This can require plain old detective work. Talk to friends or associates of your opponent. Talk to his competitors, his secretary, his janitor, his co-workers, and anyone else with relevant information. If possible, try to discover your opponent's negotiating plan. What is he going to hit you with? The best source for this type of info might be people who have negotiated with him in the past.

You can also coax a lot of information directly from your opponent. Use questions, reflections, self-disclosures, and direct requests for information to push your opponent to reveal more of his position than is wise. Observe his nonverbal cues such as tone of voice or expression (these aspects of communication are less easily guarded than verbal communications). Listen for what is not said as much as for what is said (omissions can be very revealing). Carefully analyze the way your opponent presents his offer. If he states firmly, "I want $200 cash," he's probably closer to his limit than if he tentatively asks, "What do you think of $200? Does that seem fair?"

Discovering all this information obliges you to approach negotiation with an information seeking frame of mind. Prior to and during face-to-face negotiation, you should listen a lot, empathize a lot, question a lot, and talk very little.

Here are a few suggested phrases designed to keep your opponent babbling uncontrollably.

> Interesting, I hadn't looked at it that way. How did you come to realize that? (Information request)
>
> I'm sure dealing with this isn't easy. What is such and such (or so and so) like? (Reflection/question)
>
> Tell me why you want to do X instead of doing Y. (Information request)
>
> Why is X important to you? (Question)
>
> It sounds to me like you feel... (Reflection)
>
> Which would you prefer, X or Y? (Question)
>
> You're saying that you need... (Reflection)
>
> I don't understand. (Information request)
>
> I want to make sure I understand this. Explain to me why... (Information request)

Another trick for gathering information is to play dumb. Act confused and helpless, appear to have trouble understanding, stammer, use the wrong words, ask for help. Playing dumb convinces your opponent and others that you are no threat. He feels he has the advantage and lowers his guard. He talks more, he listens less, he puts aside caution, and as a result, he's more vulnerable. Rural people have been using this technique to get the best of city slickers for ages ("Well, golly gee, mister, I'm just a pore country boy, this is all too much for me. Could y'all 'splain that again?").

Silence is another tool you can use to push others to disclose too much. As we've discussed, silence in a conversation makes most people very uncomfortable. Even when they know they should keep quiet, that awful void in the flow of words is so unnerving that they find themselves blabbing uncontrollably just to make it go away.

Begin your information gathering process as early as possible. Don't wait until you are face to face with your opponent in the actual bargaining encounter. Advance preparation separates the pros from the amateurs. A great deal of info simply can't be obtained at the last moment.

For example, if you want to buy a new car, look into the dealership's situation before you talk to a salesman. Research the dealer's costs for the car you want. Find out whether business is good or bad, whether inventory is high or low, their cash flow, whether they've met their weekly or monthly quota, their reputation for price cutting, and so on. Use these facts to determine the strength of the other side.

You might be thinking, "How would I ever find out all that info?" It's not as hard as you think. You just start contacting people and getting them talking. For instance, a salesman might not tell you that business is bad, but a service rep or the girl who answers the phone at the switchboard might.

What's the point of all this information mining? Knowing your opponent. Find out what kind of person he is, what his situation is, and then modify your approach to take advantage of his weaknesses, strengths, and needs. He'll be more likely to concede if you know what buttons to push. Now that you've educated yourself about your opponent, you can decide how to plan your tactics.

If your advance fact harvesting has been thorough and successful, you should be in a good position to predict what his position will be, what style he'll use, and what moves of your own will be most effective.

Look at the situation from your opponent's point of view. What will he respond to positively? What will motivate him? What can you give that will induce him to give something in return? Why should he meet your needs? It is critical to stay focused on these questions. As with persuasion, if you get too wrapped up in your own needs, you'll never find your opponent's pressure points.

Please understand, you aren't focusing on your opponent's needs because you want to give away the farm. Paradoxically, you are going to use his needs to get what you want. Sure, this sounds a bit underhanded, but remember, this is competitive negotiation; your opponent is trying to do unto you as you do unto him.

Below are some common needs you can use to influence people and obtain concessions.

The need to obtain a reward or escape a penalty—If your opponent believes you can reward or punish, don't disabuse him of that notion, even if you really can't deliver. Also, avoid declaring precisely what you will or won't do. Let 'em worry and wonder. Make the uncertainty work for you. Finally, keep in mind that rewards are inherently more potent persuaders than penalties. "I'm offering you a pretty large one-time order. If you give me a better price, I might be able to give you a big chunk of our company's regular business."

The need to be good to good people—One of the best ways to get concessions out of people is to make them like you. One of the worst ways to get concessions is to make them dislike you. Never come on with threats, impatience, aggression, derision, or whining complaints. Who wants to give a present to an obnoxious jerk?

The need to avoid losing out to a competitor—Always let your opponent know that he isn't the only one who is after what you're offering. To win what you have, he will have to compete with others. "I've been offered $20 more across the street," or "Of course, when I explained my plan to George, he loved it."

The need to go along with the group—Confront your opponent with the combined support (or opposition) of a group (business associates, family members, mutual friends, etc.). Most humans hate being on the outside looking in. "Greg, come on! Bill, Jim, Alice, Nick, even Joan, think this is a great idea," or "Both the other department heads have signed on. And you know Jake, he'll get the boss's support for sure. Now's the time to sign on. You don't want to be left behind, do you?"

The need to bow to an expert—Non-experts hate to disagree with an expert; the risk of being wrong or looking foolish is too great. If you are an expert, or if you can effectively sound like one, your opinion will carry much greater weight. Another option is to get an expert to support you. "I'm an accountant, and I have to tell you, this lease is out of line with current industry standards and charges," or "Mother raised six kids, they all turned out fine, and she says to do it this way."

The need to obey rules—If possible, show your opponent that rules, custom, or precedent are on your side, not his. "Look, it's right here in the company manual. I can't offer you more without getting permission from corporate," or "We can't make a change like that without a lot of turmoil. The employees expect us to do this the traditional way."

The need to avoid wasted effort—We all hate to expend a lot of time and effort and then walk away with nothing to show for it. The willingness to make concessions increases with each passing minute of involvement in a negotiation process. For this reason, a favorable agreement often cannot be gained until your opponent has invested a substantial amount of time and effort.

As a result, it is to your advantage to drag the process out. Talk at length. Make the other guy explain everything in detail. Leave and come back the next day. Break off to consult others. Repeat what's already been discussed. If you bog down on a primary issue, leave it behind temporarily and settle smaller, easier issues; then return to the primary issue. After all this blood, sweat, and tears, no one is going to want to end up with a deadlock. Your opponent will now be willing to make concessions he wouldn't have considered early on.

The need to feel virtuous—Confront your opponent with a moral quandary he can only resolve properly by conceding to you. This plays on his need to feel that he is a good person. "If you don't go, mother won't know anyone there. You don't want her to feel out of place and lonely all evening, do you?" or "If I'm not assigned at least three assistants to help me on this project, I won't have time to continue volunteering at the clinic."

The need to get some sleep—Most inexperienced negotiators give up too quickly. They are too willing to believe an opponent's claim that he will never ever make a concession. Hang in there, work your opponent, wear him down. In time, a person who previously declared that he was immovable will concede simply because he's worn out.

One other important point about the categories of needs discussed above. Initially you will familiarize yourself with them in order to use them. However, a side benefit of familiarity with these methods is that you will know it when somone uses them on you. The manipulative power these techniques have over you is greatly reduced when you recognize them for what they are. Whenever others attempt to influence you, stay alert for efforts to use your needs against you.

Now that you've discovered what your opponent's needs are and decided on a plan of attack, it's time to consider your own requirements. What is your goal, your preferred outcome? What will be your opening bid or request? What is the minimum that you will accept without breaking off discussions? On the assumption that your opening bid will be refused (very probable), what degree or kind of concessions are you willing to make? What can you afford to trade away, and what is essential?

Although the actual negotiation will be a dynamic experience in which previously unconsidered ideas and options may occur, it's always best to have carefully thought through your position beforehand. If you do this, you'll be better prepared than your opponent.

On the other hand, even though you have a plan, it is important to remain flexible as the negotiation unfolds. Be open to new ideas and maintain a creative frame of mind. Adopt the attitude that there are numerous possible solutions, some of which haven't even been discovered yet. Don't fall in love with your initial plan. If you approach a negotiation with the idea that there is only one way of doing things (namely, your way), you'll inevitably encourage resistance in your opponent. You'll also close off some potentially attractive options.

When you begin discussions with the other party, put aside making your case initially and concern yourself with setting the tone for the negotiation. Even though this is a competitive negotiation, you should establish a climate of politeness, respect, and rational discussion.

Try initially to move your opponent toward a cooperative or collaborative atmosphere. Presenting an open and fair demeanor tests the waters. Temporarily avoid discussion of the negotiable issues, choosing instead to chat about neutral matters such as family, pastimes, sports, whatever. If you aren't well acquainted with the person, this allows you to get to know each other as people and begin to build trust. If your opponent challenges you aggressively from the outset, try to avoid being drawn in and attempt to deflect the conversation to less provocative matters. Use any break in your opponent's offensive to push for a more co-operative encounter.

Cooperation is fine, but if your opponent is determined to compete, you have to compete as well. For many people, the competitive aspects of negotiation themselves are rewarding. They enjoy the contest. They may also believe they are so skilled in the gamesmanship of negotiation that playing hardball is where their best advantage lies. Since collaborative negotiation is founded on trust and teamwork, an opponent determined to compete forces you to follow suit. Fortunately, you're going to be prepared to deal with such a contingency.

Determining your opening offer or request has considerable importance in competitive negotiation. Your opener sets the tone for the rest of the encounter. Asking too little will make you popular with the opposition but won't get you much of a deal. Perversely, an opener that is extremely low can make your opponent wary. He begins to wonder if something is wrong or defective with your offering. Asking way too much brands you as unreasonable and sets a tone of uncooperativeness, assuming that the negotiation doesn't break off then and there. The best opener is higher than the other side will agree to, but not so high that he feels you aren't concerned with fairness.

Remember, your opening offer needs to allow room for you to make concessions and still achieve your goal. Why do you need to bother with working through a series of concessions? Why not just tell the other side what your bottom line is and then stick to it?

For one thing, if you negotiate well, you'll probably get more than your bottom line. Furthermore, a prolonged process in which each side gradually reduces its initial requirements has a powerful psychological effect. As discussed above, people are more likely to make the concessions necessary to find agreement when they have a lot of time and effort invested. And in the end, when an agreement has been struck, both sides will value it more and feel greater satisfaction if they had to work hard to achieve it.

Also, a tough opener throws cold water on any unreasonable expectations the other side might be harboring. It drives home the reality of the situation to an opponent dwelling in a fantasy world.

Finally, a drawn out process allows time to build a relationship, to generate the trust and understanding that nurtures cooperation. It takes time for both sides to really understand the pressures and interests affecting the opposition. This understanding can't be arrived at in a brief encounter. It is, however, critical for creating an atmosphere in which concession and creative thinking come more easily.

Here are a few pointers on planning your opener and any subsequent concessions that might be required. First and foremost, your initial offer should not provide clues as to your absolute limit.

For example, suppose you are negotiating with a car salesman over the price of a used car. If the sticker price on the car is $10,000, and your opening offer is $9,500, what does this relatively high offer tell the salesman? It tells him that you aren't playing hardball. It tells him that either your expectations aren't very high or that you are hungry for a deal. He knows you aren't going to put up much of a fight, so he can safely concede very little. However, if your opener had been $8,000, he can't really be sure whether you'll be tough or not, but he suspects the he's going to have to make some serious concessions to close the deal.

Also, as in poker, don't let your words or expression give your limit away. If you say, "I'll be glad to hear other offers, but what about $500 for starters?" you sound like a softie. Your opponent knows you will come down quite a bit. Everything you say and do should be designed to convince the other party that your opener is very close to your limit (even though it's not) and that any concessions by you will be minor.

In determining your opener, ask yourself how badly your opponent needs what you have. Consider how many other sources he has. If you want to trade money for a car that's very popular, the dealer has lots of other sources for the money you are offering, namely multitudes of other buyers. Your ability to get big concessions will be low. But, if you are negotiating for a model that's selling slowly, the dealer has few other sources of money (few buyers), and your bargaining power will be substantial.

The way you play your concessions can inadvertently reveal a lot to a watchful opponent about your limits and intentions. If your opening offer of $500 is refused, and you quickly come back with a big concession, an offer of $750, your opponent will assume that your actual limit is probably around $1000 or higher. Having assumed $1000 is your limit, your opponent will hold out for that amount. On the other hand, if your concession is small, an offer of $550, your opponent will assume your upper limit is probably only $600, maybe $650. Big, quick concessions tell the other side that your opener was a long way from your limit. Small concessions made after much delay tell the other side you don't have much left to give.

When conceding, try to trade away items that are low in value to you, while pushing the other side to give up items high in value to you. Auto dealers are experts at this. They may, for instance, convince you to give up further negotiation on price (important to them) in trade for free undercoating and floor mats (items which cost them next to nothing).

Negotiation by definition involves disagreement, and disagreement can easily lead to emotions like anger, frustration, and impatience. These and all other emotions that would be perceived by the other side as an attack should be avoided, even when the other guy becomes insulting or hostile. There is no greater advantage in negotiation than the ability to remain cool, calm, and collected no matter how frustrating the situation.

One way to increase the odds of keeping your emotions under

control is to keep your self-esteem separate from the negotiation process. In other words, you must avoid believing that failure to succeed in a negotiation means that you are a failure. If you identify too strongly with the issue at hand, you may perceive any criticism of your position as a criticism of yourself, and that's when your emotions fly out of control. Keep this in mind—you are not the issue, and the issue is not you.

If your opponent believes you have insulted him, judged him, or abused him, a strange thing happens, a thing that has been the root cause of many a failed negotiation—the issue switches from the original negotiated subject to one of personal rivalry. Both sides now become fiercely, uncompromisingly, and unreasonably competitive. A person might compromise or concede on an impersonal matter, but if his ego and self-respect are at stake, he will never give an inch of ground.

In the early stages of the negotiation, the period in which the tone of the encounter is being set, you should be the picture of cordiality. You are warm, friendly, relaxed, empathetic, a good listener. You value your opponent's opinion, you show him respect, you even admit to error if necessary. You are just a regular, likable person.

The point of all this non-aggressive behavior is to lower the other guy's defenses. The less energy he spends defending himself or attacking you, the more likely he is to cooperate, look for common ground, and accept reasonable offers. Your behavior sets the tone for his behavior. If you are reasonable, more than likely he will be too. That's human nature. The abrasive, fast talking manipulator causes people to recoil, be on their guard, and assume the worst.

Another goal of the pleasant-person approach is to humanize yourself in the eyes of your opponent. Not uncommonly in negotiation, your opponent will see you as little more than a roadblock lying between him and his objective. The initial moments of the negotiating encounter are your chance to show him that you are a real person with pressures and problems just like his. It will be harder for him to be dishonest or unfair to you if he has some human connection with you.

Describe your situation or problem in personal terms, how it affects your life, and how you feel about it. "I need to get this payment down below $350. I'd never enjoy the car if I had to write a check higher than that every month. My wife is already after me to cut family expenses. If I come home with a monster payment, I'll never hear the end of it." Remember, if your opponent perceives you as a "customer" or "number 26" or "the caller on line 3," he'll find it a lot easier to burn you than if he perceives you as a real, live human being.

Also keep this in mind—your ability to negotiate wisely and rationally declines in direct proportion to how much you crave what you are negotiating for. A good negotiator has to be willing to walk away in order to achieve the best deal for himself. If you absolutely must have something, your opponent is sure to sense it. His concessions will dry up, and you'll have to pay big time to possess your heart's desire. Unless it's unavoidable (a rare situation), always go into a negotiation with a willingness to say no if you can't get a good deal. This attitude allows you to take the calculated risks that will most likely result in a favorable transaction.

Two final points to remember. First, even if your opponent has declined the collaborative approach to negotiation, you should continue to present yourself and your case in an unemotional, respectful manner. Your opponent may want to compete, but that doesn't mean he's immune to the influence of being treated well. You can still profit from setting a fair and open-minded tone for the encounter. Second, while you may already have done considerable fact finding about your opposition, remember to maintain your detective's frame of mind. The negotiation itself is usually the richest source of usable information, and you will probably discover new insights that require you to change your plan on the fly.

As you initiate serious negotiation, begin to describe your position. Give your opponent the facts you want him to have, your opening offer, and how you believe both of your interests are affected. Present yourself in a firm, confident way. Speak in a fluid, organized manner that is easy to understand and communicates that you know what you are talking about. If you are defensive, nervous, or ill prepared, the other guy will almost certainly interpret your behavior as weakness.

Let your opponent talk all he wants. The more he talks the more you learn. As for yourself, watch what you say. Avoid giving away any information your opponent could use against you. For example, if you're under the time pressure of a deadline, don't reveal it either by word or impatient behavior.

If your opponent comes on strong, insulting, blaming, making outrageous demands, you may feel your emotions rising. Resist the urge to counterattack. Deflect his emotionalism or aggression by welcoming and listening carefully to his point of view. By no means does this require you to agree with him, you simply respect his right to have his say (even if you think it's hog swill). "That's interesting, I had no idea you felt this way? Go on."

If the attack is directed at you personally, as opposed to the issue, respond as if his attack had actually been on the issue. By avoiding open recognition of the personal attack, you can respond to the criticism neutrally. Hopefully, this will help defuse some of the tension and allow the other person to transition to a more reasonable manner without losing face.

Him: You have sure botched up this whole situation.
You: It's true, this situation is botched up. I can see why you are concerned. Let's see if we can agree on a plan to straighten things out.

Notice how positive this response is. You're not agreeing that you are to blame, but you are recognizing his concerns. Then you ask him to think in terms of solutions rather than finger pointing.

In addition to avoiding emotional or defensive reactions to your opponent's aggressive tactics, you also need to avoid prematurely judging his actions and motives. Before coming to any conclusions, hear him out fully, ask questions to clarify, and reflect his statements. If you act on erroneous conclusions before he's fully explained himself, your negotiating tactics will probably fail. When you do state your evaluation, shy away from the word *you*. "I think there's another way to look at this" is much less threatening than "You don't understand what's going on."

If your opponent's passions are stirred up for any reason, let him talk freely. Unimpeded talk is the most efficient way for people to calm themselves down. As soon as you see the other guy's emotions rising, stop and listen reflectively. Don't resume discussions until he has talked himself out and returned to his rational self.

Once you have your opponent in a calm state, your next task is to determine specifically where your positions agree and disagree. Do you disagree on basic goals or is your disagreement one of methods (how to achieve those goals)? Make sure you know what you are negotiating about. Sounds obvious, but it's easier than you think to get confused in the rush and turmoil of vigorous bargaining.

When this process reveals areas of agreement (as it usually does), you should always take time to stress these positive factors with your opponent. Make sure he understands that there is agreement as well as disagreement. This creates goodwill and an impression that progress and forward movement are occurring.

Now we get to the very heart of competitive negotiation. All the tactics and methods described so far had one aim—finding your opponent's limit. Now we want to discuss how to persuade him to make concessions that will give us an agreement as close to his limit as possible. Meanwhile, of course, your opponent will be trying to do the same thing to you.

Your and your opponent's limit is the point beyond which either party would see no value in a deal and would break off negotiations. Your opponent might offer his car for sale at $1500, but have a lower limit of $1000. He will negotiate in the $1500 to $1000 range, but he will ultimately break off negotiations if you insist on offering less than $1000.

As a buyer, if you have an upper limit of $1400 (you'll break off if you have to pay more than $1400), there is the potential for a deal because your limit is within the seller's range of $1000 to $1500. The seller in this example wants to cut a deal as close to your $1400 upper limit as he can, while you want to cut a deal as close as possible to the seller's $1000 lower limit. If either of you persist in trying to exceed the other's limit, a deal probably won't be struck.

The art and skill of negotiation is to be more effective than your opponent in bringing about concessions. Your goal is to convince your opponent that if he wants a deal, he is going to have to make concessions and settle very close to or at his own limit. Since your opponent desires a settlement near or at your limit, negotiation becomes a battle of wits and nerve. How you win that battle is the subject of our next segment.

Serious negotiation begins with each side making its opening offer. Often, these initial proposals will be pretty far apart, which starts a repeating cycle of proposal and counterproposal in which positions converge, closing the gap between the initial offers. Usually, your opening offer is exaggerated, you don't really expect to get it, and this gives you room to make some fairly painless concessions.

However, just because you ultimately expect to concede doesn't mean you should be in any hurry to do so. Present an image of determined firmness. By word and deed, communicate to the other party that getting concessions from you will be like pulling teeth. This compels your opponent to lower his expectations and adjust his goal closer to his own limit.

People often enter into negotiations with unreasonable fantasies about what they are going to achieve. A tough opening proposal from you combined with a determined demeanor is like a bucket of cold water on the other guy's overheated expectations. On the other hand, a soft, uncertain demeanor combined with quick, easy concessions only convinces the opposition that you are weak and that their expectations are within reach.

When resisting your opponent's demands for concession, try not to rely too heavily on logical argument. Logic is rarely as effective as you might think. It may work if your evidence is overwhelming or if it clearly demonstrates how the other party's needs will be met. Normally, though, people respond more readily to their emotions than to their rationality in negotiation.

Questioning your opponent's facts, assumptions, and conclusions seems like the way to proceed but is often counterproductive. It makes him dig in and react defensively. Think about it. How many times have you been successful in logically convincing another that his position is wrong and your position is right? No one likes to be proven wrong, and they will discredit and discount even the most massive evidence to avoid being humiliated.

Logic works best when it is used to demonstrate how your opponent's needs will be met by agreeing to your proposal. You can't sell a man a Chrysler by telling him he's been a fool to even consider purchasing a Toyota. You can sell him the Chrysler by showing him how it will meet his needs—"You say you like to drink a cup of coffee on the way to work. Well, look at this, see how the cupholder swivels to prevent spills in turns or stops. Notice also how it's impossible to bump it with your arm as you drive." This kind of logic is designed to increase the buyer's desire for the car and thus increase his willingness to make concessions to get it.

Logic aside, if you want the opposition to make concessions, you're probably going to have to bring his or her emotions into play. The most potent emotion you can use to influence someone is fear, fear of losing the deal. All of the following methods are designed to increase your opponent's emotional turmoil.

Express dissatisfaction with what your opponent is offering—You don't like the color, you aren't happy about the delivery time, there's a small scratch in the lower right corner, you're not interested in the mag wheels, everyone and his brother has that same model, and so on. The message—your need to cut a deal is low. In fact, you're not even sure you're interested at all. Perhaps a substantial price reduction would make you feel better. "Why should I have to pay full price for something that isn't exactly what I want?"

Show your opponent that you have options—If your needs aren't met, you have other sources to deal with. The item is available across the street. Joe Blow gave you a better offer just two hours ago. You saw the item on sale for $20 less in the paper. If you don't get a good deal you'll just put the money in a savings account. If you don't get a refund, you'll contact the district office. "Hey, Acme is willing to take 10% off their retail price. Shouldn't I expect the same from you?"

Exhibit little desire to come to an agreement—The other guy begins to wonder if what he's offering has any value to you at all. Your concessions are stingy and come only after considerable delay. You seem patiently willing to negotiate forever. You ignore deadlines, you walk out, you want a week to think about it, etc. "Hmmm, maybe I could raise my offer from $200 to $203. Don't ask for more, I must be crazy to offer you that."

Indicate that you can't increase your offer because you are tapped out—Convince the other guy that you are sitting squarely on your limit and don't have an inch of maneuvering room. "Listen, you want more, and you deserve more. I wish I could give it to you, I really do, but I don't have another dime. I want what you've got, but I'll have to walk away if you need more. Sorry."

Place a deadline on proceedings to increase the urgency of concluding a deal—Indicate that you have to have an agreement prior to bank closing time, or that you have to leave town at noon. You can also use the other guy's deadline to bring pressure to bear. For instance, delaying a complex negotiation until your opponent has only one more day to meet a monthly sales quota.

A deadline puts additional stress on your opponent. It pushes him to make concessions rapidly in order to avoid running out of time and losing the deal. When your opponent has a deadline, you can increase his anxiety and his willingness to concede by moving talks forward at a snail's pace.

If your ability to cope with the stress of an approaching deadline exceeds that of your opponent, you have an advantage. Cultivate a flexible, patient attitude toward time and communicate that attitude to your opponent. Let him know that you have all day even if you actually don't. One way to jolt your opponent loose from his position is to present a creative new option just prior to the deadline. Like a drowning man he may grab at it to escape going home empty handed.

And don't worry too much about going beyond someone else's time limit. This is rarely the death of a negotiation. There is almost always more time available if both parties really want a deal. A fundamental rule of negotiation (and human nature) is that great deals usually aren't achieved rapidly. You need to allow time for various psychological pressures to exert their full force on your opponent. Be patient. Good things come to those who wait.

Besides using your opponent's emotions to influence him, there are also lots of other ways to play the game better than him. Below are a variety of techniques designed to blast him out of a stubborn position or satisfy his needs with creative solutions. Some of these methods use fairly subtle psychological influences to gain the desired end. Others are designed to bring out creative solutions that can be used to speed the process or break a deadlock.

When bargaining bogs down over the primary issue, temporarily leave it behind and work on settling secondary issues in which it will be easier to find agreement. This generates feelings of progress and goodwill and also increases your opponent's investment of time and effort. All these factors will ultimately influence him to make concessions on the primary issue. They also make it harder for him to allow the negotiation to break down and fail. For example, you might put aside the primary issue of price in order to settle secondary issues like how soon the item will be delivered.

Here's another method that focuses on secondary issues. Pick an issue that is unimportant to you and make a big deal of it. Once your opponent has been led to believe you place high value on this issue, you can then trade it for something that has real value to you. Your opponent feels masterful because he believes he has forced you into a major concession, and you feel satisfied because you got what you really wanted at less cost. For example, when buying a new car, you might complain bitterly that the dealership doesn't have a red version of the model you want. You let them know that you might reluctantly settle for the blue model that's in stock if its price were cut substantially. In fact, blue is your favorite color.

As first mentioned in the chapter on persuasion, getting people into a pattern of saying yes can make them feel more cooperative. As you engage in give and take with your opponent, watch for opportunities to induce him to say yes or agree with you. Whenever you sense a positive reaction on his part, immediately ask a question or make a statement that will evoke a positive verbal response. Your question or statement should be built around the needs of your opponent so that it will be difficult for him to disagree. Positive responses generate feelings of goodwill and progress that encourage further cooperation and concession.

For example, suppose you are negotiating with your boss for some new office equipment.

Boss: I know you need a new computer, but it's too expensive. (The boss's response is partially positive. Follow up with questions and statements that reinforce this area of agreement.)

You: You agree that my current computer is outdated?

Boss: Yes.

You: I'm sure you want to see an increase in my productivity.

Boss: Sure.

You: With a more powerful computer and improved software, I could probably set up a program that would automatically do all the purchasing forecasts that now take me two days. In all, I think a new computer would free up almost two days a month. If I can prove this to you, would you make the purchase?

Boss: If you can show that big of an efficiency increase, I will.

Note that this method works because of the positive momentum created by appeals to the boss's own needs, appeals that almost force him to answer affirmatively. The technique isn't as effective if your appeal focuses on your own needs. "My old computer is so slow it's a real pain in the butt. You don't want me to be stressed out all the time, do you?" Unfortunately, this statement doesn't give the boss a clear picture of how he might benefit by agreeing. He's likely to answer, "Sounds like a personal problem," and then depart.

If... or *What if...* are powerful phrases you can use to explore new proposals, possible options, and creative alternatives. "If I go to a play with you, would you go to the drag races with me?" or "What if I buy twelve instead of two? Would that convince you to give me a couple of free ones?" Notice that this phrasing doesn't necessarily commit you to the described trade. The wording is tentative, exploratory. If your opponent says yes, you might answer, "What if I buy fifteen, would you give me five freebies?" *If* and *what if* are great ways to feel your opponent out, find his limits, priorities, and soft spots.

Controversial ideas or big departures from what's expected can be risky in negotiation. People are usually wary and somewhat defensive in competitive negotiation. They may react badly to surprises. They're not sure what this unfamiliar new plan represents and may decide that the safest course is to reject it.

A radical new proposal usually involves change, and change is something people often need time to accommodate to. Whenever you have a proposal or offer that you think will come as something of a shock when first introduced, it is best to present it early in the discussion rather than later. Make it as non-threatening as possible (refrain from asking for any kind of commitment at first), a mere suggestion. Then casually bring it up several more times as negotiation progresses. "Here's a thought I just want to throw out as one possible solution. I'm just trying to brainstorm all the options. What if we were to...?" Given time to think about it, get familiar with it, and talk about it, your opponent will find it less and less threatening. By the end of the negotiation, after multiple exposures, he may be more likely to seriously consider it.

Because of the restrictions on openness and candor that characterize competitive negotiation, the suggestions or demands made by your opponent often do not reveal his true underlying need or interest.

Suppose you are a renter, and you ask your landlord if you can get your carpet cleaned. He says no, it's too expensive. You might respond by screaming that it's been two years since it was cleaned, and you're a good tenant and expect better treatment than this, blah, blah, blah. The landlord still says no. Or, you could probe for his true interests. You ask him a number of questions about why he thinks it is too expensive and eventually learn that he plans to install new carpet whenever you move out. He doesn't want to spend money cleaning a carpet that's going to be replaced.

Now that you know his true interest, you can plan your next move accordingly. "That carpet is in better condition than you think. If it gets a good cleaning, you could probably keep it and avoid the big expense of replacement." This approach hits the bull's-eye of the landlord's self-interest, and he is likely to be much more receptive to it. By always seeking out additional information, you may find the key to a deadlocked situation.

People who don't like negotiation or have a macho attitude about it often hit their opponent with an ultimatum early in the encounter. Their hope is to force a quick capitulation and avoid all that confrontation and time wasting. "Look, let's skip all the baloney. Sell me the couch for $250 or I'm out'a here." An ultimatum may work, but the odds aren't good, especially if it's given too early in the process. Remember, it takes time to negotiate a good deal. There are no shortcuts.

Ultimatums work best when given toward the end of the negotiation process. At this point, the other guy has invested a good chunk of time and effort and the gap between initial offers has probably been closed somewhat by mutual concessions. In other words, everyone involved has a bigger stake in avoiding a collapse of discussions.

Additionally, it's wise to forget the macho, in your face style of ultimatum. The most effective ultimatum is barely recognizable as such—"John, I know this couch is worth more than $250, but $250 is all I have. If you say no, I'll understand."

How do you handle an opponent who refuses to make concessions or becomes frustrated and aggressive? What do you do if discussion bogs down or deadlocks?

Always keep in mind that your opponent's position or offer reflects his needs, not yours. If bargaining slows or your opponent becomes aggressive in an attempt to move talks forward, you should concede only if you feel your needs will be met by doing so.

If your opponent is a rabidly competitive negotiator, he won't concern himself with your well being. He may view you as a potential victim and attack your position with threats, bullying, belligerence, extreme demands, emotional tactics, and accusations—"Why are you trying to cheat me?" or "I guess you aren't smart enough to recognize a good deal when it's right in front of you."

Under intense attack, you may be tempted to concede simply to get out of an unpleasant situation. Don't do it. Insist on an outcome that meets your needs. Failing that, you should terminate discussions. Concessions should never be made for the wrong reasons.

One way to discourage an opponent from using rough tactics is to cease discussing the negotiated issues and instead discuss how the issues are being negotiated. "Excuse me, I'd like to point out that you are raising your voice and preventing me from explaining my own views. I'm going to discuss this calmly and listen to your point of view. I hope you'll do the same for me." Be careful not to become abusive yourself as you describe the other party's crimes and misdemeanors. Describe the behavior, don't attack the person. For instance, "Arguing isn't going to get us anywhere," as opposed to, "You are a loudmouth jerk."

Using this method puts the spotlight on the other guy's objectionable behavior and makes a direct request for fair play. You are negotiating the rules for the process of negotiation. Usually this approach is successful. If it isn't (some people don't feel comfortable with more civil methods, or they just plain enjoy conflict), you have several options. You can break off discussions, you can bring in a neutral third party negotiator, or you can hang in there.

If you choose to hang in there, don't fight back by adopting your opponent's heavy-handed methods and manners. Stay calm, reasonable, and fair. Avoid retaliation, name-calling, and losing control.

Why, you might ask, should I be pleasant when my opponent insists on being obnoxious? If both of you get nasty, the negotiation will simply degenerate into a brawl, accomplishing nothing. If you persist in a firm but polite and reasonable manner, you'll be better able to analyze, plan, and respond intelligently. The overall encounter will be more rational, and your civil manner may in time shame your opponent into tempering his tactics. He might even find your cool and calm manner unnerving.

How do you handle deadlock? The best general solution is to start asking questions, listen carefully to the answers, and then be creative with the info you glean. As we've already seen, successful negotiation depends on knowing what will motivate your opponent. Frequently, deadlock results when you misunderstand your opponent's needs or have failed to identify them. The answer is to explore his point of view more intensely via questions, reflection, and listening. Try to empathize with your opponent's position. Imagine yourself in his shoes, subject to his pressures and goals.

Even with skilled detective work, you still may not be able to induce your opponent to give you the key to his heart. If that's the case, you have to depend on guesses and creative thinking. For example, suppose you are at a consumer electronics store trying to buy a new DVD player. The model you want is priced at $350, but you don't want to pay more than $325. For fifteen minutes you've tried every tactic you can think of to convince the salesman into lowering the price, but he adamantly refuses. Now is the time to make some empathetic guesses about his situation and seek a creative solution.

You haven't been able to get much info from the salesman, so you have to use some guesswork. You speculate that the salesman is motivated more by his sales commission than by the reasons he's been stating. He doesn't want to lower the player's price because the profit margin on the player is the source of his commission. The lower the profit, the lower the commission the store will pay him.

To resolve the problem, you suggest a new way to effectively reduce what you pay without reducing the salesman's commission— "Tell you what, I'll buy the recorder for $350, but you give me two DVD movies for free. Deal?" The salesman agrees because the free peripheral items won't reduce his commission. You found his need and showed him a way that both of you could get what you wanted.

Creativity is an often overlooked element of skilled negotiation. Seek out new angles and new ways of looking at the situation. Ask yourself what else you have that the other party might value. Ponder whether there is a different combination of offerings that might have unexpected appeal to your opponent. Brainstorm with him. Ask him directly, "Are there any options we haven't explored?" Many a deadlock has been broken by a creative new idea.

Suppose you ask your boss to let you work on an important upcoming project, but he turns you down. At first, he claims that he has all the people he needs, but with questioning it becomes clear that he doesn't think you have enough experience. Now you have to be creative. You can't convince him by saying, "Gee, boss, I'm sure I could do it."

Instead, you start looking for something you can offer the boss that will calm his fears over your inexperience. You might offer to take a class at the local college, play a less central role in the project, work under close supervision, or demonstrate your ability in some fashion. Discussing these proposals might bring out further ideas if you continue to think creatively. Eventually, if you are persistent, you may find the right combination of ideas and get the boss's approval.

To wrap up our discussion of competitive negotiation, let's consider what you will do when all the issues are resolved and you and your opponent have come to an agreement. First, restate all that was agreed to, write it down if necessary. Second, define the elements and requirements of the agreement with enough detail that all parties know exactly what's required of them. Fuzzy, ambiguous settlements lead to dispute, poor execution, and opportunistic behavior. Finally, if appropriate, make a future appointment to get together and discuss the success of the agreement. This puts all parties on notice that their performance will be assessed at a specific time.

Now let's look at the friendlier, more satisfying, and often more productive techniques of collaborative or cooperative negotiation.

Many people see the world as a place where you grab the biggest chunk of the pie that you can, before someone else does. Others see it as a world where working cooperatively with others will increase the size of the pie, allowing a bigger piece for all. While one person bases his tactics on the fear of running out, the other acts on the assumption that collaboration creates abundance.

What is wrong with competitive negotiation? As it usually occurs in the real world, there is little concern for the well being of the other side. The goal is personal victory, not mutual benefit. The emphasis is on outwitting the opponent. Lack of a conscience can be an advantage, because the negotiator is stalking his prey, hoping to catch him unawares, and seize all that he can.

In competitive negotiating, feelings are disguised, facts are held back, the degree of needs and the needs themselves are hidden. Nothing that could be used against the negotiator is given out. To further his position, the negotiator exaggerates, creates, and mixes and matches the facts to the best of his scheming ability.

However, even when a competitive negotiator is victorious, he may be creating a debt that will require payment at a later date. The loser may feel resentful, he may seek to sabotage the winner's victory, and worst of all, a healthy relationship may be permanently destroyed. In fact, in its nastier forms, competitive negotiation is best avoided in situations where you have a continuing relationship with the other party (as with family, friends, and business associates). The used car salesman feels safe with his competitive tactics because car buyers come and go with little chance for retaliation (even here, though, a buyer can retaliate by buying his next car elsewhere).

Collaborative negotiation is superior in many ways to competitive negotiation, however, it takes two to collaborate. If the other side won't agree to the cooperative, trusting, respectful methods of collaboration, then you are forced to compete. If you drop your guard with a predator, you are probably going to get eaten.

Collaborative negotiation requires that you pull down most of your defenses and throw open your arms. The focus is on meeting the needs of both parties through teamwork and mutual problem solving. The hope is that the combined creative and cooperative thinking of both sides will lead to new options that will satisfy the requirements of all concerned. You proceed from the belief that the needs of the participants aren't necessarily in opposition, and consequently there is no need to grab what you can and run.

Certain conditions have to be met for collaborative negotiation to work. One is that all parties have to believe that mutual benefit is possible. Or, better yet, all parties need to believe that greater benefit will be created through cooperative teamwork than by an every-man-for-himself approach. Sometimes these conditions aren't met. The car salesman may feel that he has such a pronounced advantage over the typical customer that he won't be able to make as much money if he is open and cooperative.

Many times, though, collaborative negotiation has more application than you might think. While the narrowly focused car salesman might not see the advantage, the dealership's general manager would do well to take a wider view. He ought to understand that while hard-nosed sales tactics sell cars at a higher price, in the long run the resentment customers feel over their rough treatment could lead to fewer car buyers long term and reduced profits in other areas.

Customers who got a raw deal on their auto purchase might decide to have their car serviced elsewhere. They might buy all their parts and accessories elsewhere. They might buy their next car elsewhere. From the manager's perspective, the increase in profit from the hard sell of one car is outweighed by the loss of service, accessory, and repeat business later on. To prevent this, he might instruct his salespeople to negotiate the sale of vehicles in a more collaborative manner. The moral here is to examine a situation or problem closely before you conclude it requires a competitive approach.

A relationship of trust is another condition that must be met in order for collaborative negotiation to work. First you build a relationship, then you build mutual trust on the foundation of that relationship. In collaborative negotiation, trust is required because both parties need to reveal information they would usually keep secret in competitive negotiation.

An open, trusting exchange of information about your situation and needs can be risky. In a competitive environment such information might be used against you.

It takes time to build a relationship that allows you to reveal information without fear that it will be used to undermine your position. Forming that relationship often must precede the actual negotiation by weeks or months if possible. The more lead time the better, trust and openness do not happen overnight. The way must be paved by a prior pattern of fairness, respect, reliability, and just plain friendliness. You have to listen to the other party, show concern for his views and welfare, and prove yourself to be someone who is not a threat. The other person has to believe that your goal is to find solutions that will benefit all concerned, not to exploit his weaknesses.

Also use whatever time is available prior to a negotiation to analyze potential differing interests and their causes. Try to experience the other person's requirements. Try to understand the factors that influenced the development of his position.

If you don't have a lot of lead time (or none) prior to actual negotiations, relationship building becomes more difficult, if not impossible. The other party's natural caution may lead him to interpret your efforts to create an open, trusting atmosphere as an attempt to sucker him. Still, it's always wise to attempt to coax the other side into proceeding along cooperative lines. If they refuse, you'll have to fall back on competitive methods.

If the other party appears willing to proceed collaboratively without a familiar relationship, a little caution is advisable before you reveal all. True collaborative negotiation is a team problem-solving activity that involves creatively working through problems by the candid exchange of information and ideas.

Unfortunately, if the other side is an unknown commodity, precipitous disclosure of all your classified info could be too much of a temptation for your opponent. A weak or new relationship has little power to constrain people. A salesman you've known for ten minutes is far more likely to betray you than a longtime associate. As a result, you should move forward cautiously in a collaborative negotiation that lacks the underpinning of a solid relationship.

Until the other side's trustworthiness is proven, begin by offering non-critical information and limited concessions. Then watch how the other side responds. If he responds with openness and concessions of his own, you can feel safer in revealing more and making bigger concessions. If he offers nothing of value, then continue to be cautious.

You can also use *if...*, *what if...*, and trial-balloon statements to explore the other side's reaction to various proposals. "If I were to... Would you be willing to...?" or "What if we decided to... Would you agree to...?" or "Well, I've considered doing... What do you think of that idea?" These statements are phrased so that you can avoid committing yourself. They allow you to claim you were merely hypothesizing if the other guy's reaction tells you he is competing, not collaborating.

In collaborative negotiation, whether the relationship is established and strong or new and fragile, it is important to keep the focus on the goal, not the way the goal is to be accomplished. Make an effort from the beginning to get all parties thinking in terms of ends, not means. It's usually easier to reach agreement on ends than means, and that agreement sets a positive tone for following discussions.

Initially, it is best to avoid the topic of means entirely. If people are allowed to blurt out their ideas or plans early on, they will invest their egos in them and be less flexible and open-minded about other ideas. Collaborative negotiation requires a greater willingness to look impartially at the ideas of all participants, accepting or rejecting them on the basis of workability, not ego.

One last point, collaboration is not the same as compromise. Collaboration's aim is to fill the needs of all participants fully. Compromise, by comparison, springs from the competitive mindset of shortage. In compromise, everyone gives up something, and no one's needs are fully met.

Suppose, for instance, that you are a manager who has assigned an employee to the night shift. The employee comes to you and asks to be taken off night shift because it's too hard on his family. You are short handed, however, and can't get by with fewer workers in the late hours.

If you were to compromise, you and the employee would agree that he would work the night shift only three times a week instead of the usual five. You both give up something—you don't have as much help as you'd like at night, and the employee still has to be way from his family for a substantial amount of time.

In collaborative negotiation, you and the employee look for a solution that meets both your needs fully. After collaboratively going back and forth over a number of options, the employee suggests that perhaps another employee who doesn't mind night work might be found to take his place. The next day you talk to several other employees and find one who is unmarried and doesn't mind the night shift because he can make more money than in his daytime position. Net result, no one compromises, no one gives up anything. The original employee no longer has to work at night, and you the manager have all the late help you need. Everyone is happy.

This ends our investigation of negotiation. Unless you're an extraordinarily giving, self-sacrificing person, it's unlikely that you'll be able to get through a single day without negotiating something. Whether you bargain competitively or collaboratively, developing your skills will ensure that you get more of what you want out of life.

Chapter 10:
Business Talk

Business is primarily a social activity. It is social in the sense that it is a function of the interactions of people. Sure, its ultimate goal is to make money by producing some manner of good or service, but 99% of the time, business success requires the effective, cooperative, and coordinated efforts of human animals working in groups. A key lubricant that keeps all those cooperative and coordinated efforts running smoothly is conversation. A common cause of failure or stunted achievement in business is poor communication skills.

This chapter draws on all the skills we've looked at previously in this book but focuses and interprets them for the requirements of the business world. The purpose is to help you get ahead, get things done, cut the frustration, and increase your leadership abilities. No matter how lowly your position, you can still exercise influence, effect change, and build achievements if you know how.

Many people, especially introverts, like to believe that with top-notch technical skills, they can probably skate by with minimal social skills. Not likely. Today, there are virtually no jobs in which your work would be so independent, isolated, or exclusively technical that human interaction would be a low priority.

Okay, you think, what if I'm so good at my job, so productive, that I can write my own ticket? People would have to take me the way I am because I'm so valuable. For one thing, few people ever become that valuable and irreplaceable. Also, individual productivity isn't as important as you might think. If you aren't socially skilled, your ineptitude will eventually drag down the productivity of others. In addition, your superiors and co-workers probably place considerable value on a friendly, socially stable working environment.

Most important of all, significant achievement almost always requires you to acquire and organize the support of others, and that requires social and communication skills.

If you are a social misfit, sooner or later people are going to say, "Yeah, he's skilled in his area, but who needs the aggravation?" Before long, you're being cut out of the office information loop. You get the brush off when you need help or advice. People undermine you in subtle ways. Your fellows stop sharing gossip with you because you are the gossip. Increasingly, you are out of touch. And then the day comes when cutbacks have to be made, and you find yourself on the street wondering what happened.

Even if your poor communication skills don't get you ousted, you may notice that none of your technical superiority seems to matter at promotion time. Repeatedly you find yourself passed over in favor of people who are less creative and knowledgeable than you. How can that be? Smart as you are, capable as you are, your boss just doesn't think you "have what it takes."

While technical capability is highly valued at lower levels, it becomes less of a factor for determining your future at higher levels. Managers aren't technicians—managers manage people. With each step up the management ladder, your people skills become increasingly important. No people skills, no movement up the ladder.

The higher you rise in an organization the more important it is that you be able to empathize, motivate, persuade, and communicate clearly. You have to know when to laugh, what remarks are inappropriate, how to control your nonverbal communication, and how to interact with a wide variety of personalities. Most of success or failure arises from the quality of one's people skills, and the largest element of people skills is communication skills. Your technical abilities cannot help you lead or motivate others. Your technical abilities alone will never get you a table in the executive dining room.

As you read the rest of this chapter, understand that the material here is for everyone who makes a living in the business world. Unless you're a kid, a retiree, or heir to a family fortune, this means you. These are general principles that apply whether you are a clerk or a vice president. If you want more specialized or in-depth information than our necessarily brief overview can provide, there are multitudes of books on business communication and career management at your local library or bookstore.

Let's begin our discussion of business communication with a look at perceptions. Most of us assume that others perceive us as we perceive ourselves. If we feel friendly, we assume others see us as friendly. If we are angry, we assume others know we are angry. Sadly, assumptions like these are frequently incorrect. Worse, not only are our feelings inaccurately read, but our meaning is often misinterpreted as well. To further complicate matters, misperceptions often go undetected until that nasty moment when we discover that mistakes, damaged relationships, and wasted effort have resulted.

Most of the time there is going to be some divergence between how you see yourself and how others see you. With many of us, that divergence will be substantial. For example, you may think of yourself as direct and frank, while co-workers see you as brusque and rude. Or, you may believe you are careful and thoughtful, but others find you to be waffling and weak-willed.

Why is it that we are so often unaware of the image others have of us? We not only communicate our thoughts and feelings poorly but also comprehend the feedback from others poorly. Most of us are seriously oblivious to the reactions of the people around us. We ignore their hints, dismiss their critical little jokes, and miss the expressions on their faces and the tone in their voices.

Most of us only notice the most obvious declarations of others. If a colleague or superior subtly or indirectly refers to a problem, we miss it, ignore it, or assume it's no big deal rather than explore the situation. And when the problem explodes into the open, we yell, "Where did this come from? Why didn't you say something?" And the other person yells back, "I did, I did, I told you a thousand times!" In truth, there's almost always valuable feedback being given to us, but we rarely tune in long enough for it to register.

Even if we're relatively aware, few of us want to hear criticism. We have a nice, safe, comfortable image of who we are, and comments or evidence to the contrary are unwelcome. When bad reviews do come in, we have a number of techniques for dismissing them. We tell ourselves that people are out to get us, or the situation was to blame, or it's no big deal, or we are surrounded by idiots, or it wasn't our fault, or that's just the way we are. We use our brain to distort what we see and hear until it fits our preconceived ideas of who we are.

The most popular avoidance mechanisms are denial and blame. Our denials come instantaneously. "That's not true," we cry. "I do too care about your opinion," we bleat. "I am not angry all the time," we scream…angrily. Our blaming also comes effortlessly. "If you'd seen what Bill did, you'd understand why I was so sarcastic," we declare. "Sure I find fault, there's a hell of a lot to find fault with around here," we insist.

Or, we may admit to the basic facts but claim our behavior was justified. "Well, I suppose I did yell at him, but he deserved it. You have to yell to get his attention." In other words, sure there was yelling, but it wasn't bad yelling, it was good yelling. No need for self-examination here, the responsibility is the other guy's.

And sometimes we're right, sometimes the fault isn't in us. Not all criticism is fair, accurate, reasonable, or without ulterior motives. But, there's often a grain of truth we don't want to recognize, even in ill-considered criticism. We all have a strong need to see ourselves as okay, but that need can block the process of becoming a more effective and promotable person.

Few of us ever make an active effort to explore just how others perceive us. Our communication problems persist, unrecognized, and we are baffled as our career progress slows or flounders. Without a solid understanding of the way we come across to others, we can never hope to improve the interpersonal skills that are crucial to workplace success.

So, what do you do to discover how your superiors and co-workers perceive you? And, once you identify your communication failings, how do you change without doing violence to who you are?

First of all, don't assume that you only have to cinch up your image with those who count, those who have a powerful influence on your career, such as your superiors. You need to communicate and interact efficiently with *everyone*. Good general interaction in the workplace is seen as an indicator of deeper management skills such as leadership, decisiveness, teamwork, and clear thinking, all of which are used by your superiors to evaluate your promotability. Believe it, poor interaction and communication skills, even with the most junior office clerk, stir up trouble that eventually gets back to your boss. When he has to sort out these problems, your star dims considerably in his eyes.

Here are some pointers you can use to identify the way you are perceived by others and to zero in on problem areas.

Increase your awareness of how co-workers and superiors respond to you—Watch their expressions, listen to their tone of voice, and observe their body language as you interact with them. Think about the underlying meaning of their jokes, hints, and indirect references—commentary you previously would have disregarded ("He was only kidding."). Seek out patterns of similar responses to you from different people on different occasions. For instance, if you notice that on several occasions you have had people kiddingly mention that you are sarcastic, it may be something to look into.

Increase your awareness not only of others but also of yourself—Try to stand apart from yourself and see yourself as others do. You want to have a kind of out-of-body experience in which you detach yourself from your preconceptions of who you are and impartially assess how your words, expressions, and body language are actually affecting others.

Ask questions and probe for reactions—Talk to people about the way you come across. You want to nail down people's reactions on the spot if possible—"Are you satisfied that I'm giving you a fair hearing?" or "I'm sorry, I was staring out the window as I listened. Did you think I was ignoring you?" or "I can be pretty direct about how I feel. Do I come across as impolite or unfeeling?" or "I guess I tend to think out loud. Do you feel like you are being lectured?" or "I know, I'm changing my mind again. I suppose it seems indecisive to you?" Of course, some people will have a hard time giving you their unvarnished opinion. Try to reassure everyone that you truly are looking for honest feedback and won't react badly to criticism.

If on-the-spot probing isn't enough, make a formal appointment with co-workers you trust—Tell them you really want to improve your communication skills, and you need them to give you an honest appraisal of your habits and abilities. If you are really courageous, you might call together a group of fellow workers (perhaps even your boss) to present their feelings and perceptions. Scary but effective.

Find out what standards others, particularly superiors, are using to assess you—This one can be a real revelation. You may assume that your boss is deliriously happy with your performance because you are the top salesperson in your office. You can almost smell that promotion to district manager. But, alas, while your boss feels that sales skills are important, his primary standard for a district manager is the ability to motivate others. Your blunt, demanding manner and poor listening skills rule you out as management material in his eyes, no matter how high your personal sales go. Many people fail to advance in their organization because they never fully understand how they are being assessed.

When you have your annual or biannual performance review with your superior, pay attention—People commonly disregard certain negative or warning observations that come up in these meetings. "Oh, they say that to everyone. It doesn't mean anything," you may tell yourself. Don't let this happen. Focus on all critical comments. Ask your superior to expand on them, give you examples of the behavior in question, and tell you how significant they are to your career. And crucially important, ask what would be required of you, specifically, to eliminate the problem.

Once you've determined the communication and interpersonal deficiencies that you need to work on, you are often faced with the daunting task of changing deep-rooted behavior patterns. These behaviors are habitual, often learned in childhood. Making matters more difficult is the seeming paradox that even the worst behaviors have their benefits.

Bad habits usually have some underpinning of benefit in order to survive. Despite their long-term damaging effects on your career, negative interpersonal habits often have short-term rewards that need to be understood if you are to successfully eliminate them. For example, the bully enjoys the control over others that his intimidation gives him. The faultfinder craves the feeling of superiority he gets when lecturing and gossiping. The indecisive person values the avoidance of responsibility and confrontation. These benefits, along with force of habit, make efforts to change difficult and uncomfortable. While attempting to alter your ways, you have to continually fight the gravitational pull of your old and disreputable, but comfortable, practices.

Remember that you are not changing your basic personality. If you are overly aggressive, for instance, you aren't going to change yourself into a mild, nervous little mouse. You are merely going to substitute firmness and assertiveness for abrasiveness and displays of temper.

In time, your new healthier habits will seem just as natural and spontaneous as the old damaging ones. As an analogy, over time a car may take on a nasty front-end shimmy that makes it hard to live with. Fixing this problem doesn't change the type of car it is. If it was a sports car before, it's still a sports car after, but now it does its job more effectively.

The best way to ease the transition from old habits to new is to formulate new behaviors ahead of time so that they are available when you need them. Then, when you are interacting in the real world and feel one of your disfunctional habits coming on, you will have the new and improved behavior already for use.

These alternate positive behaviors should be planned in advance, written down if necessary, and even practiced in front of a mirror (so you can work on your facial expression and manner). Such responses should be short and simple. Something you can blurt out with a minimum of thought when you begin to get yourself into trouble. "I'm sorry, I'm too impatient sometimes. Tell me how you feel about this plan."

Let's look at some common communication and behavior problem types and formulate alternative responses that will be more effective. A characteristic of almost all the alternatives is increased respect for the other person and his or her point of view. Frequently, these new behaviors also disclose to the other party that you know you need to improve and are trying to do so ("Look, I know I can be…").

The Black and White Thinker—Has a hard time seeing gray areas or middle ground. Thinks his way is the only way and therefore sees little profit in listening to other points of view. May make statements such as the following—"We're getting distracted here. There's only one way to go, so let's get on with it," or "Look, this is a financial matter pure and simple, so why don't we treat it as such and move on?" or "Why are we worrying about John's feelings? Let's do the right thing here. John will get over it." Here are some alternatives—

> I'm not sure I fully understand your view. Would you go over it again? (then listen)

> That's an angle I hadn't considered. Let's talk about it and see if it might work.

> Sorry, sometimes I'm too single-minded. You've pointed out some factors I hadn't considered.

The Nice Guy/Gal—Inclined to sidestep conflict or anything that might be negatively received by others. Has a difficult time saying no. Indecisive and unable to make a decision unless there is already wide agreement. Usually unassertive and viewed by others as pleasant but weak. Prone to statements such as the following—"Sure, no problem," or "Um, I'm not sure, what do you think we should do?" or "Yeah, I can have that report for you by tomorrow" (even though tomorrow is virtually impossible), or "Oh, I don't think I could tell John that. Why don't we just wait and see if matters improve on their own?" Here are some alternatives—

No, that's not workable. I know you want me to agree, but it's my job to set limits.

I often say yes and regret it later. I do understand your difficulties, but I need to think this over and get back to you later today.

I understand that you want it by Friday, but that would require me to delay other time-critical projects. The earliest it can be completed is Tuesday.

This issue does need to be addressed. I'll look into it, and make a decision by the end of the day.

Rough and Tumble Bully—Harsh, aggressive, and often sarcastic or insulting. Never hesitates to confront or "tell it like it is." Hates to compromise or give ground. Happier making demands than requests and highly intolerant of opposition. May make statements similar to the following—"Look, I know what I'm doing, mind your own business," or "You don't need to know why, just do it," or "I want to know why you've been talking to Jim about this. If you're trying to shoot me down, there's going to be trouble," or "Hey, this is settled. I don't need you screwing things up with a lot of half-baked ideas," or "What the hell's your problem?" or "I need these reports every Monday by noon, on the dot. If you can't do the job, I'll get someone who can. Comprende?" Here are some alternatives—

Okay, I know I can come on too strong. Let's back up, tell me how you see the situation.

Let me explain my reasoning.

If you've been talking to Nick, you must have some doubts. What concerns you?

I think I understand the situation, but tell me how you see it.

Listen, it's important for me to have these reports by Monday
noon. Let me explain why, and then I'd like to hear any
problems you might have delivering.

The Contrary Griper—Given to faultfinding, complaining, and
focusing on the down side of any issue or plan. Sees the glass as half
empty. Would rather blame than solve. Often has difficulty seeing the
difference between describing a problem ("We need more secretarial
help.") and complaining about it ("Why is it that we never have the
help we need? Management could care less."). Makes statements
such as—"This won't work," or "Our customers will never listen to
this," or "Management doesn't want our opinion, so why give it," or
"I've seen this a million times, and it always ends up being a big
waste of time," or "This is Jack's fault. He couldn't make a decision
if there was a gun to his head." Here are some alternatives—

I know, I know, I have a hard time seeing the possibilities here.
Help me out, sell me.

This is a problem, but if we look into it further, we may find a
way to resolve the matter.

Sure, this is upsetting, but let's forget about who's to blame and
focus on what's happening and how we can fix it.

Jack's a good employee but this situation is giving him trouble.
How can we help him out?

The Emotional Outburster—Uses temper or tears to achieve ends in
a calculated way or has difficulty exercising control over basic emotions. Outbursts are used to intimidate, gain sympathy, or keep others
off balance. If the outburst is an unintentional reaction to a situation,
if may be due to a misinterpretation of others' motives, unreasonable
expectations about how life should work, or job stress.

In the short term, emotional outbursts can be effective; others will
often be quite cooperative in an effort to escape the uncomfortable
situation. However, the long-term result is often catastrophic for a
career. People rarely forget, and some never forgive, any serious loss
of control or extreme emotional behavior. The outburster is seen as
weak in self-restraint, unpleasant or impossible to work with, and
lacking the strength and leadership skills required for promotion.

If your emotions sometimes get out of control, how can you

contain them and repair the damage of a flare-up? Try to identify in advance the situations or people that will push you over the line and then make a special effort not to let things get out of hand. If you feel yourself losing control, call for a break and go get a drink of water or take a brief walk. Most important of all, try to assess the seriousness of situations as rationally as possible. On close inspection, is the consequence of the circumstance truly horrible and worthy of strong emotions, or is it realistically not that big of a deal?

A common reason for becoming emotional is a misunderstanding of the motives or attitudes of others. Many such problems can be avoided if the situation is clarified by probing.

> I noticed you frowned when I gave my opinion. Do you disagree?
>
> Tell me what happened. I've heard some rumors, and I want to get your side.
>
> I'd like to talk with you about your meeting with Jack. I have to tell you, from my point of view it seems like an end run.

If, despite your best efforts, your temper does get away from you, don't pretend it never happened. Make an immediate effort to explain and patch up any relationship the outburst may have damaged.

> I'm sorry, I have a lot of time and effort invested in this project, and I let my emotions get out of hand.
>
> Jane, I feel bad about some of the things I said during our meeting. We're all doing our best to solve this production problem and some of the things I said weren't helpful.
>
> Okay, I'm starting to get upset here, and I don't want that. Let's take a break, and then I'll tell you why this bothers me.

These are some of the major categories of interpersonal problems. Being effective at work means having sound relationships with your colleagues. Every time you show disrespect, teach someone a lesson, kick some butt, take revenge, make so and so look like the idiot he is, slap down an opposing viewpoint, or let your natural inclinations run rampant, it's probably a personal setback. You lose allies, create enemies, and damage your reputation, even when you are right. Long term, such behavior creates liabilities that you eventually have to repay in lost career opportunities.

Perhaps the best way to motivate yourself to improve and control your behavior is to keep your goals in mind. Place your objectives and self-interest front and center in your consciousness and then refuse to do or say anything that doesn't move you toward those predetermined goals. Convince yourself, believe in your heart of hearts, that any unwise behavior on your part will allow others, perhaps even your enemies, to control your future, block your dreams, and exercise power over you. Remember, a winner sets a goal, makes a plan to achieve it, and then follows through without distraction.

If you have a reputation for any particular communication flaw, don't expect your struggle to change to be immediately credited or even recognized by your colleagues. Their definition of who you are took a long time to form, and it will take a long time to alter. Don't become discouraged or give up. In the end, only ongoing repetition of your new behavior will ultimately convince others that you have indeed changed.

Make your attempts to change as high profile as possible; let others know what you are doing. "I know I've got a temper, and I'm making an effort to get it under control. So if I call a break when we're discussing a sensitive issue, don't think it's odd or that I'm not interested."

Let's look now at another aspect of work communication. Most workplace environments throw you into contact with large numbers of people who have widely varying communication styles. Without really knowing it, most of us assume that others communicate in the same way we do. This belief is usually wrong and a common source of discord. For instance, if your style is slow-paced and analytical, you will probably clash with a person whose style is direct and action oriented. We all have communication needs, and when those needs aren't met, there is great potential for conflict, misunderstanding, and ineffective working relationships.

Power, the ability to achieve your ends in the workplace, flows in part from your skill in meeting the communication needs of colleagues. Using the right communication style in each interaction is the difference between influence and impotence. What you say may be profound, but if the way you say it is awkward or inappropriate, your brilliance may have little impact.

Most of us have a particular communication style that feels most natural to us, and as a result, we use it with great consistency even though we deal with widely varying persons and situations. Despite this, it's important to understand that you do have the ability to alter your dominant style in order to meet the needs of others. In fact, adapting your style to successfully interact with different types of people is a key element of influence and leadership. It is just the kind of talent that your superior will look for when he or she is considering who to promote.

In order to increase your communication flexibility, you first need to study yourself carefully. Few of us have ever really given much organized thought to how our communication style is unique or different from those around us. Once you have a handle on your own style, analyze the styles of the people with whom you regularly associate. Over the longer term, you'll develop your ability to quickly determine the communication styles of mere acquaintances or even strangers.

The capacity to size people up in a short period of time and then design your approach accordingly will give you a huge competitive advantage over others. Once again, meeting the communication needs of others will greatly increase your influence over them.

Below are three categories of characteristics that you can use to define your and others' communication styles.

CATEGORY 1—*"Let's get down to business."*

Action oriented, dislikes details and excessive analysis, prefers to cut to the solution or bottom line

Concise and to the point, avoids chit chat, impatient

Not warm or supportive, usually unemotional and businesslike, not given to personal disclosures

Sees the function of conversation as primarily practical, deemphasizes the social side of talk

Thinks in simplified, black and white terms, has difficulty recognizing the importance of gray areas or subtleties

Honest and straightforward, often to a fault, may offend with unvarnished opinions, expects the same from others

Won't take time to give clear, particularized instructions, will tell subordinates what to do but not why

May have unreasonably high expectations

Gives orders, makes demands rather than requests, hates to explain or justify

Expects organized presentations, intolerant of segues, side issues, rambling, or digression

Uses absolutes ("This always happens," or "Management will never listen to us.")

Doesn't listen well, not interested in the views of others, often interrupts

CATEGORY 2—*"Let's think this through."*

Talkative, detail oriented, sometimes to the point of boredom, may give you more info than you need or want

Likes to analyze, consider all the options, and look at issues from every angle

Slow to act or decide

Needs to win and prove he is right, has difficulty admitting error

Argumentative, enjoys debate and matching wits with others

Confident of his skills and analysis, defensive when criticized

A natural performer, enjoys the limelight

Rambling, digressive, often elaborates on irrelevancies

Comments are often so disorganized and detour filled that the listener may become confused and miss the original point

Uses facts, knowledge, an aura of certainty, and loaded questions to control others

Speaks with confidence and certainty that results from his detailed analysis and study

Tends to lecture, often in a superior, patronizing tone that offends

Often a perfectionist, inflexible

May use pretentious vocabulary

Often uses hypothetical situations to explore an issue. ("If we were to…then…")

Poor listener, but if forced to hear you out, can be persuaded by solid logic

Often susceptible to praise and compliments

CATEGORY 3—*"Can't we all just get along?"*

Hates and avoids conflict or confrontation

Believes in the value of social interaction, friendly and polite

Needs to socialize before getting down to business

Likes to exchange stories of personal experiences and problems unrelated to work

Wants to be liked, makes an effort to develop and maintain relationships

Will accept mediocrity, partial solutions, and unacceptable behavior in order to avoid strife

May use personal disclosures to create atmosphere of closeness and openness

Will request rather than order or demand

Often uses seemingly innocent questions to lead you to a preferred conclusion

May tell you what you want to hear in order to maintain peace

Has difficulty expressing opposition, may allow silence to be falsely interpreted as agreement

Observes and listens well, stays in the background, says little in meetings

Reluctant to put forward an opinion, especially if controversial

May seem shy or weak, often ignored

Rarely uses absolute statements, tends to qualify and soften ("maybe," "I'm not certain about this, but...," "Tell me if you disagree," "You know more about this than me...," "could," "might," "I'm sorry," etc.)

Never reacts or speaks spontaneously, tests waters first, may conceal true thoughts and feelings

Unassertive, can be intimidated (but will hold a silent grudge)

Indecisive unless preferred option is widely supported and approved by others

Note that these classifications are not rigid. An individual's characteristics will usually cluster predominantly in one primary category but will also be found scattered through the other two as well. Also, because many of these characteristics are not positive, a good deal of personal honesty is often required in order to acknowledge some of them as your own.

Once you've developed a good understanding of your own communication style, you will have a better understanding of how you come across to those around you (whose styles you have also studied).

Suppose you are a man of few words, a person whose response to a difficulty is to formulate a plan of action and put it into effect, now. If the plan isn't perfect, you figure it can be modified and perfected as you go along. You are a Category 1 person. Your current problem is that you need to obtain the support of a Category 2 person. That person's style is to analyze at length, perfect a plan theoretically before using it in the real world, and generally waste your time with a lot of irrelevant, time-wasting discussion (as far as you are concerned). How do you win over such a person (let's refer to him as Mike)?

If you charge in and try to force Mike to act before he's gone through his usual step-by-step analysis, he will resist you. So don't. Start with the expectation that Mike will have to be given more time than you think is reasonable. Let Mike talk, let him go through his methodical process. Listen and refrain from making pained faces and fidgeting in your chair.

Convince him that you are part of his process too. Give him all the informational detail he will feel he needs to do a proper examination of the problem. When you do offer an opinion or plan, back it up with detailed reasoning and be willing to repeat that reasoning as many times as necessary to give it the appropriate emphasis. Finally, try to lead Mike to your own conclusion by the manner in which you organize and emphasize the facts, thereby convincing him that the solution was at least partly his idea.

Another example. Assume you are a Category 2 analyzer, and you need to influence a Category 1 man of action named Joe. If you want to effectively persuade Joe, you need to control your propensity for rambling, long-winded, and sometimes condescending soliloquies. Joe has no tolerance for all that time-wasting talk. He'll become irritated, cut you off, and make some kind of excuse to flee the scene

("Gotta go, big meeting in five minutes.").

If you want to influence Joe, you have to speak concisely and quickly, cut the dead wood from your presentation, and talk primarily in terms of action and solution rather than analysis. Don't attempt to argue or match wits, approach him in a spirit of practicality and joint problem solving

How about the agreeable, social, Category 3 individual who avoids conflict and controversy? How should this person be approached? It's easy to assume that this type of person is weak and easily intimidated, and therefore little care need be exercised in the approach used. This would be a mistake.

A Category 3 person may be mild mannered, but if you abuse him, he will resent it and look for a chance to pay you back. Moreover, just because a Category 3 person won't readily express opinions doesn't mean he has nothing to offer. Draw him out, get his input. Finally, although he may not openly disagree with you, if you don't genuinely persuade him, he won't actively support you. In other words, take the time to win him over. Here's how.

Plan to take time to do a little socializing prior to getting down to business. Ask what his kids are doing or how his golf game is going, and so on. Once you've brought up the problem at hand, don't come on with demands or strong opinions. Instead, be warm and nonthreatening. Be patient, listen to him, try to relieve his concerns and fears. If possible, describe the issue in human terms as opposed to technical terms.

If you feel he isn't saying everything that's on his mind, probe gently. "How does this idea strike you? or "What would you like to see done here?" Try to lower his perception of risk. Tell him you are only looking for input, nothing is set in stone. Ask him to speak hypothetically. Use reflection, personal disclosure, and anecdotes to encourage him to open up and become part of the process. Most important of all, don't become confrontational. If you press hard, he may tell you whatever you want to hear just to get rid of you. Later on, however, you'll find he isn't really supporting you or following through.

As we work with people of different communication styles, we get to know their quirks and habits, we make allowances and learn to cope with their peculiarities, and that's all well and good. However, simply understanding another's needs isn't the same as making an effort to meet those needs. To really increase your communication effectiveness, you must consistently design your interactive styles to appeal to others' communication requirements (this is true for people anywhere, not just the workplace).

Now that you understand the mysteries of perceptions and communication style, you are ready to learn how to handle some of the most common workplace trials and tribulations. This next section deals with problems that eventually plague everyone who works for a living—dealing with difficult or emotional people, handling complaints, confronting others, criticizing, arguing, dealing with superiors, and asking for a raise.

When someone comes to you in an emotional state, how do you avoid making matters worse? How do you help the person calm down and work rationally on the problem? If you handle an emotional situation poorly, it can result in an unresolved problem or a disabled relationship, or both.

The first rule for handling the emotions of others is to keep your own emotions in check. You may be mightily tempted to argue or lash back if the emotion is directed at you—don't do it. Try to refrain from saying anything but the most minimal and innocuous responses. Until the person has calmed down, there isn't much you can say that will have a salutary effect anyway. So, just let him or her talk (or rant). If the person is angry, your calm, non-reactive response will go a long way toward dissipating his rage.

Instead, use your time and brainpower to patiently listen and try to understand the other person's experience. Attempt to learn something. Listening means gathering information, and that information may ultimately lead you to a response quite different from your initial reaction. Let the person talk himself out. As he verbalizes, his emotions will dissipate. If you say anything at all, make some kind of empathetic response that acknowledges his concern—"I see why you feel this way, I would too if I were you," or "It's true, this does seem to be happening way to often."

Avoid recommending a solution. Once the person has calmed down and can think soberly, talk to him in his own style, reflect what he has said back to him ("You believe this problem happened because…"), and use questions to guide him toward his own solution.

To get him to start thinking of a solution, ask questions such as

"What are the factors that cause this sort of problem?" or "How do you think we can best work this out?" To help him think critically, ask questions such as the following—"What factors might cause your plan to fail?" or "Can you think of any other solutions to this situation?" If you have a hard time getting concrete responses, ask, "What can I do to help you resolve this situation?"

Don't judge. Statements like "You shouldn't have done that" or "If you weren't so inflexible, this never would have happened" close off communication and stir up an emotional hornet's nest. Concentrate on what happened and how it can be fixed, not on blame and recriminations. Further, try to keep the discussion focused on the present and future as opposed to who's been negligent and generally rotten in the past.

If the person is protesting some dreadful crime he blames on you, compel yourself to ignore the attack and focus instead on what happened and what can be done. Insist that he be specific about his complaint. Ask for the who, what, when, where, and why of the matter. Don't let him get away with general statements like "I'm sick of the way you always make things harder for me" or "You never keep me informed." Ask for the details. "How exactly have I made things harder for you?" or "What facts have I kept from you?"

Listen to him closely and then respond in a manner that shows respect. Using a reflective response lets him know you've listened and understood. "Okay, Jim, I believe I see your concern, and I want to respond. Let me know if I've misunderstood any part of your position."

A great tool for dousing the flames of your attacker's anger is to admit error and take the blame for some aspect of his complaint. Usually, when a problem occurs and complaints are directed at us, there probably is some aspect of our behavior that contributed to it, something we could have done better. Don't admit fault if you truly weren't responsible, but don't insist on being perfect either. Own up to an error or judgment lapse forthrightly and you'll get credit for being fair minded, honorable, and willing to learn. "You're right, I should have informed you sooner about this change of policy. What can I do to help you out of this jam?" A simple statement like this often takes all the fight out of the other guy.

Reflection is a great method for discovering an underlying complaint. For example, suppose you receive the following specific complaint—"You never arrive on time for my meetings, and I'm sick of it." A reflective response might be—"You think I'm being disrespectful of you and your program because I come in late." If the person disagrees with your reflection, he will explain his true grievance. If he agrees, then you know you're on target and can answer more accurately. "I do value your efforts. My situation is that our biggest client habitually calls me every day at 3:00, just when your meetings start. What can we do to solve this?"

In some situations, a person's emotional upset may not be quite as involuntary as he'd like you to believe. He may find it advantageous to exaggerate the intensity of his emotions in order to intimidate you, throw you off balance, avoid an issue, or generate sympathy. This can be an effective tactic because few of us have ever really learned how to handle overwrought people.

The best response is to use the same techniques recommended above for genuinely emotional people. Stay calm, listen patiently, reflect their concerns, and respond respectfully. Most important of all, refuse to take the bait and be drawn into an argument or angry response. Firmly and patiently defend your position until the other person realizes his emotionalism isn't working.

Remember, being respectful to the other person and recognizing that he has a problem doesn't mean that you are necessarily agreeing with him or admitting blame. Nor does it mean you will necessarily give him the satisfaction he demands. "I see what you're getting at" says that you understand, it doesn't say you are the cause or that you agree with the other party's position. But, it does go a long way toward making the other person feel he or she is getting a fair hearing.

What if you are the person who wants to make a complaint? How do you best approach someone with criticism or a request for change? First, go back and read the earlier chapter on assertion. Then look at the following additional pointers.

When you feel a colleague has let you down or behaved in an unfair manner, your initial and natural response may well be anger. A good rule of thumb for such situations is that your natural and spontaneous reaction is almost always counterproductive and should be reined in before it goes public.

Solving the problem is your true goal, and for that you are probably going to need cooperation. If you decide to strike a blow for truth and goodness with a gloriously unrestrained castigation of the offender and all his ancestors, you may feel potent and righteous, but you can forget about cooperation. Before you take action, always ask if your planned approach is going to help solve the problem or incite emotional resistance. It's always better to first ascertain the reasons for someone's objectionable behavior and then attempt to bring about change by motivation rather than attack.

Here are some suggestions for confronting or criticizing a fellow employee or subordinate.

Don't act on your assumptions—Before you judge or decide on a course of action, interview everyone involved and gather information from any other sources. Most of us have a natural tendency to jump to nasty conclusions. A thorough investigation often reveals that the other party's behavior was not as villainous as originally thought.

Don't beat around the bush—A common reason for failing to obtain what we want from people is the lack of a well-defined request or statement of the problem. Don't make a vague, indirect appeal and hope they'll figure out what you want. You may hold back fearing rejection, opposition, hurt feelings, lost support, and so on. All these things are possible, but most of the time we are far too delicate in our requests for change or action. Be polite and respectful, but direct.

Make sure the problem really is theirs and not yours—You have to be honest here. Does the other person's behavior cause concrete trouble for you or is it just something you don't happen to like? If someone's desk is a mess but his work is good, you probably have no real business trying to impose your ideas of orderliness. Learn to live with it.

Avoid public criticism—If you decide that you must criticize someone, never, never, never do it in front of others. Public criticism creates maximum resistance and destroys working relationships because it creates the greatest loss of face for the criticized party. If you are a superior who does this to subordinates, it can ruin moral and employee concern for company welfare. One way or another, a person publicly criticized will find a way to get back at you.

Don't present yourself as perfect—Soften criticism by admitting to your own fallibility. Before you describe the other's failings, tell him an anecdote or instance of your own failure. This basically tells the other person that even though you have a complaint, you don't think you are better than he or she is.

Avoid the word **but** *in criticism*—We often try to soften a critical comment by prefacing it with a compliment which we then snatch back with the word *but*. "You led the group well, but you didn't really give the others enough opportunity to contribute ideas." When you use this phrasing, the other person feels your compliment wasn't genuine and only served to pave the way for criticism. Instead, give more weight to the praise by making it very specific, omit the word *but*, and then cite areas that need improvement. "You showed real leadership in your meeting. You brought out the key points in your opening, kept the group focused, and finished on time. In your next meeting, work on giving others more opportunity to contribute. Good job."

Avoid using the word **you** *in criticism*—Think of the word *you* as a knife thrust. Each time *you* is used in a criticism, the other person feels he is under personal attack and defends himself. Instead, talk about *it*, the *situation*, the *problem*, or the *concern*. It's much easier to hear that a situation is bad than to hear that you are bad. Rather than say, "You messed up the Robinson account," say, "Let's discuss the problem with the Robinson account."

Talk about what happened rather than intentions—Face it, you may think you know what someone's intentions were, but in reality you're only guessing. As with the word *you*, telling people that their intentions were bad makes them feel personally attacked and ends all constructive discussion. Rather than say, "You hand in these reports late just to make me mad," say, "When these reports are handed in late, it puts me under a lot of pressure."

Don't back the other person into a corner—Give others a way to save face. Your attitude should be one of finding a solution to the problem, not defeating, embarrassing, or blaming others.

Never make a threat you can't back up—Threats are rarely a good idea; they should always be a last resort. But, if you do make a threat, be certain you have the power and guts to carry it out. Otherwise, you'll end up looking weak and foolish.

Here is the general procedure for criticizing or requesting a change of behavior in the workplace.

1. Pick a good time and place. Don't approach the person when he is pressed for time or under stress. If the problem was an incident in which emotions ran high, it will probably be wise to wait until tempers have cooled before confronting, whether that's an hour or a day. Don't wait too long though; timely discussion is the most effective. And, choose a setting that's private, one in which you will not be overheard or interrupted.

2. When you do meet, describe the facts of the problem and how it is negatively affecting you. Avoid blaming, personal attacks, your opinion of his intent, and anything that might be interpreted as disrespectful.

3. Ask the person to explain what happened from his point of view. Get his reasons and motivations. Please note, this is not the time to let your attention drift or plan your next comment. Listen and learn. It's not uncommon to discover facts that change the whole complexion of the situation. After listening, reflect your understanding of his or her meaning.

4. After hearing the other person's full explanation, state your position and needs. At this point, give the other person the chance to find his own solutions. As stated previously in this book, people will be more willing to cooperate and follow through if solutions are theirs and not imposed by others.

5. Negotiate a mutually satisfactory solution and agree on specific action to implement it. If necessary or appropriate, make an appointment for some future time to review implementation progress. Knowing that performance will be checked at a subsequent meeting is a great motivator for change.

Suppose that despite all your efforts, you cannot resolve a problem with a colleague and have to take it to your superior. How do you effectively present a difficulty to a boss whose plate is probably already full of problems?

First, be conscious of how you come across to your superior. Regardless of the words you use, if you seem demanding, impatient, whiny, emotional, rigidly one-sided, and so on, you will probably weaken the credibility of your case and reduce his motivation to help you or side with you.

Next, design your appeal to be compatible with your superior's style of communication. If he or she is a person of few words, organize a concise presentation. If personable, take time for some small talk before bringing up your problem, and to the degree appropriate, state it in human terms (vs. facts and figures). If analytical, include lots of detail and analysis stressing facts and figures. Finally, if possible, show your boss how helping you to solve your problem will also lighten his load. Aim your approach at his needs and his point of view.

Begin the discussion by defining the problem. Stick to a factual description at this point, no opinions, blaming, complaining, or self-justification. Avoid side issues or poorly organized comments that might distract him from your main point. Cite specific instances of the problem and find ways to emphasize the key issues. Keep your main point squarely in front of him so that he doesn't have to work too hard to understand or recognize it.

Once you've described the facts of the problem, lay out your conception of the causes. Again, skip the blaming and complaint. Give him a businesslike, straightforward analysis that's big on specifics. Vague generalities won't move him. The causes you cite should support the next phase of your presentation—recommending solutions.

The best way to get ahead in business is to be known as a problem solver. Never go to your superior empty-handed. If you are ready to present him with a problem, you should also be ready to offer him a solution.

If you habitually offer excuses, complaints, and blame for others, your boss will eventually come to regard you as an ineffective pain in the neck. If instead, you have a reputation for solutions and carefully considered ideas, he'll regard of you as an asset. You'll seem productive, reasonable, fair-minded, and thus more credible and worthy of help. (Note—While it's generally not a good idea to present a solution to the person you're criticizing, it is okay to offer your proposed solution to a mediating third party, such as a superior.)

Your superior always has the option to choose a solution different from the one you offer. Even if he does, he knows you made an effort rather than just dumping the problem on him. Depending on his personality, it might be good to indicate that you aren't trying to force your plan on him. "If you'd like to hear it, I've put together a possible solution to this problem. Of course, I'd like to hear your ideas and get any advice you might have." Such a non-demanding and respectful statement makes it easy for your superior to respond by asking to hear your plan.

You can also motivate your superior to take quick action by giving him a compliment to live up to. For example, if he's a procrastinator, you might urge him to act quickly by saying, "You've always been a manager who knows how important it is to catch problems early, so I've put together a plan that can resolve this situation before it gets out of hand." Explain your solution, and then, if appropriate, ask him pointedly if you can implement it. Having just received a compliment as a decisive leader, he will find it more difficult to respond with hesitation and doubt.

Now let's discuss that common and much beloved workplace institution, arguing. In any situation involving confrontation, criticism, high emotions, or differing priorities, the potential for argument is high. It's hard to resist. Everyone involved will just be itching to annihilate any opposing views. Unfortunately, regardless of how emotionally satisfying it can be, argument rarely furthers your goals. Worse, it not only undermines the cooperation you need to achieve your goals, but may also create active opposition.

One problem with argument is that while your actual purpose may be to prove your idea right, you end up putting more effort into proving your opponent wrong. Argument inevitably attacks the other person's intelligence and sense of importance. Quite naturally, he will oppose such an insult. It's not likely that someone will come over to your side after you've suggested that his brain operates at significantly lower wattage than your own.

Avoid communicating by word, tone, or expression that others are wrong. Start by listening to the other side. Train yourself to delay the usual knee-jerk verdicts that we humans love to form in the first ten seconds of another's presentation—"That's BS," "What an idiot," "This is ridiculous," "Give me a break." Make an effort to actually understand the other person's position. Who knows, maybe you'll find that you agree.

Even if your opinion is already known, show others that your mind is still open and that you value their input. "I've looked at this carefully but I can't see every angle. Tell me how you see it." This gives others recognition and respect, lowering emotions and raising the willingness to concede and cooperate.

If the other person states his opinion first, listen and show interest. Fight the urge to tell him his idea stinks on ice. Begin your counter opinion something like this—"Hmm, that's interesting, I hadn't thought of it that way. Let me tell you what I've been thinking and then get your reaction." This response is appreciative and avoids stirring up a defensive reaction that will lock the other person into his position.

You may never get complete agreement, but the potential for concession and cooperation is much higher if argument is avoided. You may not experience the joy of crushing the opposition with your smart-bomb logic, but your true goals, the success of which will determine your personal success, are more likely to be met.

And speaking of success, let's look at a few guidelines for successfully coexisting with your superior.

When a situation requires that you go to your superior for advice or a decision, always keep your focus on meeting or accomplishing goals. Arrive with a concise description of the issues, your best opinion or solution, and a clear statement of what you need. As we've said before (numerous times), leave the complaints and blaming elsewhere. Whenever your superior comes into contact with you, you want him to think problem-solver, not problem-causer. If you want to advance your career, you should lighten his load whenever possible.

To make a big hit with a superior, find out what problems are keeping him or her awake at night and then try to devise solutions. For example, if you discover that your boss is under pressure from above to cut expenses, look around for cost cutting ideas. If you find anything he can present to his superiors, anything that lowers his stress, you'll be a hero.

One common cause of strain between superior and subordinate is misunderstanding. Many bosses have difficulty defining exactly what they want. They assume you already know, or they feel they've already explained fully when they haven't. Unfortunately, even if the misunderstanding was entirely the boss's fault, you lose. That's one of the advantages of being the boss. If you want to stay out of trouble, it's up to you to make sure you have a clear definition of his expectations and goals, your authority, your responsibility, and any deadlines.

If your boss is vague about these things, you have to force him (politely) to clarify. "What areas exactly should be covered in this report?" or "What will it take for you to consider this problem solved?" or "How long and how detailed of a report are you expecting?" or "How much time and effort should I give to this project?" or "Is it all right for me to bring Bill in to assist me?" or "Who will be using the information in this report?" or "When do you expect this on your desk?" Ask questions and keep asking them until you have a well-defined picture of what is expected. Anything less is risky.

Here's an important survival tip. Any time you make a mistake or have a setback, make sure that you are the first one to reveal and explain it to your superior. By being the first, you may not avoid repercussions, but they are sure to be milder than if you delay and word reaches your boss through someone else. Quick reporting of problems combined with a plan for resolution makes you look trustworthy and even capable.

We all make mistakes and have problems; it's how we handle them that defines us. If you stall and your boss discovers the difficulty through some other avenue, you seem to be covering up or letting things drift. Plus, now the boss is probably embarrassed; he didn't know what was going on under his nose. That will make him doubly angry. Finally, by reporting an error yourself, you will surely put a more favorable spin on it than someone else would.

Suppose you've handled your job so well that you think you deserve a raise. What's the best way to get it from a reluctant boss who's trying to cut expenses?

First, reread the chapter on negotiation. Then consider these points.

The number one rule for obtaining a raise is to ask for it. That's obvious, right? Perhaps, but many people either can't steel themselves to confront their boss or assume he already knows they deserve a raise. You may deserve it, but companies are usually quite fond of money, and they won't necessarily give it up without a push. Ask!

Many of us ask for a raise because a year has gone by, and we figure that's reason enough to get a raise. Your superior, on the other hand, may feel that if you are no more productive now than twelve months ago, you don't deserve a raise (other than an inflation adjustment). So, the best way to justify a raise is to point to your accomplishments. Ideally, you should try to quantify your performance—"I brought in fifteen more accounts this year than last year." Quantifying works because it's easy to understand and difficult to dispute.

Another method is to point to improvements cited in your formal performance review (if you have one). If last year's review said you needed to increase your technical knowledge of widgets, point to the two classes you took in widget system design at the local college. Or, point out that previous criticisms of your communication skills had ceased to be a factor in the most recent review. Show that you deserve more compensation because you are a more valuable employee.

Prior to asking for a raise (one or two weeks before), try to give your boss something he or she really wants. For example, if your boss is plagued by concerns about customer service complaints, show him that you have the best customer service record and hand him a report listing your methods for handling the ten most common customer problems. If this is useful or takes some pressure off the boss, your chance of getting a raise increases.

Finally, if all else fails, offer your boss a deal or a trade. Get his commitment to give you a raise if you meet certain goals within a specified time period. You might say, "Okay, boss, if I can increase my production by 10% in the next two months, will you give me a 10% raise?" or "Would you be willing to give me the raise I've requested if I can bring in six new accounts before June 1rst?"

This approach encourages a fair play response from your superior. "Sure, if you make the extra effort, I'll give you a raise." On the other hand, never imply that you'll withhold performance unless you get your raise.

In summary, if you want a raise, show easily recognizable proof that you deserve it. In order to be sure you will have such proof when you need it, formulate a plan of action and keep your eyes open for opportunity.

As I wrap up this chapter, I want to make two final points—one relates to persuasion, the other relates to appreciation.

In the workplace, good persuasion skills are a major element of that elusive quality we like to refer to as leadership. Attempts at persuasion in the workplace often violate a basic rule of salesmanship—keep the message simple and easy to understand. In our haste and need to persuade, we often throw every justification we can think of into the mix. The result is a loss of clarity and direction. In the confusion, the listener can't distinguish critical points from minor ones and may never grasp the thrust of your logic.

Proven leaders consistently show the ability to distill complex ideas into simple, even overly simple, messages that persuade because the main point is instantly understood. To drive a point home, leaders use analogies, metaphors, and humor to highlight a concept and relate it to the listener's everyday life. "Listen, Joe, I know you like to go fishing. Think of our clients as trout, and our product flow as the river. If our product flow dries up, even briefly, those client fish of ours don't just take a break from swimming, they die. They're gone for good. Consistent availability of our product, 100% of the time, is critical. See what I mean?"

Humor is a wonderfully effective way to get a message across while lowering resistance. "The other problem with drying up a client fish's river of product is that even if he survives, he's sure as hell going to look for another river to live in."

Sell your ideas with a little showmanship. If your presentation is dry and boring, your idea may seem dry and boring too. Careful though, don't get carried away and say something so outrageous that you violate the culture of your company. Still, try to wake your audience up.

For instance, make a seemingly wrong or crazy statement and then watch as your listeners hang on your every word to see how you explain yourself. "This company is like an old hunting dog. By that do I mean we like to lay in the shade and scratch ourselves? No. Do I mean we have fleas? No. We are like an old hunting dog in the sense that we have a vast store of hunting experience that we can draw on to outwit our younger opponents. We may not run quite as fast as the pups, but we don't have to, we're smarter than they are. My plan makes use of our staff's long-term experience to…" Believe me, people will pay attention when you use this technique. Just make sure you can pull it off without getting in trouble.

Now let's look at appreciation. Success in the workplace inevitably involves gaining the cooperation of others. You may think your job is fairly independent, and it may be, but from time to time, daily, hourly, or even constantly, most of us have to call on others to help us attain our goals. You never know which person's assistance might suddenly become critical to your success. If these people resources are to be available when you need them, you have to maintain quality relationships.

Appreciation is one of the basic fuels that keeps relationships running. It makes people feel important, needed, and admired. Unfortunately, most of us take the contributions of those around us for granted. After all, they get a paycheck for what they do. The effort they make is a responsibility, not a favor, so why thank or compliment them?

The answer is best understood by asking yourself how you respond to appreciation. If you're like most people on this planet, you find it very motivating. It makes you glad you did a good job for the person who praised you, and it encourages you to do so again in the future. It also makes you like the person who went out of his or her way to take note of your accomplishment.

Make your praise specific. Avoid praise that's general and vague—"Good job," or "Super effort," or "Keep up the good work." Instead, clearly identify exactly what it was that you liked. "John, your analysis of the reasons for our production slowdowns was right on target, very insightful."

Want to double or triple the impact of your appreciation? Offer your praise in front of others. "I think you should all know that John's report on production slowdowns was fantastic. We're all going to benefit at bonus time because of his efforts. Thanks, John." If that doesn't make John feel good, nothing will. And, you can bet the next time you need a favor or help from John, you'll get it.

Aside from simple praise, let people know you are thinking of them and want the best for them. Remember their birthdays. Ask about the wife that's in the hospital or the son that just went away to college. Go to lunch with them periodically. Make time for some non-business social chat now and then. If someone needs help or advice, offer it.

In short, be friendly. Let the people around you know that you see them as human beings, not just cogs in the company wheel. Quite aside from making work a more pleasant place to spend a third of your life, all these efforts are like deposits in the bank. If you don't make deposits, the day comes when you want to make a withdrawal and find your account is closed. If you've built close relationships, you have a reserve of trust, respect, admiration, and affection that makes it a lot easier to wield influence and obtain cooperation. Start making deposits in that goodwill bank account today.